Broken Icarus

The 1933 Chicago World's Fair, the Golden Age of Aviation, and the Rise of Fascism

DAVID HANNA

Prometheus Books

Guilford, Connecticut

(PB) Prometheus Books

An imprint of Globe Pequot, the trade division of
The Rowman & Littlefield Publishing Group, Inc.
4501 Forbes Boulevard, Suite 200, Lanham, Maryland 20706
www.rowman.com

Distributed by NATIONAL BOOK NETWORK

British Library Cataloguing in Publication Information Available

Library of Congress Cataloging-in-Publication Data

Names: Hanna, David, 1967– author.
Title: Broken Icarus : the 1933 Chicago World's Fair, the golden age of
   aviation, and the rise of fascism / David Hanna.
Description: Lanham, MD : Prometheus, 2022. | Includes bibliographical
   references and index. | Summary: "In Broken Icarus, author David Hanna
   tracks the inspiring trajectory of aviation leading up to and through
   the World's Fair of 1933, as well as the field of flight's more sinister
   ties to fascism domestic and abroad to present a unique history that is
   both riveting and revelatory"— Provided by publisher.
Identifiers: LCCN 2021046387 (print) | LCCN 2021046388 (ebook) | ISBN
   9781633886766 (cloth ; permanent paper) | ISBN 9781633886773 (epub)
Subjects: LCSH: Aeronautics—History—20th century. | Aeronautics and
   state—History—20th century. | World politics 1933–1945. | Century
   of Progress International Exposition (1933–1934 : Chicago, Ill.). |
   Fascism—History—20th century.
Classification: LCC TL515 .H253 2022 (print) | LCC TL515 (ebook) | DDC
   629.13—dc23
LC record available at https://lccn.loc.gov/2021046387
LC ebook record available at https://lccn.loc.gov/2021046388

∞™ The paper used in this publication meets the minimum requirements of American
National Standard for Information Sciences—Permanence of Paper
for Printed Library Materials, ANSI/NISO Z39.48-1992.

FOR KATIE

We'll always have Rome . . .

And this fairy-like apparition, which seemed to melt into the silvery blue background of the sky, when it appeared far away, lighted by the sun, seemed to be from another world and to be returning there like a dream—an emissary from the "Island of the Blest" in which so many humans still believe in the inmost recesses of their souls.

—Hugo Eckener

Listen to the music of the sky with its mellowed tubes of pride, the buzzing drills of miners of the clouds, enthusiastic roars of gas, hammering ever more intoxicated with speed and the applause of bright propellers. The rich music of Balbo and his transatlantic fliers hums, explodes, and laughs among the blue flashes of the horizon.

—F. T. Marinetti

When you fly a balloon you don't file a flight plan; you go where the wind goes. You feel like part of the air. You almost feel like part of eternity, and you just float along.

—Jeannette Ridlon Piccard

The Century of Progress is ahead of us and not behind us.

—William Randolph Hearst

Contents

A Note on Sources

This book was by far the most complex project that I have undertaken to date. There were so many strands that needed to be followed, understood, then woven together into a digestible whole that told the story I wanted to tell. As much as I have included in this book, that which I left out could fill entire shelves with additional books on the subject matter. There are times when, as a historian, one is frustrated by a paucity of source material—for this book, it was the opposite. I often felt overwhelmed by the amount of material available, and making sense of it all while also trying to be as thorough as possible wasn't easy. My aim in writing this book was to try and capture the Zeitgeist of this era, using the World's Fair, aviation's Golden Age, and the rise of fascism as lenses through which to gain an understanding of it. It is not an attempt to write a definitive account of the fair or any of the main figures that are featured in this book. There are a number of secondary sources that I would highly recommend to readers who are interested in pursuing these topics in greater depth. Cheryl Ganz's book, *The 1933 Chicago World's Fair: A Century of Progress*, is the best book written to date on the 1933 Chicago World's Fair. The late Claudio Segrè's biography of Italo Balbo is the most informative and well-written book in English on this controversial figure. Balbo himself wrote a number of volumes in Italian on his air voyages. The late Douglas Botting's *Doctor Eckener's Dream Machine* is an excellent dual biography of the man and his airship. Eckener's memoir, *My Zeppelins*, is also available in English, and is a great read. He was a bit of a poet. If you want to understand in detail the first "Space Race" of manned ballooning in the 1930s, David DeVorkin's *Race to the Stratosphere* is the definitive account, while Tom Cheshire's *The Explorer Gene* is an outstanding multibiography of an extraordinary family—the Piccards.

Prologue

The 1930s conjure still-painful images: the great want of the Depression—the drawn and haggard faces of men and women lacking comprehension of why their world had been knocked out from under them—contrasted with the exuberance of frothing crowds motivated by self-appointed national saviors dressing up old hatreds as new ideas. The downcast, the beaten, the hypnotized, and the enraged typified the age. Or so it seems in retrospect. But there was another story that embodied mankind in that decade pregnant with foreboding. In the same year that both Adolf Hitler and Franklin D. Roosevelt came to power in Germany and the United States, respectively, the city of Chicago staged what was, up to that time, the most forward-looking international exhibition in history. Instead of trying to re-create an idealized neoclassical past, as its predecessor in 1893 had done, the 1933 World's Fair's organizers, architects, scientists, and artists looked to the future, unabashedly, as one full of glowing promise. The Technicolor vision of the future they produced could not have contrasted more sharply with the gritty black-and-white economic and political realities that surrounded them. And yet, they were undaunted.

No technology loomed larger at the fair than aviation. And no persons at the fair captured the public's interest as much as the romantic figures associated with it: Italy's internationally renowned chief of aeronautics, Italo Balbo; German zeppelin designer and captain, Doctor Hugo Eckener; and the husband and wife team of Swiss-born aeronaut Jean Piccard and Chicago-born aeronaut Jeannette Ridlon Piccard. To underscore this, the 1933 Fair's official promotional poster prominently and explicitly featured an aviation motif. This was for a reason. If one was forward looking in 1933, one gazed skyward. It spoke to the inner Icarus in all of humanity.

Italo Balbo during his first trip to the United States (1929). *Alamy Images.*

In the summer of 1933, the trans-Atlantic flight of Balbo's famed gleaming-white flying boats, and their subsequent precision landing on Lake Michigan in front of adoring crowds, provided perhaps the signature event of an eventful fair. This was a time when aviation had outgrown its early, awkward age—interrupted by World War I—but still possessed a certain elitist quality personified by aviators such as Charles Lindbergh, Amelia Earhart, Bessie Coleman, Antoine de Saint Exupéry, Jean Mermoz, and Ernst Udet. This golden age of aviation and its high priests and priestesses portended to many the world over that a new age was dawning—an age when man would not only leave the ground behind, but also his uglier, less admirable, heritage of war, poverty, corruption, and disease. Pilots were the heroes of the age. And perhaps no one more comfortably assumed this mantle than the amiable, goateed, black-shirted, charmer from Ferrara, Italy. Italo Balbo was both a product of his times, and one who shaped them. In his person, two of the main, and most attractive, fashions of the 1930s—aviation and fascism—merged seamlessly. It was only later in the decade, as the hysterically enthused youths were turned into jack-booted monsters perpetrating any crime in the name of nation or race, that Balbo's political creed was discredited—his legacy in Chicago and elsewhere forever tarnished. But for a moment in 1933, this all lay in a future that still seemed so promising. No one then could have known that 60 million would perish in a war that would dwarf the earlier 1914–1918 conflict.

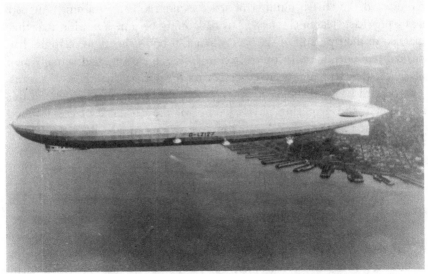

The _Graf Zeppelin_ over San Francisco (1929). _Alamy Images._

Three months after Balbo's flying boats returned to Europe, Hugo Eckener piloted the world-renowned *Graf Zeppelin* north from Brazil to Chicago. Its presence graced the fair with an indescribable sense of wonder and inspired those in attendance with Eckener's dream of a more peaceful and technologically advanced world—a world connected by giant airships (looking like "silvery fish," according to Eckener) running nearly silent among the clouds. By 1933, the problem that presented itself to Eckener in realizing this dream was not so much technological as it was political. With the rise of Adolf Hitler and the Nazis to power, Germans and German Americans were forced to confront ugly truths and make difficult choices. For Eckener, the trip to the 1933 World's Fair represented an opportunity to make a final public display of his contempt for Nazism. Facing the possibility of denunciation to the Gestapo for his lack of enthusiasm for local Nazi sympathizers in Chicago, he was eventually marginalized by Hitler as the official head of Germany's fleet of airships. Yet his brilliant vision for the future continued to inspire many the world over. The tragedy that befell the *Graf Zeppelin*'s sister ship, the *Hindenburg*, four years later seemed to confirm that without Eckener's direct guidance, his dream could not be sustained.

For Auguste and Jean Piccard, flight meant ascension into the heavens above. Rather than traveling from city to city above the Earth's surface, the two brothers seemed to want to break free of the Earth itself; to go higher than any human beings had ever been and attain what Icarus had failed to reach. Their manned aeronautical capsules, attached to gas-filled balloons, represented the true beginning of space exploration. By training, Auguste was a physicist; Jean a chemist—but ballooning became a passion that they married to their pursuit of science. Albert Einstein's theory of relativity had posited that cosmic radiation existed in space. As no one had actually *been* in space, this had not been observed, or measured, directly by humans. The Piccard brothers looked to change this by breaking free of the Earth's atmosphere and acquiring physical proof of the existence of cosmic rays. This required ascending to heights in excess of ten miles above the Earth's surface. The genre of science fiction literature had existed since the days of Jules Verne, but these men weren't just reading about the future. They were making it.

Ultimately, the Piccard attempt at a height record in 1934 would not be a brotherly endeavor, but rather a shared accomplishment of Jean and his wife—Chicago native Jeannette Ridlon Piccard. When Dow Chemical (which had assisted the Piccards in designing the capsule to be used for the record ascent) heard that a woman—and a mother no less—would be sharing the risks with her husband of high-altitude flight, it required the Piccards to remove the company logo from the craft. On the other hand, as Jeannette trained to pilot the balloon in the months leading up to the ascent, Orville Wright endorsed her efforts by serving as an observer during her practice flights. Jeannette Piccard was not merely attempting to break altitude records; she was breaking important social barriers as well. She and Jean were

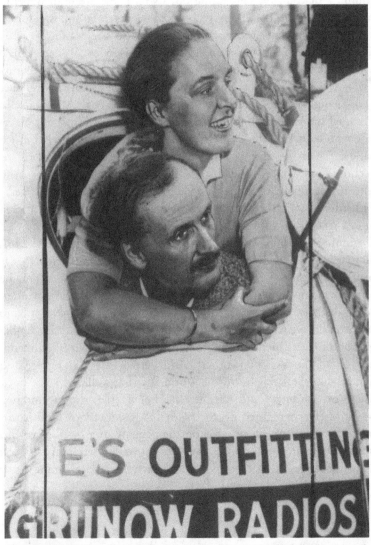

Jeannette Ridlon Piccard and Jean Piccard after their record-setting flight into the upper reaches of the stratosphere in 1934. *Courtesy of Bertrand Piccard.*

true partners. They were going up. They might not return alive. And the world was watching. These pioneering aeronauts blazed a trail for those that followed, as attested by Jeannette's work with the National Aeronautics and Space Administration (NASA) later in her life.

Today we are navigating both the relentless advent of new and exciting technologies, as well as the appearance of authoritarian-style political leaders in a number of countries, including our own. These are both hopeful and uncertain times. As in the 1930s, technology seems to be almost a force with a life of its own, perhaps more so. Yet there is also a retreat into a national, ethnic, and racial tribalism that defies a progressive view of man. This book aims to serve as both an inspiration and a cautionary tale. Fascism combined with advances in aviation technology to level large swaths of the cities of Madrid, Shanghai, and London before, in the hands of the Allies, leading to the eventual nuclear annihilation of the cities of Hiroshima and Nagasaki. No one who witnessed the impressive Italian Fascist planes flying in formation above Chicago's distinctive skyline in 1933 could later fail to see the connection. The Cold War–era Space Race too had its origins in Chicago and the Soviet Union in 1933–1934, as Russian aeronauts competed with the Piccards to reach the outer limits of the stratosphere, thus anticipating *Sputnik*, Yuri Gagarin, John Glenn, and the Apollo program.

Beginning in 1893 with the first World's Fair held in Chicago, historical forces embodied by rapid technological advances and frightening new political philosophies had been gathering momentum for decades, before converging on the shores of Lake Michigan forty years later. A young boy attending that first fair with his parents, coming again as a grown man to the second, would have witnessed breathtaking change in the interim, embodied by aviation pioneers such as Alberto Santos-Dumont, Count Ferdinand von Zeppelin, and the Wright Brothers. And perhaps he may have witnessed firsthand the unspeakable horror of World War I as well. Yet what lay ahead was more extraordinary and terrible still. For a brief, shining moment in the midst of that benighted decade of the 1930s, a city of tomorrow, and all the hopes it embodied, teetered on the edge of an abyss that yawned so ominously before it. It was only in the skies above that humanity still seemed fully capable of breaking free, avoiding cataclysm, and claiming its noble heritage from Icarus.

CHAPTER 1

On the Edge

In the spring of 1933, Germany's propaganda minister, Joseph Goebbels, arrived in Rome to arrange the details of the first meeting between his master, Adolf Hitler, and Italy's Il Duce, Benito Mussolini. He arrived in style. Ensconced aboard the giant airship, the *Graf Zeppelin*, Goebbels descended from the skies like some queer, elfish genie. The *Graf*'s captain, Hugo Eckener, held a low opinion of its VIP passenger and the noxious ideology he propagated. Perhaps, then, it was no coincidence that his trusted lieutenant, Ernst Lehmann, commanded the airship on its flight to the "Eternal City" instead. Lehmann was a professional. The airship's landing required all his attention, and the theatrics were a symptom of the wonder this creation engendered, something to which he had long since become accustomed. The Nazis clearly hoped to highjack this for their own purposes. For Eckener, stunts such as this were forcing him closer to having to make a choice between decency and expediency. He wasn't always going to be able to beg off these unpleasant interactions with high Nazi officials.

The rise of Adolf Hitler to absolute power earlier in the year had occurred with dizzying speed once the aging President Paul von Hindenburg had appointed him chancellor. Hitler had never won an election, but his rogue political party had been brought into the circles of power by the political right in Germany, in the hope that it could be contained and used. It turned out to be the other way around. With the Brownshirts holding torchlit vigils and marching through the streets chanting *blut und Boden* ("blood and soil"), the Nazis terrorized their opponents and insisted on using their swastika emblem as the national symbol. Hitler's will to power would now embody the national will as well. Coverage of giant rallies, and an endless barrage of chauvinism, half-truths, and outright lies poured forth from cheap

1

new mass-produced radios. The evil marketing genius behind this campaign was Goebbels. Perhaps of all of Hitler's lackies (who ran the gamut from the urbane intellectual, Albert Speer, to near-moron, Rudolf Hess), Goebbels was the most in tune with Hitler, and the most effective (and therefore dangerous) advocate/enabler for his twisted worldview. His trip to Rome aboard such an indisputable and virulent symbol of German technology and aeronautical skill held significance, which he fully understood. And Rome was not just any city; it was, after all, the Eternal City, the great imperial city of ancient Rome. Not for nothing had the Nazis adopted the Roman imperial eagle for their standards on display at rallies and other public events. The Fascist salute with the right arm outstretched, at a slight angle with palm down, was not merely aping Mussolini's Italy; it was making an explicit connection between the Third Reich and the glory that was Rome. Hitler's Germany (and by implication, not Mussolini's Italy) would be the new Rome, whose world mastery, like that of her ancient forebears, would last one thousand years. Swept up with the speed and totality of Nazi political success in Germany, it was easy to see why someone like Goebbels could actually believe nonsense such as this. And what is propaganda anyway, but national or ideological mythmaking? Goebbels's visit looked to shape that myth. In a speech he made during that period, he was quite explicit about this, but he went beyond it to mine and cultivate old hatreds and suspicions of his fellow Germans toward their Jewish neighbors:

> A good government cannot survive without good propaganda. Nor can good propaganda without a good government. If Jewish papers think they can intimidate National Socialists. I tell them, beware. One-day our patience will end and then we'll shut those lying Jews' mouths.[1]

Anti-Semitism would prove to be the line that Italo Balbo would not cross in his endorsement of the Fascist life. In his own time, he was a world-renowned celebrity aviator and probably the world's best public face for fascism as an ideology, in the world. But he was not a racist, and thus being chosen by Mussolini to be his official emissary, to stand beside the king, and to welcome this raving bigot to Rome must have been a trying experience. In a film produced at the time to commemorate the giant airship's visit, one can readily sense the awkwardness of the meeting.[2] This would be repeated throughout Balbo's career as an aviator and then as a colonial governor—he would make nice because Il Duce willed it, but his heart clearly wasn't in it. Neither was his head. He would long be a (quiet) critic of an Italo-German alliance, fearing Italy would simply become a puppet of the Nazis, with likely destructive results for his country.[3] That said, he shared with the Nazis their disdain for leftists and liberal democracies, arguing in a similar fashion to Goebbels the expediency of propaganda for controlling the masses: "Propaganda is the instinctive need of the convinced. . . . It appears absurd that others do not think like me."[4]

Photo taken during Joseph Goebbels's 1933 visit to Rome. Goebbels is third from left; Italo Balbo is fourth from left. *Getty Images.*

Goebbels, perhaps sensing Balbo's discomfort, insisted on having Italy's world-renowned air minister ascend for a cruise above Rome in the *Graf*. Balbo had accompanied King Victor Emanuel III to greet their German guests, but he clearly outshined the uninspiring representative of the House of Savoy. Photographs taken of the giant airship hovering over the Eternal City provided a powerful juxtaposition of the past and the future, as St. Peter's Basilica, the Colosseum, and the Palatine Hill fell under its shadow as it flew overhead. For his part, Balbo was not particularly fond of airships. His countryman, Umberto Nobile, had crashed the airship he was commanding during an Arctic expedition just a few years before, with tragic results. Italy had to call on the efforts of an international team, along with the resources of its own Aeronautica, to rescue the survivors. And for what? Balbo questioned the utility of such enterprises, never mind the risk. But the *Graf* held a certain allure. Hugo Eckener and Italo Balbo were certainly aware of each other. Three years earlier they had been asked, along with Charles Lindbergh, to provide testimony before the League of Nations' Committee on Communications and Transit, in Geneva. The topic was air transport cooperation. The three eagles cumulatively made a compelling argument for an international air transit system, in which zeppelins, land-based aircraft, and seaplanes would complement rather than compete with each other.[5] It was a promising beginning. Both Eckener and Balbo knew they shared a common destination later that year—Chicago. It was an exciting time, but it was also one fraught with anxiety.

Soon after the rendezvous in Rome, Balbo headed north to his base at Orbetello on a lagoon near a remote peninsula on the Tyrrhenian Sea. Named Scuola di Navigazione Aerea di Alto Mare,* it began operations on New Year's Day, 1930.[6] Balbo's pilots were some of the world's finest. Over the past five years they had completed three great aerial cruises flying twin-hulled Savoia-Marchetti seaplanes: two to either end of the Mediterranean, and the most ambitious, a trans-Atlantic crossing to Brazil. Though not without cost, the success of the 1931 expedition to Brazil had not only catapulted Italo Balbo to truly worldwide fame, it had also convinced the Italian government to back his long-planned Chicago project. Now, he and his pilots and their crews were readying themselves to cross the North Atlantic to the World's Fair on Lake Michigan. It would test both their skill and the technology at their command. As May blurred into June on the blue waters, practice

---

* "The High Seas Air Navigation School."

flights increased in frequency, and night flights and celestial navigation became *de rigueur* for what Balbo called his "aristocracy of the Aeronautica." He claimed the base maintained a monkish, quasi-religious atmosphere, and yet Balbo had his own personal field tent furnished with polar bear and lion skins, pitched in a grove of dark green pine trees. Here under the stars with a beach and the peak of Monte Argentario nearby, he lived what he termed an "aboriginal life" with—it was rumored—his beautiful mistress. But always he donned a dinner jacket in the evening. America consumed his thoughts. He had visited it once before.

In 1928–1929, Italo Balbo had visited the United States with his wife and a number of aides to present a paper at an international aviation conference in Washington, DC. He decided to take advantage of the opportunity to make a coast-to-coast tour of the country. Presaging what was to come, he was invited to visit an aeronautical exhibition in Chicago as an honored guest. The "Windy City" with its famous downtown "Loop" was utterly unlike anything in Europe: Its size, pace, the height of its buildings. In fact, everything he experienced in America—particularly the country's scale—made a lasting impression on Balbo. While in the Midwest, he and his wife had stopped in Dayton to meet Orville Wright, and then stopped in Detroit to meet with Henry Ford. Ford was an odd mix of ruthless businessman, socially-minded progressive, and vicious anti-Semite. According to Balbo biographer, Claudio Segrè, the Italian aviator found Ford "a charmer whose directness in appearance and manner Balbo found delightful."[7] Ford would later play a critical role in advancing aviation and space exploration in connection with the 1933 Chicago World's Fair.

Balbo toured U.S. military bases and was impressed with the skill of American pilots. It might now seem strange that the U.S. military would have allowed such close inspection of its facilities and methods by a Fascist air minister. In 1941, of course, the two countries would go to war. But in the late 1920s up through of the creation of the Rome-Berlin Axis in 1936, this inevitable collision was in no way self-evident. As historian R. J. B. Bosworth remarked, Fascist Italy at this time had a "fascination with aspects of the U.S. mission in the world" and until "very late in its history . . . did not reliably place the USA among its certain foes."[8]

During this transcontinental odyssey, Balbo also felt keenly his transplanted countrymen's pride in having remade their lives anew in the New World and their sense of quiet humiliation about the country they had felt forced, by want, to leave. He longed to return, but this time not as an observer of America, but as a discoverer of new air routes to her shores, and as an unarmed conqueror of her skies. Chicago's World's Fair, which by its announced opening in May 1933 was being held against all the odds in the bleakest days of the Depression, was his vehicle for realizing this vision. Chicago knew something about hosting world's fairs. Balbo was sure the city would know how to frame his achievement—if he could pull it off.

―――∞∞∞――――

As soon as the *Graf Zeppelin* left Rome, Balbo's thoughts returned to the upcoming mission. The seaplanes he and his men would be flying were Savoia-Marchetti's latest upgrade, designated with an X by the Sesto Calende–based company. Also, for the first time. Balbo would have directional gyros and artificial horizons—manufactured by Sperry of the United States—installed in the instrumental panels on the flight decks. Everything that needed to be done was being done, but there was always the unconsidered factor, the "unknown unknown" that can drive leaders mad with anxiety. But the objective was worth it. This could prove to be the greatest World's Fair of all time—he understood this. After another day of training and training again, and again, making sure all of the pieces were steadily coming together, then turning in for the night, and in that nether world between wakefulness and dreams, one image appearing over and over again in his melting consciousness, Chicago . . .

CHAPTER 2

White City

Most cities are, to a greater or lesser degree, products of their geography, but in Chicago's case it is even more pronounced. In the late seventeenth century, the French explorer Louis Joliet noted that the spot where the city now stands was the shortest portage between the watersheds of two great rivers: the St. Lawrence and the Mississippi. Native Americans, of course, had long recognized this and used this route. The South Branch of the Chicago River is just a few miles from the Des Plaines River, a tributary of the Illinois River, itself a tributary of the Mississippi. The land itself is low and marshy. Decades later, a trading post was established at this location by Jean Baptiste Point du Sable, a farmer and entrepreneur of mixed French and Haitian ancestry. In 1803, the U.S. government fortified the post and named it Fort Dearborn. It was the site of a terrible massacre in the War of 1812. Its future didn't look particularly promising, but then events hundreds of miles to the east would create the impetus to take this strategically significant spot and transform it from a muddy, isolated outpost into a front-rank New World metropolis.

The Erie Canal, completed in 1825, was the greatest American engineering achievement of its time. The vision and money to make this a reality came from New York, whose leaders recognized that by connecting Lake Erie to the Hudson River, New York could siphon off the commerce that would inevitably have been centered in New Orleans. The Crescent City was ideally suited by geography to become the great metropolis of North America, but it wasn't to be. New Yorkers exploited the economic opportunities of the Upper Great Lakes for themselves. Buffalo, at the western terminus of the canal on Lake Erie, was the first settlement to boom. But the unimpressive, underdeveloped site at the mouth of the Chicago River

7

on Lake Michigan soon attracted even greater attention in the east. If a canal could be completed across the valleys and through the mountains of upstate New York, why not a canal connecting the Chicago River and the Des Plaines? Once completed, a project such as this would allow New York commerce to penetrate into the very heartland of the Mississippi Valley, and compete with the merchants of St. Louis, Memphis, and New Orleans in their home markets. It was audacious. It was thrusting. It was fabulously successful.

From its earliest origins as a recognizable American city (shortly before incorporating itself in 1833), Chicago was to a certain extent a creation of New York. Many a New Yorker, as well as a fair showing of New Englanders, came west and speculated in Chicago real estate. It was a good bet. To say that Chicago was a "colony" of New York would, perhaps, be stretching the evidence. However, it wouldn't be entirely inaccurate, either. With New York money underwriting its development, the city by the lake took hold and thrived. Its first mayor was New Yorker turned real estate mogul, William B. Ogden. Within a matter of a few decades, it had become one of the largest cities in the Western Hemisphere. The famous fire in 1871, which laid the city flat, in fact allowed for a rebuilding on an even grander scale. Architects of great talent were drawn to this seeming *tabula rasa* to design a modern city, with modern buildings. The skyscraper was born.

But this growth had a cost: pollution, noise, unsafe streets and transit, and glaring socioeconomic inequalities between native-born and immigrant, black and white. The infamous Haymarket Bombing of 1886 had shaken the city to its core. Real fear of an anarchist revolution triggered an ugly, reflexive backlash against political radicals and the foreign-born. There was a sense that Chicago was careening out of control toward the twentieth century. Both utopian socialists and utopian capitalists earnestly tried to find solutions to the myriad ills affecting their society. A yearning to create a model of the possible was—at least partly—one of the main motivations behind the proposal for a World's Fair to be held in Chicago in 1892. Ostensibly, the fair would commemorate four hundred years since Christopher Columbus's first voyage to the New World in 1492. In reality, the more urgent present was what occupied people's minds. In the event it wasn't until 1893—a year that would signal the beginning of a serious economic downturn in the country—that the World's Fair opened its gates to the public.

—∞—

The fairgrounds largely reflected the genius of architect and urban designer, Daniel Burnham, and the venerable urban landscape artist, Frederick Law Olmsted. The location of the grounds was situated in the southern part of the city along the lakefront at Jackson Park, with its central Court of Honor constructed around a lagoon-like "Grand Basin," adding a water theme to the experience of millions of fairgoers. The buildings and statuary were made to be temporary—a vision of what could be, but not a reflection of what was. Burnham, influenced by the neoclassical style in vogue in the École des Beaux-Arts in Paris, emphasized a brilliant white façade for the exterior of the fair. Inside its various halls and buildings, however, the most modern technologies and forward-looking innovations were on display for an optimistic and curious public. The exhibits within the Electricity Building in particular vividly demonstrated the wonders of this new god-like power source with men like Thomas Edison, George Westinghouse, and Nikola Tesla personally involved. The world was changing, fast. The neoclassical style gave people the illusion of an ennobling continuity with the past and tradition. At the same time, their world was being altered in ways that were both exciting and unnerving. And it was clean, safe, and free of the incessant racket of daily life in downtown Chicago, just a few miles away. The "White City" provided both a model and an illusion. People wanted to believe it was the way of the future, while being willfully blind to the deeper societal ills that produced that which they feared. At this time there was a real belief in the efficacy of intelligently designed buildings, parks, and esplanades to shape people's behavior. As historian Donald L. Miller has emphasized, many at the time possessed "a deep faith in the transforming power of good surroundings" and saw Burnham's efforts as "an antidote to social disorder."[1] This was important, if naïve. It was also important that the fair was held where it was held—in the country's interior.

The 1893 World's Fair & Columbian Exposition held in Chicago was the city's first attempt at welcoming the rest of America and the world to the shores of Lake Michigan. For better or worse, it established the aesthetic sensibility of the era with its vision of neoclassical architecture spearheading urban design (in the process, it set back modern, progressive styles for decades, according to architects such as Louis Sullivan). Be that as it may, this fair defined an age and inspired an entire generation to think on a grand scale of what might be. Edward Bellamy's utopian novel, *Looking Backward*, published five years before the fair, had motivated many across the country to aspire to a better world—one in unmistakable contrast to the Dickensian realities one faced in almost any city of any size at that time: polluted water and air, homeless children, dangerous labor agitation, and cruel suppression of the same by rich capitalists. The fair's White City offered the millions that entered its stucco mirage a glimpse of the type of society envisioned by Bellamy. Its mix of the cosmopolitan, the genteel, and the salacious would also inspire emulation.

To be sure, Chicago's 1893 Fair wasn't the first world's fair to capture the public's attention on a grand scale: the fairs in London in 1851, Philadelphia in 1876, and, perhaps most famously, Paris in 1889, inspired millions of people. The nineteenth century had proven to be a time of unparalleled, substantial, and often intimate change. Someone born in Europe in 1800 grew to adulthood in a world that had more in common with the ancient Greeks and Romans than with the world he would live in just a few short decades later, in middle age. The world was also becoming a smaller place. The process, started by the very person the 1893 Chicago Fair was memorializing, had accelerated with the advent of steamships and transoceanic telegraph cables. Imperialism—now an ugly word—was then all the rage, as the more technologically advanced countries imposed their will on the less technologically advanced. Exoticism was the inevitable companion of the imperialist impulse as the world shrank and the "Other" became objects of curiosity and, unfortunately, derision. Exhibits such as "Eskimo Village" and "Dahomey" objectified the Other for the mostly white fairgoers. The line between cultural enlightenment and leering exploitation was blurred by fairs like those in Paris or Chicago. People wanted to be ennobled, but they also wanted to be titillated, and ultimately to have their own sense of superiority confirmed.

Daniel Burnham enlisted a youthful entertainment entrepreneur, Sol Bloom, to oversee the Midway Plaisance exhibits and attractions. Eventually shortened in the popular lexicon to the "Midway," this pedestrian thoroughfare connecting Washington Park to the west with Jackson Park and the lakefront to the east, provided fairgoers with a less rarefied experience than the White City beyond. Part carnival, part cultural exhibit, the Midway brought together the furtive, if not sleazy, sideshow experience and mixed it with exhibits from institutions as reputable as Harvard University and the Smithsonian. It was a roaring success. Fairgoers longed for the rarefied air of the Court of Honor, but after a certain point they found they couldn't breathe. The Midway allowed them to let their hair down and have some fun. Shocked, conned, and, yes, perhaps enlightened, denizens of the Midway raved about the experience. Sol Bloom's "Street in Cairo" introduced Americans to the "belly dance," and a stein of the Pabst Brewing Company's freshly awarded blue ribbon–winning pilsner let them take the edge off a long afternoon. In retrospect, this Jekyll-and-Hyde aspect of the 1893 Fair was clearly a crucial component in its overwhelming success. The high and

Visitors look down at the centrally located pool in the White City (1893).
Alamy Images.

the low; the genteel and the *demi-monde* maintained a sort of equilibrium that summer, which made it all work. In the end, it was estimated that over 27 million people crowded the fairgrounds in Jackson Park and the Midway Plaisance.* One of them was eleven-year-old Franklin Delano Roosevelt. The scion of the colossally wealthy Hyde Park Roosevelt and Delano clans, young Franklin traveled to the fair in his family's own private railway car.[2] Chicago in the summer and fall of 1893 was simply the place to be.

Another person attending the fair had taken a different path to see its wonders close up. In the middle of an economic depression that had gripped the country starting in early 1893, Elias Disney gained employment as part of the veritable army of laborers and skilled craftsmen hired by Daniel Burnham to complete the vast civic undertaking in time for its May Day opening. Disney was fortunate to find work as a carpenter at the fair site erecting the awe-inspiring—albeit temporary—structures of the White City. He would share stories of what he considered to be one of the great privileges of his life[3] with his four sons, including the youngest, Walter, or "Walt." The seeds of both the "Rainbow City" of the 1933 Chicago World's Fair, and of Walt Disney's "Experimental Prototype City of Tomorrow" in Orlando, Florida, were sown here.

---

* Fourteen million of them came from abroad. This is all the more impressive when one considers that Chicago was located deep in the interior of the North American continent, and to reach it required a long journey by rail after a long journey by sea.

Mindful of the great success of Gustav Eiffel's tower at the 1889 Paris World's Fair, the 1893 Chicago Fair's organizers looked to engineer George Ferris to design an attraction that would bring visitors into the skies at a height, and in a way, they never would have previously experienced. His giant "Wheel" did just that. Taking fair visitors 264 feet into the sky at its apex (this height—over twenty stories in diameter—greatly exceeds most contemporary Ferris wheels), the attraction was a sensation. The enclosed, rotating platforms held up to sixty people at a time.[4] The view was spectacular, indeed unlike any vista most paying customers had ever beheld: the blue of the lake, the glaring white of the fair, and the dingy, gray throb of modern Chicago with its decidedly *un*-classical buildings crowded in the Loop,* reaching skyward. In a larger context, this desire to rise to giddy heights anticipated the age of flight.

The Wheel was firmly affixed to the ground, but balloons straining at their tethers along the Midway offered the adventurous the ability to truly break free from earthly constraints. A ride in a "balloon" was a first-rate thrill. The ability to rise and descend had been mastered for some time by the late nineteenth century, but horizontal motion was essentially at the whim of the elements. To say this was controlled flight was pushing the definition of the term. This uncertainty about where one would end up increased the thrill. French author Jules Verne had previously mined this material in his novel *The Mysterious Island*, whose plot revolves around a group of marooned passengers aboard a balloon gone astray. Later L. Frank Baum transformed a wayward balloonist into the "great and powerful" Wizard of Oz inhabiting a wondrous "Emerald City." His departure from the Emerald City is also in a balloon, borne away by natural forces not fully within his control. But what if one could ascend into the skies and control the direction of one's "airship"? Yes, what if?

To try and answer this question, pioneering French American engineer Octave Chanute—then collecting and disseminating information on gliders, in particular—assembled the first International Conference on Aerial Navigation, to be held in his hometown of Chicago. This meeting of aerial enthusiasts at the 1893 World's Fair established a mechanism for a collective effort to achieve powered flight sooner rather than later. With an eye toward sharing what was known at that time, Chanute wrote *Progress in Flying Machines*. Published in 1894, it would become a go-to guide for would-be aeronauts (including Wilbur and Orville Wright). And throughout the 1890s, Chanute and his team worked to perfect a glider among the windswept sand

---

* Chicago's congested downtown business district.

dunes of Lake Michigan's south shore. After much trial and error, they tasted success. Chanute's boxy wing design with both vertical and diagonal trusses became the basis for the design later adopted, and refined, by the Wright brothers.

By the end of the decade, intrepid inventor-aeronauts on both sides of the Atlantic had begun to make the technological leaps that would enable true controlled flight. First in Paris, as Brazilian Alberto Santos-Dumont pioneered the use of a powered "lighter than air" ship. Then in Germany, with Count Ferdinand von Zeppelin's more ambitious airship. And, finally, with the Wright brothers' successful experiments with heavier-than-air flight at Kitty Hawk, North Carolina in 1903.

"Captive" balloon and the Ferris wheel at the World's Columbian Exposition, photographed by Charles Dudley Arnold (1893).

The World's Fair ended in the autumn of 1893. Within weeks the grand, abandoned halls of the White City had become home to a large population of homeless men, squatting along the lakeshore looking for any shelter they could find. The economic depression worsened; the carefree joys of summer replaced by the grim realities of capitalism's latest catastrophic failure. Unsurprisingly, fire eventually engulfed what remained of Chicago's beautiful mirage, sparing the city the expense of having to formally dismantle it. It would be another forty years before Chicago rose again to welcome the world.

CHAPTER 3

Black Shirt

Italo Balbo was born in 1896 in Ferrara, Italy, three years after the first Chicago Fair ended. Ferrara had once been quite important in Italy's history as the seat of the powerful d'Este family during the Renaissance. Its location, on the Po River between Venice and Bologna in a fertile area called the *Emilia*, ensured it would remain a town of some significance, if not necessarily brilliance. Balbo's parents were schoolteachers. But there was a martial tradition, as well as a faded aristocratic lineage, on both sides of his family tree. One of his great-grandfathers had served under Marshal Murat in Napoleon's Russian campaign, and had fought his way across the Berezina River during the famous retreat of 1812.[1] His maternal grandmother was a *contessa*. For the young Italo Balbo, the desire to reawaken the past glories of his family and his town fed his ambition. Later, an English journalist would describe Balbo as a "reincarnation of the militant and magnificent Italian princes of medieval days."[2] It's hard to escape the conclusion that Italo Balbo would have fully embraced this description. He was, if nothing else—and from quite an early age—a romantic. It was this quality more than any other that would define his future path. Without it, he would never have achieved what he ultimately did.

———— ∞ ————

As a student, Italo Balbo imbibed the mythology of his country's founding: the near messianic zeal of Giuseppe Mazzini; the swashbuckling exploits of Giuseppe Garibaldi in his cape, fez, and red shirt of revolution and *Risorgimento*. The republican values of secularism and democracy (albeit in the imperfect form of a constitutional monarchy) were the Founders' heritage to Balbo's generation. There was much to take pride in, but there was also the shame of the undeniably massive outflow of Italian *emigranti*, primarily to the United States. Too poor to make a go of it in modern Italy, between 1900 and 1914 there were an estimated 400,000 emigrants *per year*.[3] For many Italians, America, not Italy, was the land of opportunity. Cities such as New York, San Francisco, and Chicago would soon boast Italian populations to rival those of Naples or Rome. This was not part of the grand vision of nineteenth-century romantics and progressives such as Mazzini and Garibaldi. Italy, late to the game of nationhood and great power relations, would need to test itself in Europe and abroad to prove itself to its own people.

Balbo's father hung maps throughout the family's home. This meant that Italo and his brothers and sisters were keenly aware of the world's geography. Countries such as the United States and Brazil (another prime destination for *emigranti*), for instance, were not mere abstractions to them. Their worldview was expansive and grounded in knowledge. But *patrie*, love of homeland, was emphasized even more by their schoolteacher father.

The Darwinian worldview popularized by the followers of Herbert Spencer and Friedrich Nietzsche would also become part of the youthful Balbo's education. This dark vision justified the domination of the weak by the strong. Or perhaps, to put it more accurately, the domination of the ordinary by the extraordinary. It had earlier roots in romanticism, certainly. But this was now wrapped in a pseudo-scientific analysis that attracted many influential figures, including the poet and playwright, Gabriele D'Annunzio, as well as the fiery socialist journalist, Benito Mussolini. The flamboyant D'Annunzio found in the exploits of aviators such as Frenchman Louis Blériot something that transcended man's less admirable qualities, as he saw them: the petit bourgeois inclinations toward material comfort and safety, the casual acceptance if not embrace of corruption (both monetary and moral), and the weakness (both physical and moral) of faint hearts. In the waning years of the Belle Époque, these men seemed to welcome some sort of crisis that would allow them, and those like them, to rise in fulfillment of this prophetic vision. The teenage Italo Balbo was equally moved by this new race of flying men. In 1910, he had avidly followed the successful attempt by the Peruvian pilot, Geo Chavez, to fly over the Alps. He mourned Chavez's loss—a result of an accident that occurred when he was descending to land his plane in Milan. The following year, Balbo helped tend one of the signal fires for an air race between Bologna and Venice. And in 1913 he penned a pamphlet to immortalize the life and death of the young Ferrarese pilot, Roberto Fabbri. Balbo's heartfelt words in eulogy of Fabbri would prove to be eerily prophetic regarding his own life: "to salute from on high his beautiful sleeping city and awaken it with the thunder of his powerful motor, making his white aircraft soar around the manly towers of the Castello D'Estense."[4]

⟋⟍

The assassination of Austrian Archduke Franz Ferdinand on June 28, 1914, triggered a series of events that led to a cataclysmic war. Europe, divided into two alliances, brought all of the awful power harnessed by the Industrial Revolution against itself. Italy, initially allied with Imperial Germany, at first stayed out of the terrible conflict. Though technically bound to the German kaiser and his ally Franz Joseph, the aged emperor of Austria-Hungary, Italy's position in 1914 was more ambiguous than it appeared at first glance. Though it had conflicting interests in North Africa with France on the Allied side, it had larger unresolved territorial issues with the Austrians that harkened back to the eighteenth century, even earlier in fact. Thus Italy's "natural" opponent was its ally's ally. The consensus in the summer of 1914 was to sit it out. In fact, if public opinion had been paramount, this is what Italy would have done (much like Spain, its neighbor across the Mediterranean, did—and profited handsomely). However, social and political pressures channeled by a vocal and truculent minority created a climate for intervention that became increasingly difficult to resist. Italo Balbo agitated in support of it. Why? It seems that he was driven primarily by a desire to see Italy engage in a great struggle for its own sake and to regain its "unredeemed" territories on the Adriatic Sea and in the Tyrol from their Austrian overlords. The former speaks to his fundamental immaturity at the time. To the eighteen-year-old Balbo, war was an opportunity to test oneself, and one's values, rather than a horrific and avoidable waste of human life. This talented but restless student was genuinely stirred by the call to arms. Benito Mussolini, thirteen years Balbo's senior, was also stirred to act. It was partly a political calculation on his part, but it was also ideologically driven. Mussolini was attracted by the futurist credo of poets such as D'Annunzio and F. T. Marinetti, calling for men of action to lead the way in the age of machines. These powerful creator-scientist-revolutionaries would be the living, breathing expression of Nietzsche's *Übermensch*. Bound by no moral code or bourgeois notions of the rights of mankind, these "superior" men would lead and the inferior masses would follow. War would open the path to this new order.

Ultimately, the louder, more violent minority got its way (a lesson Mussolini learned very well), and the government negotiated with the Allies for Italy's entry into the war in May 1915 (on quite favorable terms). Italo Balbo volunteered almost immediately. D'Annunzio and Mussolini would also serve.* Balbo had studied mathematics, science, and Latin and had passed his examinations for the Lyceum diploma in 1914, thus singling himself out for officer candidate school and a posting to an elite Alpine regiment.[5] As Italy entered the charnel house of trench warfare in the peaks above the Isonzo River, the savagery loosed against the Austrian enemy following the near-fatal disaster at Caporetto in 1917 created a new kind of man. Shock troops and trench raiders known as the Arditi would strip naked and paint their bodies black before swimming the frigid Piave River to kill via sudden strangulation or thrusts with a dagger. These young men—some of them ex-convicts released specifically for this sort of duty—loved war, relished violence, and respected no one. Their banner was a black flag bearing a skull and crossbones; their slogan, *Me ne frego* (literally "I don't care!" and in spirit, "Fuck it all!")[6]; their future in postwar Italy, uncertain.

Italo Balbo distinguished himself in battle in the final great offensive of the war on the Italian Front—the offensive that ultimately broke the back of the Hapsburg Empire at Vittorio Veneto. For his actions in the bloody assault on the Monte Grappa, and the follow-on assault on Monte Valderoa in late October 1918, he received two silver medals and one bronze medal.[7] In light of his future political and military career, this is important. Balbo led men, successfully, in bloody fighting to achieve an objective. His future chief, however, had not. Benito Mussolini volunteered for an elite Alpine unit, and was posted to the Isonzo Front, but saw no combat. He was not an officer, and though wounded, it was as a result of an accidental explosion during a training exercise, not enemy fire. For months after being released from the hospital, he continued to use the crutches he'd been given. In fact, he used them long after he actually needed them. These two were different men. However, their experience of the war and disillusionment with the peace would bring them together in a shared purpose.

Woodrow Wilson promised a new order in Europe based on self-determination, enforced by an international peacekeeping organization. Rome welcomed him, initially, and was moved by his insistence on paying homage to Mazzini. But the good feelings did not last long. For Gabriele D'Annunzio and Benito Mussolini, the Versailles Treaty represented a "mutilated" peace where the victor (Italy) was treated as a second-rate country. Postwar eco-

---

* D'Annunzio would participate in some of the most daring Italian exploits of World War I. Mussolini was injured in an accident, and was never in combat.

nomic chaos and the rise of Bolshevism in Russia created a climate of crisis on the streets of Milan, Rome, and other cities and towns. Veterans and police battled deserters and peasants waving the banner of the Red Leagues. Into this political and social maelstrom, Balbo (veteran of the ferocious assaults on Monte Grappa in 1918) inserted himself as a champion of veterans and *patria* in his hometown of Ferrara. It was in the cafés of Ferrara and Milan, Turin and Siena, that fascism as a distinct political philosophy was born. The Arditi were its willing shock troops; the skin-headed D'Annunzio, now wearing an eyepatch said to mask a wound incurred in combat, was its bard; and Mussolini, its political genius.

The Adriatic port of Fiume became the first flashpoint in the struggle against this new internationalist order. Awarded by treaty to the new state of Yugoslavia, Fiume's status was not recognized by Italian ultranationalists. They marched on the city (whose population contained a sizeable Italian minority) with D'Annunzio at their head, snorting cocaine, preaching free love, and endorsing the revivifying qualities of the use of violence.[8] D'Annunzio, in many respects the real progenitor of fascism, had early on grasped the power of flight in the realization of Nietzsche's "superior man" and had transferred from a torpedo-boat squadron to the Ministério da Aeronautica during World War I. In one of the most daring feats of the entire war he flew over Vienna, dropping leaflets on the city's residents demanding their immediate surrender.[9] This convergence of aviation, propaganda, and the cult of the superman was a powerful political weapon. Others would take note.

Benito Mussolini, the savvy and connected ex-journalist, humored D'Annunzio's grandstanding in Fiume until the city ran out of food.* Then he returned with vigor to the task of building an actual political party out of the movement spawned by the war and the unsatisfying peace that followed it. The Fascist Party, posturing as the only force able and willing to stand up to Bolsheviks and bandits, adopted the black shirts of the Arditi and sought battle in the streets and power in Parliament. Though only a relatively small minority, men such as the charismatic and handsome Italo Balbo were able to impose their will on the majority, and win. In 1922, they launched a *putsch* grandiosely named the "March on Rome." In the event it was more publicity stunt than *coup d'état*, but it had the same effect. On October 29, the king invited Mussolini to form a government. The ugliness of the trenches, the chauvinism of nationalist bullies, and the roots of a cult

---

* D'Annunzio's farewell speech in Fiume on December 31, 1921: "The night is dark, but each of us has a flame in his hand.... Soon the new year will begin.... A death's head crowned with laurel clenches its teeth over the naked dagger and stares fixedly from its deep eye-sockets into the unknown. To whom does the unknown belong? To us—*a noi*" (quoted in Gallo, *Mussolini's Italy*).

of personality had been brought into the highest chambers of government. Italo Balbo had personally beaten fascism's opponents with his bare fists, and with clubs. He had burned their homes and businesses. He had forced them to drink enough castor oil to simulate drowning, and then laughed as they shit their pants.* His star, too. would rise.

Two years after the March on Rome, Mussolini's henchmen murdered his most vocal critic, the Socialist politician, Giacomo Matteotti. Historian Max Gallo later explained the context that led to this violent act:

> When he [Mussolini] went out, he used a red sports car that he drove fast and recklessly, and in these simple satisfactions that he allowed himself one could already discern the man drunk on his own success, amazed to have made his dream an even larger reality than his imaginings, astonished at being the equal of the greatest. The feeling of being the incarnation of destiny, already quite intense in him, became a firm conviction, shored up by the opinions of the most varied notables and by newspaper campaigns—and those not

---

* Castor oil is made from castor beans, a powerful laxative.

The March on Rome. Benito Mussolini in the center; Italo Balbo second from right (October 29, 1922).

only in Italy. In such a climate, such a man, with such a past and his aspirations for totalitarian power, could no longer tolerate opposition and opponents.[10]

Matteotti was a brave and principled patriot who very publicly exposed the Fascists' systemic voter fraud and voter suppression tactics that had allowed them to gain more power in Parliament. There was much debate then, and much since, over whether Mussolini actually ordered the "hit" or simply in a Henry II–like lapse of judgement had a "Will no one rid me of this priest!" type of moment on which his violent, sycophantic lackeys were only too eager to act. Matteotti's decapitated, naked corpse was discovered by the roadside. The outrage over this murder was widespread and deep. Mussolini himself, momentarily paralyzed by events, expected Parliament to move against him. The monarchy wavered in its support. But nothing happened. Parliament lacked the cohesion and the leadership to remove Mussolini from power. And the king was timid. Once Mussolini realized he wasn't going to be arrested—the thought of resigning in disgrace over the murder of this decent man never seemed to have seriously entered his head—he then moved to turn the tables on his parliamentary opponents, and rammed through a special election law that "legally" allowed a minority (the Fascists) to govern as the majority. Democracy in Italy was effectively dead.

Italian writer Ignazio Silone documented what these new political realities meant in his novel, *Bread and Wine*: "Either we had to submit to it or be crushed by it, either serve it or rebel against it. Once upon a time there were middle ways. But after the war, for our generation, those ways were shut."[11] One of the notable characteristics of Fascist brutality in its Italian incarnation was its use of sexual violence against the wives and sweethearts, sisters and daughters of Socialists, Communists, and liberal, democratic-minded opponents of the regime. Silone recounts a gang rape of the wife of a leader of the Red Leagues that took three hours.[12] Why raise this issue? Did Italo Balbo perpetrate crimes such as these? Given what is known about the character of the man (and much was written about him, and by him), it is difficult to imagine him doing so. On the other hand, he attached his star to the movement that enabled—even encouraged—actions such as these. What responsibility, then, does he have? This is an important question if one is going to look honestly at Italo Balbo's role in aviation history, and twentieth-century history more broadly. Robert Wohl of the University of California, Los Angeles argued that for most people, it was "easier to ignore him than to grapple with his contradictions."[13] The late Balbo biographer, Claudio Segrè, was even more explicit:

I have tried to bring my subject to life and to do him justice. As his contemporaries found, and as my sources, written and oral, testified, he was a likeable man blessed with intelligence, charm, courage, enthusiasm, and humanity. He was also a pillar of a corrupt and cynical regime, the friend and collaborator of a demagogue who led his nation to catastrophe. In these pages, the reader may at times succumb to Balbo's charm and fascination as I did. Nevertheless, I have not forgotten the real nature of the regime that Balbo promoted and served so well—and I hope the reader does not either.[14]

⸺ ◦◈◦ ⸺

The 1920s then represented a watershed in Italian history—the "choice" Ignazio Silone had articulated wasn't really a conscious choice at all, but rather simply acclimating oneself to the new order. For its opponents, it was a cruel time. For Italo Balbo, however—one of the chief architects of fascism's rise to prominence and then dominance in Italy—the Twenties were a time full of unique opportunities. With Mussolini firmly ensconced in power, and increasingly looking the part,* Balbo eagerly assumed his new post at the Ministério da Aeronautica in Rome (first as undersecretary, then as general of an air fleet, and finally, air minister). Initially, the appointment was greeted with a degree of curiosity, not unmixed with skepticism. Balbo possessed great energy, but he was not known as a pilot. In fact, it was not a given that he would—or would need to—learn how to fly in order to direct the air ministry. To his credit, Balbo made a concerted effort to master the skies. Like his hero Garibaldi, he was a "man of action." And it fit perfectly with his Fascist credo; as Italian journalist Guido Mattioli put it, "Every aviator is a born fascist."[15] But perhaps more importantly, flying spoke to him as a man—as a human being.

Fascist Italy had already produced an aviator *par excellence* in Francesco De Pinedo, who on his own piloted a Rome–Melbourne–Tokyo–Rome flight in 1925.† This round-trip air journey of 34,000 miles captured the public's attention. The desire for speed, as well as distance, pushed the Ministério da Aeronautica to achieve victory in the popular Schneider Trophy seaplane races in 1926, with Italian pilots flying the distinctive Macchi M.39 and besting their American counterparts.[16]

Balbo demanded much of himself and of his subordinates. Pilots whose individual skills were notable, but whose egoism or social transgressions were also notable, were cashiered. He appreciated De Pinedo's wealth of experi-

---

* His personal wardrobe was now stocked with multiple uniforms of various hues.
† De Pinedo's mechanic accompanied him, but did not pilot the aircraft.

ence in organizing long-distance air voyages, but not his insistence on solo enterprises of this nature. What Balbo wanted was a professional Aeronautica that worked like a well-oiled machine. Unlike almost all of the other giants of aviation's golden age, Balbo emphasized *groups* of planes conducting long air voyages, working as part of a team, rather than the lone eagle. The military application of this type of coordination was lost on no one involved in aviation. Yet, there was a sense of adventure to it all that appealed strongly to Balbo's sensibilities as well. His vehicle would be the twin-hulled flying boat with its cockpit directly below its giant propeller. The commercial possibilities of sea-based air travel also played a part in his thinking. Today, land-based jet-engine aircraft dominate commercial air travel. That future was by no means foreordained in the 1920s. Looking at these giant seaplanes, it is not difficult to imagine why many once believed the future of commercial aviation belonged to them.

Savoia-Marchetti S.55 Flying Boat. Notice the Fascist symbol painted on the tip of each hull.

In 1928, Balbo led the first of the four aerial cruises that would make his name in aviation history. Cruising the western Mediterranean after departing his base at Orbetello, located on a lagoon bounded by a mountainous and densely wooded peninsula on the shores of the Tyrrhenian Sea, Balbo demonstrated his aeronautical principles in action and in so doing became a willing tool of Fascist propaganda. Sixty-one seaplanes carrying over two hundred pilots and airmen demonstrated a coordination and skill that impressed everyone who witnessed them in action—taking off, flying overhead, and landing gracefully as twin hulls parted the waves. Balbo himself understood his limitations as a pilot, and made it standard procedure to fly with more experienced men in the event he felt overmatched by conditions. But he loved flying! What had started as a position, had become a passion. This first cruise took the Italians to the Spanish naval base at Los Alcazares via Sardinia and Mallorca, then a return leg via Puerto Alfaques and Berre on France's Côte d'Azur. An undertaking of this scale, with all Europe watching, was a major test for Balbo. Mussolini was willing to give him the opportunity to realize his aeronautical ambitions—after all, they suited Mussolini's vision for *his* Italy, and their realization would be *his* success—but failure would be Balbo's alone. And it nearly struck. As aviation historian Robert Wohl later recounted:

> Several of Balbo's technical advisors had warned him against undertaking such a foolhardy enterprise. . . . And indeed a storm at the normally calm base of Los Alcazares near Cartagena nearly fulfilled their prophecies. Only after an Olympian struggle of nearly four hours were Balbo and his men able to secure their planes amidst swells that reached nine feet and winds of sixty miles per hour.[17]

The following year Balbo cruised the eastern Mediterranean, with the Soviet port of Odessa as his final destination. This was a longer air voyage, with a fleet of seaplanes scaled back from sixty-one to thirty-five aircraft. Balbo and his men flew via Taranto, Athens, and Istanbul up the Black Sea coast, and then crossed into Soviet airspace. The fact that fascism had been, at least partly, birthed as an antidote to communism could not have been lost on someone like Balbo. A career black shirt and ex-Squadristi leader, Balbo had personally engaged in violent acts against "reds" back home. Now he was the futuristic leader of an expedition sent to make contact with a mysterious and alien pariah regime. Russia had always represented a bit of the unknown to western Europeans, but this was now enhanced tenfold since the frightening revolution and bitter civil war there. It was interesting that the Soviets reciprocated the Italians' desire to meet, however fleetingly, in that ancient port city. Balbo viewed his Bolshevik hosts more sympathetically than he had anticipated, remarking on their shared disgust with liberal democracies. On the other hand, as his biographer Claudio Segrè explained:

> He was also glad to see traces from time-to-time of pre-revolutionary Russia. They allowed him to escape from the "oppressive atmosphere of bolshevik uniformity" that gave the city a barracks-like air; he wondered at the "perverse mania" that the revolution had for rendering life "uncomfortable, ugly, squalid."[18]

This visit to Stalinist Russia was an odd interlude that proved that even the most extreme ideological polarization was no match for the excitement of heroic aviation. No one better exemplified this heroic streak more emphatically than the American pilot, Charles Lindbergh. The year before Balbo's first Mediterranean cruise, Lindbergh had successfully piloted an airplane he called the "Spirit of St. Louis" across the Atlantic Ocean to France, alone. News of his accomplishment stunned an increasingly jaded world soaked in alcohol and fueled by speculative fortunes. The combination of knowledge, skill, bravery, and audacity that Lindbergh displayed made the champagne taste a little sweeter, for a time.

The great hero of the age: Charles Lindbergh, with his famous airplane (1927).

Lindbergh was no fascist, yet. However, to many he was the purest embodiment of Nietzschean philosophy. His reception at Le Bourget airport in Paris on the night of May 21, 1927, touched off a wild celebration that degenerated into hysteria bordering on anarchy. For his part, Lindbergh demonstrated remarkable restraint and ease of manner in the face of a press and diplomatic crush that would have overwhelmed even more experienced and sophisticated men. His visit to the Arc de Triomphe to pay silent homage at the Tomb of the Unknown Soldier rekindled the flame of Franco-American relations that had gone cold in the haggling over repayment of debts incurred during the 1914–1918 war. Lindbergh seemed to many to have elevated himself above the masses, both figuratively and literally, by his actions. As Robert Wohl explained, "The Superman had passed from the philosophical and literary imagination into technological fact."[19] The future was now.

In Chicago, the Twenties had roared particularly loud. And the champagne had been supplied by a brutal, enterprising son of Italian *emigranti* named Al Capone. To many Americans, when one thought of *Italy*, one thought of columned ruins, Renaissance artworks, and the pope. But when one thought about *Italians*, one thought of Al Capone. The pride some Italian Americans found in Capone's ability to operate with impunity in Chicago was offset, however, by the shame of having their most famous son be a gangster, bootlegger, and murderer. But Italo Balbo provided an alternative. For Italians and Italian Americans, he embodied a new, more dignified, and heroic Italian identity, one that was based on science and technical skill, not violence (it goes without saying that his earlier transgressions in support of Mussolini certainly weren't emphasized by his admirers).

Balbo's refashioning of the Ministério da Aeronautica as a modern, forward-leaning institution was convincingly on display at the air ministry's new headquarters located in Rome's Castro Pretorio district. Learning from his time in America, and his discussions with Henry Ford, Balbo insisted on open, bright workspaces where glass replaced walls whenever possible. Efficiency, professionalism, and transparency were the watchwords of the day for the 1,200 employees working under his scrutinizing eye. The Mediterranean tradition of lunch at home, followed by a brief nap before returning to work, was replaced by an elegant, if severe, canteen where everyone had to eat standing up. There were no chairs! No cubbyholes either, so work that was piling up couldn't be hidden from supervisors.[20] Coughing, sneezing, blowing one's nose, all were frowned upon in the workspaces and in the canteen.

Air Marshal Italo Balbo. *Alamy Images.*

Employees were expected to brush their teeth before returning to their duties (Balbo was even thoughtful enough to provide a toothbrush and toothpaste, just in case one didn't get the hint). It all smacked of the martinet. Yet it also pointed to someone refusing to run a casual workplace—someone who was aiming to be serious about all aspects of what he was trying to do, and to be taken seriously by the world.

On a more somber note, the handsome ministry building featured a list soon after it was inaugurated of the names of all the Italian airmen who had died in accidents, or in combat. The names were etched in stone in the large arched main entryway to the building, leading to its inner courtyard. Anticipating sculptor Maya Lin's later Vietnam Veterans Memorial in Washington, DC, the names are simply listed in chronological order of when each airman was lost. There is no designation for rank, or hierarchy of fame—De Pineda, Italo Balbo, Mussolini's son, are indistinguishable from their brother airmen. This, to a very large extent, embodied the collective ethos that Italo Balbo was trying to instill in the Ministério da Aeronautica. The tradition has been maintained ever since. It's quite moving to see it in person. There are a lot of names. Too many.*

In 1930, Italo Balbo organized his most ambitious aerial cruise to date. The plan was to fly, via Africa, nearly five thousand miles from his base at Orbetello to visit the great coastal cities of Brazil: Salvador de Bahia and Rio de Janeiro. The distance across the Atlantic from Africa to Brazil was daunting, but this had already been traversed. No, it was the scale of his conception—

---

* According to Italian aviation historian Gregory Alegi, "In Balbo's time, an airman died every 1,000 hours of flying. In an often overlooked measure of the progress, fatalities have dropped to less than one per 100,000 hours. Probably less fascinating than breaking a speed record, but much firmer grounding to make aviation universally accepted." Alegi, "Ninety Seconds over Tobruk," *Aviation Historian* no. 13, October 15, 2015.

The Aeronautica Building in Rome. Note the ancient Roman ruins in the foreground—the building is located in the Castro Pretorio neighborhood, which has seen a continuous military presence on the site since the days when the emperors' Praetorian Guard had barracks there. *Courtesy of the Aeronautica Militare.*

twelve giant Savoia-Marchetti S.55 flying boats—that captured the imagination of the public, and of his boss, Il Duce.

The air route from Europe across the Strait of Gibraltar to Morocco, then down the western coast of Africa to Dakar, had already been established by the famous French air company, Aeropostale, in the 1920s. Known simply as *La Ligne* ("the Line") by its employees, it made the delivery of intercontinental air mail, if not ordinary, at least regular. Ultimately, it expanded its service to South America, delivering mail via express steamers across the Atlantic to Brazil where its pilots then flew the mail down the coast to Uruguay and Argentina. By the late 1920s service had reached Paraguay and crossed the Andes to deliver mail to Chile. The pilots of La Ligne became legendary in their own time. Perhaps the most famous of these was Antione de Saint Exupéry. This was largely though not exclusively due to the beautiful, spare prose he wrote about his experiences in Africa and South America. He is best known to modern readers for his novella, *The Little Prince* (set in a desert after an aviator is forced to make a crash landing). Within La Ligne itself though, it was his counterpart, Jean Mermoz, who was lionized above all others for his skill and bravery in delivering the mail. And it was Mermoz who pioneered the direct delivery of air mail from Senegal to Natal on the northeastern coast of Brazil in 1930, in a flight of over nineteen hours' duration. Mermoz would later lend his celebrity to the French variant of fascism by joining the Croix-de-Feu political movement. Saint Exupéry himself would flirt with fascistic ideology, if not its politics, throughout the 1930s before rejecting it altogether. Mermoz's death at sea in 1936, in what would have been his twenty-fourth trans-Atlantic crossing, stunned the world of aviation. He was greatly mourned. It was this same route that Italo Balbo hoped to exploit to bring an "armada" of Savoia-Marchetti S.55s to Brazil.

There was a business angle to Balbo's ambitious plans as well. Italy's aircraft industry hoped to make inroads into the new markets of Latin America. The "flying boats" with their twin hulls, allowing room for both passengers and mail, could compete for lucrative potential contracts with businessmen in Rio and Santos, Montevideo and Buenos Aires. In fact, the plan was to sell the Savoia-Marchettis and leave them in South America, returning by ship back to Europe once the locals had been suitably impressed.

On December 17, 1930, Balbo's much reduced armada of twelve seaplanes (with two additional planes and their crews in reserve) and fifty men left their secluded base at Orbetello and headed west across the Tyrrhenian Sea. Balbo, impatient to be off, had ignored warnings of a cyclone in their path and nearly lost the expedition before it started. He and his pilots battled through a storm that gave a savage beating to the Savoia-Marchettis. The air

Antoine de Saint Exupéry (left), and Jean Mermoz (right). DR / *Succession Saint Exupéry-d'Agay*

voyage would take four days before resuming the cruise. Balbo had learned a crucial lesson regarding meteorology.[21] Better to wait until conditions improved and be delayed than to go ahead, weather be damned, and not arrive at all.*

After jumping off from Los Alcazares to cross from Spain to Africa, the Italians made their way down the coast of Morocco, then to Senegal, and finally to Boloma in the Portuguese colony of Guiné. For Balbo's seaplanes to

---

* Later, when stuck in Iceland en route to Chicago in 1933, Balbo showed he had learned this lesson well by not continuing the cruise until the weather permitted.

reach Natal without being forced to make a water landing en route required each to carry a fuel load far greater than those they had previously carried. In addition, of course, the engines powered by this fuel would need to get the aircraft into the air carrying the men, supplies, water, and the weight of the aircraft itself. Trans-Atlantic crossings had been achieved both before and after Lindbergh's pioneering solo nonstop flight. Far more, however, had failed. And none of them had involved this many planes of this large a size. As daunting as the 1,864 miles of ocean ahead of them were, it was the takeoff that caused the greatest consternation. This was not for the faint of heart. Balbo intended to leave in the early morning hours to take advantage of the moonlight and the more favorable cooler temperatures for liftoff. But on the date set (January 5, 1931), clouds veiled the moon and in the tropical blackness the pilots had to rely on their altimeters to tell them where they were relative to the ocean they were leaving below. It was then that tragedy struck, when one of the seaplanes, its engine overheating due to the tropical temperatures and the strain of lifting so much weight into the sky, exploded in the darkness below. Four airmen and their craft vanished without a trace off the coast of Africa. Two seaplanes still remained to take off. Letting the motors cool first, they attempted to gain the sky, but one of the planes lost airspeed and slammed into the sea, killing another crewman. Twelve planes were headed west into the night, while two that had flown with them through the cyclone and down the African coast would not. Five brave Italian airmen were dead. This night would bring home to Italo Balbo and his men the grim truth that what they were doing might very likely kill them.

The strain of that journey into the darkness, knowing the ocean that they couldn't see was ever-present below them, must have tried the nerves of every man involved. Training, technical knowledge, and skill all played a role, certainly—but will cannot be underestimated when calculating the factors that led to success. Fuel powered the powerful engines, but will powered the men. Six hours into the journey, the sun began to shed its first rays from behind them to the east. As it so often does, the sunrise buoyed the spirits of Balbo and his men. Ultimately two more aircraft had to make emergency landings at sea due to overheating. The Italian government had had the foresight to assign vessels as minders for the seaplanes in the event of an SOS call. One of these was towed to Natal to join its sister planes, but the other sank in the South Atlantic. This time, fortunately, there was no loss of life. Too many had already died.

Reaching the coast of Brazil brought a great sense of relief and accomplishment, but it was bittersweet. Cameramen filming the expedition captured a pensive Balbo standing aboard the wing of his craft, his dark black hair cropped close on the sides, wearing a black shirt and suspenders, a cigarette dangling from his mouth above his now-famous Vandyke beard.[22] He looked every bit the swashbuckling adventurer, missing only perhaps an earring to complete the effect. Brazil lay at his feet; his fame was now of the intercontinental, not just European, variety. The ten remaining Savoia-Marchettis would prove to be more than sufficient to make an impression in the land of samba.

The appearance of the giant white formations in the azure tropical skies caused a sensation in the Brazilian public and press. For Italian Brazilians, the wonder was complemented by a sense of buoyant national—Italian—pride. The staggering tide of impoverished Italian *emigranti* who had left Italy beginning in the 1880s had not only gone to North America; they had also come to Brazil and Argentina in large numbers. Vast coffee plantations—the source of much of Brazil's wealth—had begun the transition from slave labor to hired hands in the late nineteenth century as the country finally moved toward emancipation. But this was labor-intensive work. The Italians were in for a shock when they realized they were trading poverty for back-breaking serfdom. They brought with them radical political ideologies and eventually were seen as undesirable, and ungovernable, by the country's elites, but they were there to stay. The coffee barons eventually looked east to Japan for agricultural laborers, to replace the unruly Italians. One of the scions of the coffee nobility was the pioneering aviator, Alberto Santos-Dumont. Once the toast of Paris, Santos-Dumont had retreated into reclusive anonymity as he struggled with the effects of a debilitating illness. Thus, Brazil possessed a national context for the arrival of Italian aviators and appreciated them for who they were, and what they had accomplished.

Wearing black shirts underneath their flight suits, the aviator-celebrities were also a potent symbol of fascism. It is important to note that this was long before wars of aggression and genocide had irrevocably discredited this ideology. In 1931, fascism seemed to many the world over, including in America, to be the antidote to Bolshevism. It was seen as a more virile, modern solution to the world's problems than the fusty old parliamentary and democratic institutions championed by the now-dead Woodrow Wilson. With the rise of the authoritarian Brazilian President Getúlio Vargas, Fascist Italy anticipated a strong relationship with the giant country where so many of their long-lost brothers and sisters lived.

The journey southwest down the coast became one long spectacle, as then almost all of Brazil's major cities were located along the route. The white sand beaches, swaying green palms, and towns and cities with buildings of white stucco and orange tiled roofs swept past below as the cheering crowds looked skyward at their new heroes. With stops in Pernambuco and Bahia, the Italians had some opportunity to taste the sweet Southern Hemisphere midsummer air. But Rio de Janeiro, *Cidade Maravilhosa,** was the main, and final objective. No city in the world can boast a more stunning natural topography than Rio, with its necklace of beaches along Guanabara Bay and Botafogo Bay, its lush tropical headlands and mounts rising like jeweled green breasts from the sea. Balbo's seaplanes, gleaming white above the famed Pão de Açúcar, made one of the most viscerally beautiful landings in aviation history as they came to rest amid the calm waters of Botafogo Bay.[23] It was like poetry. And no one appreciates a poet like a Brazilian. Robert Wohl recounted Balbo's impressions, which were much in line with his hosts':

> Their arrival, Balbo later wrote, was an apotheosis in brilliant golden sunlight and empyrian blue worthy of Dante . . . Balbo was so overcome by the spectacle of this "paradise on earth" that he felt it transcended the fantasy of the greatest painters and poets who had tried to imagine paradise in the world to come. "Perhaps in creating the bay of Rio, God wanted to demonstrate that all art derived from him."[24]

Rio was then still the capital of Brazil, and its grand public buildings and thoroughfares were more reminiscent of Paris than the rest of South America (with the possible exception of Buenos Aires). Noted for its beautiful women, fast nightlife, and haunting music, the city provided endless distractions for the Italian airmen. As he had in Russia, Italo Balbo proved himself adept at representing his country in the public eye. Receptions, reviews, parties, and balls all required the optimum mixture of charm and dignity. In Brazil, a country settled by the Portuguese, the population felt a kindred spirit in Balbo, a fellow Latin with a Latin soul. Much later on, when Mussolini was flattered by Hitler's insinuations that Italians were also Aryans, Balbo, proud of his heritage, would have none of it. And perhaps he remembered his history books that he had read as a boy, recounting how his hero, Garibaldi, had come to Brazil and met his great love and fought beside the famed gaúchos

---

* Brazilian writer Coelho Neto had given the city its nickname—the Marvelous City—after his experiences living there in his youth.

for their freedom. Balbo would write about his experiences during the cruise in his book, *Stormi in volo dell'Oceano*, adding an important contribution to the literary genre produced by the aviators themselves during aviation's golden age.

In Brazil, in 1931, Balbo was indeed the man of the hour. But there was another, older figure, who also appealed strongly to Brazilians, one who more closely resembled their national hero, Santos-Dumont, in his worldview, and in his view of the role aviation could play in that better world. His name was Hugo Eckener.

CHAPTER 4

Zeppelin

Hugo Eckener was born nearly thirty years before his Italian counterpart, in Flensburg on Germany's Baltic Sea coast, in 1868. This part of Germany, known as Schleswig-Holstein, had been claimed by the Kingdom of Denmark, and it took a series of wars between Prussia, Austria, and Denmark between 1864 and 1866 to determine its sovereignty. Prussia unified Germany five years later; thus, Eckener grew up a subject of the kaiser, not the Danish king. But his hometown was much closer to Copenhagen than Berlin. The Viking seafaring spirit seemed to have been hardwired into young Hugo. He would always consider himself a "sea dog" at heart, even long after he had left the waves for the clouds. As an adolescent, he neglected his studies and spent as much time as he could on the water. Flensburg itself was set on a picturesque fjord hemmed in with forests of beech. Beyond lay the Baltic: a slate-gray and pale-blue sea whose waters have more in common with the stormy North Atlantic than the inland lake it appears to be on a geographer's map. To sail these waters alone took nerve and skill. Eckener's biographer, Douglas Botting, made a telling observation about the effect this period in Eckener's life would have on later events: "Sailing was his paramount interest, and it was through sailing that he acquired his extraordinary ability to read the weather in all its guises."[1]

When assessing Eckener's career as a zeppelin commander *par excellence*, one is inevitably drawn to his own personal accounts of his many air voyages over land and sea—and, in the process, just as inevitably realizes how much this almost preternatural grasp of wind, clouds, rain, the light of the sky, heat, and cold shaped his success. The young lad on the Baltic absorbed lessons from the natural world that could never be learned in a classroom.

The first forty years of Eckener's life corresponded approximately with the Belle Époque, a "beautiful time" for many. This more gracious, more graceful age was a time of tremendous scientific and technological progress—which, coupled with the effects of the Industrial Revolution, also led to increased material progress. Living standards were consistently rising—though not for all, or at least not at the same rate—and optimism in the potential for improvement in the human condition was widespread. Eckener eventually pursued his studies in physics and math seriously enough to earn admission to a university far to the south in Bavaria. There he indulged a wide-ranging intelligence that included courses in art, history, Medieval literature, and logic. Hugo Eckener was becoming a true Renaissance man, without any apparent conscious effort. His continued pursuit of knowledge took him to universities in Berlin and Leipzig. He dabbled in philosophy before earning his doctorate in experimental psychology. His work in this field gained him significant enough notice to be offered, at age twenty-four, a position in Canada at the University of Toronto.[2] But he stayed in Germany. Ultimately, Eckener's interest in psychology spurred him to write a book on the social effects of capitalism (a phenomenon strikingly evident and relevant in Germany at the time—his own father was a tobacco entrepreneur; his mother, the daughter of a shoemaker). But this didn't pay. Ultimately, now married, the philosopher-turned-psychologist-turned-economist took on work as a freelance journalist to meet his financial obligations. At first glance this might appear incongruous, but Eckener was a keen observer who possessed an innate ability to string sentences together—in a word, he could write.* It was in this capacity—not as a mariner, a philosopher, a psychologist, or as an economist—that he first encountered the man that would change his life forever: Count Ferdinand von Zeppelin.

Eckener had been sent from his newspaper to cover the launch of the "mad" count's "air ship" on Lake Constance near Friedrichshafen, Germany, in the autumn of 1900. Friedrichshafen is located on the German shore of Lake Constance, the border between Switzerland to the south and Germany to the north, but also the source of the Rhine River flowing from the foothills of the Alps to the North Sea. By his own admission, Eckener was initially dubious of the man and his machine, though he would come to admire his determination, if nothing else. In 1905, he again reported on one of the count's

---

* The various memoirs Eckener wrote after he had retired from public life contain some of the most beautiful passages ever written about the wonder and beauty of flight. It was this combination of the man of science and the poet that mark Eckener as a man of genius.

efforts to achieve sustained powered flight, which again ended in failure. But the count was sufficiently impressed with Eckener's evenhanded account of a mediocre showing to call on him in person with a note of gratitude. The journalist became a publicist; the publicist became a propagandist; and the propagandist became a pilot. Zeppelin may have been old and cranky, but he also was a visionary, and one with an eye for talent. Hugo Eckener would come to embody the concept of lighter-than-air ship travel the world over in the decades ahead—essentially becoming Zeppelin's heir in the public's mind. But the two men were quite different.

Count Ferdinand von Zeppelin at the helm of one of his "air ships." *Alamy Images.*

Ferdinand von Zeppelin was an aristocrat of the old school, and a career army officer. After falling out with a young Kaiser Wilhelm II in 1890 he was cashiered from the military at the age of fifty-two. Devastated, he looked to find a way to prove his worth to the Fatherland. As a younger man he had traveled to the United States to observe the Civil War, and in a side-escapade had found himself aloft in an observation balloon in St. Paul, Minnesota. The experience was a great thrill, and it seemed to have planted the first seed that would germinate later in his mind. From that point on, Zeppelin was a casual devotee of news of aerial innovation. Now, retired before his time, the count decided to act on his aeronautical interests in a more practical sense. Fancy had become a hobby, hobby then became passion, passion would become obsession, obsession became necessity. His great purpose and belief was that by devising a flying machine (which he envisioned as a balloon-like craft traveling between fixed points under its own power), he could contribute in a decisive manner to his country's military capacity. In Zeppelin's mind, his invention would enable Germany's military to dominate its enemies (such as France) in any future war. His airship, or what would popularly come to be called a "zeppelin," would be the new cavalry for a new century. Scouting far ahead of the main body of the army, a zeppelin could provide crucial battle-winning intelligence. Frankly, it's remarkable that the count was able to put his fanciful ideas into actual practice. In 1898, he began construction on the first of his airships in a village on the lake. He felt that landing on water would be gentler on his airship than bringing it back to earth ashore. The design of the LZ-1 was based on the concept of gas-filled cells creating lift (as in a balloon) but with a rigid, more durable, structure. The distinctive elongated tube appearance of the zeppelin, rather than the typical round-shaped balloon, was due to this internal rigid structure. Engines and steering mechanisms would then allow for powered flight. It was a flop. In its maiden voyage on July 2, 1900, the LZ-1 stayed aloft for all of eighteen minutes and less than four miles. Smaller, less ambitious, non-rigid "dirigibles" had already exceeded the LZ-1's performance. Unsurprisingly, the German military was cool to the concept. And yet, as Douglas Botting explained, "The crowd lining the shore and watching from boats on the water was not disappointed. . . . It had been an extraordinary spectacle."[3]

Dangerous, costly, and notoriously temperamental in anything but a calm wind, the zeppelin was also a wonder to behold. No one who saw one could fail to be moved. A zeppelin looked like a visitor from another world. For a half a dozen years the "mad" count continued in his quest, dismissed by the experts, but increasingly drawing sympathy from ordinary people. By this time, he was approaching seventy years of age, but he refused to abandon his quest. Years later, looking back on this exciting, uncertain period in the development of zeppelins, Eckener explained the secret of the count's ultimate success: "everyone underestimated the old gentleman's determination."[4]

The first one-on-one meeting between the two men was initiated by the count after his most recent disappointing effort. With a sailor's eye, Eckener had pointed out the giant airship's shortcomings in his article, but he had avoided using the dismissive tone of other critics. He was fair, and the count recognized and appreciated this in the younger man, and wanted to express it in person. A few nights later, Zeppelin invited Eckener to dinner and broached the idea of him coming to work for the zeppelin project as a public relations man pitching the airship to the general public. Eckener was game—and the rest, as they say, is history. Over time, Hugo Eckener became more than a mouthpiece; he felt compelled to take an active role in the airship program itself. What better way to convince the public than by actively participating in flights and learning how, eventually, to pilot the craft on his own? This said a lot about Eckener as a person. He wasn't just an observer; he was a doer.

In 1908, Count von Zeppelin experienced his greatest success to date with the air voyage of the "LZ-4" down the Rhine Valley to Strasbourg in Alsace. But a series of equipment malfunctions forced the craft to land, and an unexpected squall resulted in an accident that ignited the airship's hydrogen gas cells, leading to a terrific explosion. Fortunately, no one was injured, but it certainly appeared that the count was now finally, irrevocably defeated. But he wasn't. The tens of thousands of ordinary people who had lined the bridges over the Rhine to cheer the zeppelin on its journey now rallied behind his vision, donating their own funds to keep the project alive. Zeppelin clearly had touched something in the German soul. What was it: Nationalism? The spirit of adventure? Anxiety over military preparedness? Sympathy for the underdog? Likely it was some combination of all of these. For the count himself, military uses remained the priority. Regardless, people were moved. Hugo Eckener was moved as well. But for Eckener, the great sense of possibility for the count's invention lay not in war but rather in connecting the world, exploring it, sharing it. He had evolved a higher purpose in what was increasingly clear would be his life's work. Looking back, he explained that he had wanted to "combine his moral and political ideals with the purely technical."[5] By 1913, infused with cash and buoyed by popular support, the zeppelin project was a resounding success. Airship passenger service inside Germany was becoming a reality. The Belle Époque continued on. Peace and technological advancement seemed to go hand in hand. In apparent affirmation of this, Eckener himself would declaim,

"Peace nourishes; war devours."[6] But war was coming, and aviation would inevitably be co-opted by it.

Man's obsession with flight had taken on an entirely new dimension with the Wright brothers' experimental flights on a windy, remote sandbar in North Carolina in 1903. Lighter-than-air flight in balloons and dirigibles of various shapes and sizes had pushed the limits of the possible in the nineteenth century, but the brothers' bird-like design with its small gasoline-powered engine took aviation in a radically different direction. Over the next decade, pioneers such as Alberto Santos-Dumont, Louis Blériot, Glen Curtiss, and Gianni Caproni accelerated the pace of aeronautical design. Speed and distance competitions pushed the technology even further. Both land- and sea-based aircraft held their own prestigious races, with the winners claiming the Gordon Bennett Trophy and Schneider Trophy, respectively. The public followed the exploits of successful pilots as they would matinee idols, and clamored for more. But the various military staffs throughout Europe were also paying careful attention. "Aero planes" possessed great potential, but zeppelins had two important advantages: distance (range) and duration (the length of time one could stay airborne).

For the Wright brothers, there was another, darker, element at work in the air as well. Soon after repeating their successful experimental flights, the brothers sought an audience with U.S. military officials in Washington. Finding only lukewarm support at home, they then brought their aircraft to Europe and in short order found a far more enthusiastic reception awaiting them among foreign governments. By 1911, heavier-than-air aircraft were being used to bomb targets on the ground in Italy's war to wrest control of Libya from the Ottoman Turks. By 1918 they were being used to bomb civilians indiscriminately in London, Venice, and Paris. But so were zeppelins. It took time, but once Germany's government and people embraced the old count and his invention, they were convinced it could play a critical role in wartime. Hugo Eckener wasn't convinced. But by this time—recognized as the most skillful airship pilot in the fleet—he felt it was his patriotic duty to train others.

When World War I broke out in the summer of 1914, Eckener (now forty-six years old) supported his country and offered his services to the newly formed Naval Airship Division. The war provided some satisfaction for those, like Count von Zeppelin, who had put their faith in the airship as a useful and potent element in future German military operations. Eckener, in his role as instructor, took his student-pilots out over the North Sea into active combat zones. It was here, above the waves, that he felt Zeppelins could perform to their best advantage, scouting the vast spaces for enemy craft. In the titanic sea battle off Jutland in 1916, a zeppelin had provided crucial intelligence that saved the German Navy from what Eckener characterized would have been "severe losses."[7] On the other hand, Eckener lamented the loss of zeppelin crews sent to bomb England who never returned. To him, it was clear that reconnaissance (particularly at sea), not strategic bombing, was the most useful function of an airship in wartime. However, the German High Command's desire to bring the war home to civilians in Allied cities took precedence. Compared to the later mass bombings of cities from the air, by airplane, in World War II, these zeppelin raids were more psychological in their effect on civilian morale than purely destructive. But there was no doubt that there was something unsettling, even sinister, about these giant silvery behemoths crossing the North Sea at night to rain down death on the unsuspecting below.

Howard Hughes later produced a film called *Hell's Angels* (1930) that included a haunting sequence involving an airship raid on London, capturing the zeppelin's aura of spectral dread. The film's plot is nearly incoherent, but Hughes's air combat sequences are not. They transcend the film's mediocrity. To add dramatic tension to the nighttime zeppelin raid, the airship must lose weight in order to outclimb the range of enemy fire, and the result is the patriotic suicide of a number of the crew, who drop to their deaths in an attempt to save the zeppelin. It's a horrifying waste of human life. To a large degree, the same could be said of the campaign to bomb Allied cities with zeppelins, as a whole. The technological edge in the sky would shift irrevocably in favor of the airplane. Even the cover of darkness provided little protection from retaliation. After the initial shock of nighttime zeppelin raids had passed, the British military prepared countermeasures (powerful intersecting searchlights, airplanes specifically for use as night fighters, and shrapnel to be fired great distances into the sky). The effect could be devastating. The site of great, flaming airships falling to Earth became part of the English experience during the war. In response, a new generation of zeppelin designers created airships that could climb to heights far beyond the reach of searchlights and enemy aircraft. Four miles up, in the thin, cold air, zeppelin crews were experiencing conditions unknown up to that time. This remarkable leap in zeppelin technology greatly increased the giant airships' range (in one twenty-hour raid, a fleet of airships traveled over Copenhagen to London and then Paris before eventually finishing their cruise over the Mediterranean Sea). However, being so high, their effectiveness in seeing and hitting their targets was greatly diminished. By 1917, it had become apparent that large bomb-laden, multi-engine airplanes were better suited for raids on urban centers (even the count, who died that year, agreed), and zeppelins were phased out of the war. But the targeting of civilians from the air continued until 1918.

The exponentially more lethal use of aircraft in the war, and Germany's humiliation at the end of it, left Eckener shaken but resolved to continue Count von Zeppelin's work, now free of any military expedient. Those years after the war were painful for Germany. The unloved Weimar Republic had replaced the Empire. The kaiser and his generals were either in exile or discredited relics of a bygone age. Two men, more than any others, would rise in this period to offer Germans a way forward, free of the past. Adolf Hitler would use his experiences as a soldier in the trenches of the Western Front to gain credibility with his fellow veterans—many of them angry and bitter; all of them capable of shocking violence—to build a political movement aimed at national regeneration through rearmament and racial purity. Hugo Eckener rejected this. Instead, the zeppelin would be the vehicle for a renewed sense of German identity and national pride based on peace, technological achievement, and international cooperation. It was a powerful symbol. It was a cosmopolitan symbol. And the wartime innovations had made it a vastly enhanced wonder of aviation.

Eckener was the ideal man to take over the count's legacy. His understanding of the nature of zeppelin design, and its capabilities and weaknesses, was unmatched. Part of this, as has previously been mentioned, can be attributed to the many hours he spent as a boy and as a young man, sailing on the Baltic Sea. His prime directive to those he trained to become airship pilots was that a zeppelin was a "ship" and not an airplane, and as such needed to be handled in a similar manner to an ocean-going vessel. For Eckener, to travel by airship was not to "fly," but rather to "voyage." Words perhaps, but words are important. This distinction between flying and voyaging was emphasized by Eckener to all with whom he came in contact as a result of his connection with the zeppelin enterprise. And by the late 1920s, the company founded by Ferdinand von Zeppelin was producing airships of a size compatible to the more modestly sized ocean liners of the day. This size was largely due to the rigid aluminum interior over which the silver-painted fabric exterior was stretched. Enclosed inside this structure were large bags (or "cells") filled with hydrogen gas. This was the secret to the airship's buoyancy. Gondolas hung below the aluminum interior, providing rooms for a bridge, navigation, communications, a steward, and, ultimately, passenger accommodations. The view was unparalleled. In the twenty-first century, the Zeppelin Company has renewed passenger service in the *Zeppelin NT*—a hybrid of sorts between the earlier zeppelins that featured a rigid, ring-like interior filled with gas cells, to a rigid triangular interior structure inside a gas bag filled with helium. But the effect of flying as a passenger is the same. One seems to be floating above the landscape below, but not aimlessly. There is direction. It's uncanny.

—— ◦⊶◦ ——

The first zeppelin built after the war was for use by the U.S. Navy. Christened the USS *Los Angeles*, it was an unqualified success. And its personal delivery by Eckener and his crew in the first-ever trans-Atlantic crossing by a zeppelin made the "Doctor"* an overnight sensation in America, and a national hero in his homeland.

At the war's end, it appeared the dream of Ferdinand von Zeppelin was to be brought to an end—at least in Germany. The victorious Allies had imposed very harsh restrictions on German aviation, and this included airships. While aspiring aviators carried on the German tradition in airplanes, flying gliders from the *Wasserkuppe* in the early 1920s,[8] Eckener was busy trying to revive the airship project by finding a way around the Allied restrictions as well. If German expertise in zeppelin design and manufacture could be put to constructive use for one of the victor nations, then perhaps a general loosening of restrictions would follow. The opportunity presented itself as a result of German airship crews scuttling their own craft to deny them as spoils of war to the victorious Allies.† One of the Allied powers, the United States, was (it was determined) owed $800,000 for the loss of its share of the lost airship. Eckener intervened and made a bold proposal to the American military commission to construct (and deliver) a new airship to the U.S. Navy in Lakehurst, New Jersey. A craft capable of crossing the Atlantic would require a scale at least equal to the largest zeppelins built during the war. By reaching this agreement with the U.S. Navy, Hugo Eckener had resurrected the zeppelin project in a phoenix-like manner. The construction of the giant new airship commanded all the energy of those involved at Friedrichshafen. Where once Ferdinand von Zeppelin had hoped to cross a lake, now they were readying a vessel to cross an ocean. The sense of purpose must have been remarkably strong. Eckener and his team were not only on the cutting edge of lighter-than-air aviation technology; they were also blazing a potentially glorious, peaceful path toward national rejuvenation. The contrast with the odd-looking, hate-filled Nazi "Brownshirts," beginning to make their presence felt in German cities, could not have been more stark.

---

* An honorific Eckener had earned for his earlier work in experimental psychology.
† This was inspired by the German Navy's scuttling of the High Seas Fleet in Scapa Flow, Scotland, in 1919.

The voyage of the ZR-3 (later rechristened the *Los Angeles* by the U.S. Navy) from Friedrichshafen to Lakehurst in 1924 would prove to be one of the most important events in Hugo Eckener's life. Greater fame, and heartbreak, certainly lay ahead for him, but this first transoceanic crossing was a step into the unknown. It required skill, faith in science, confidence in the quality of the zeppelin team's workmanship, nerve, and leadership. It also required vision. Hugo Eckener possessed all of these qualities. On October 13, 1924, the ZR-3 ascended into the skies above Friedrichshafen and headed west across southern France. Germany's archenemy in the war was now at peace, looking from high above like a "garden":

> We looked down with a sort of sensual pleasure on the stony hills where the vineyards of Burgundy grow, and later came to the region where the Bordeaux grapes stretch across level fields in the soft sea air. How different did we find both the country and the flavour![9]

As the sun set in the west, the airship crossed northern Spain and headed out to sea. In an era still without radio direction-finders and signals, precise navigation was absolutely crucial in this endeavor. This was the human factor. The plan called for a route directly west, skirting the Azores in the mid-Atlantic. By noon the following day, Eckener and his men could see the peak of one of the Azores' dormant volcanos above the clouds:

> The beautiful scene spread out before us. A low-lying cloud ceiling covered the greater part of the ocean, but rising above it in magnificent splendour was the tremendous 7,500-foot peak of Mount Pico, on the island of the same name, along whose flanks we were gliding. A strange spectacle, this fantastic mountain isle apparently floating in the air in the midst of the ocean! Finally it vanished in the distance, and the sea beneath us was again visible.[10]

The remainder of the voyage was not as pleasant. Wind and weather (a low-pressure system over the Atlantic) forced Eckener to alter his route and head for the southern tip of Newfoundland before coming about and cruising down the coast of New England to reach his destination—the great New World metropolis of New York. That same year—1924—George Gershwin was completing his masterpiece, "Rhapsody in Blue." One can almost hear the strains of Gershwin's music in Eckener's description of the sensation of arriving at dawn and seeing New York City for the first time:

> At daybreak we were off Sandy Hook, seventy-seven hours after our take-off from Friedrichshafen. The bay and the low shore were

shrouded in a light morning mist, but the fantastic shapes of the skyscrapers towered above it and gleamed in the rising sun. The imposing picture, celebrated in all languages, which this overpowering giant metropolis of daring and enterprising spirit offers to the arriving stranger, appeared to us with a double beauty, a fairy-tale city to which we had abruptly come out of the dark, empty sea.[11]

After circling above the city, Eckener descended to the Naval Air Station at Lakehurst to be greeted by a multitude of reporters, spectators, and assorted well-wishers. In America, the zeppelin craze had begun! It would continue unabated for the next thirteen years, until it ended as dramatically as it began, in the same place it began.

———◦◦◦———

The success of the first crossing of the Atlantic by the ZR-3 provided Hugo Eckener with powerful evidence to support his vision for the future of airship travel. Back in Germany, he had expected enthusiastic support from a German government basking in his reflected glory. In this, he was disappointed. Like the "mad" Count von Zeppelin before him, Eckener had to rely on his own devices and support from the public to continue to the next step in the zeppelin project: to build the greatest airship ever constructed up to that time. And then to establish permanent, regular service between Europe and the Americas with zeppelins carrying paying passengers and mail, not bombs. He succeeded.

The *Graf Zeppelin* was a triumph of engineering, utility, and style, unmatched in the sky. Its purpose was not only to earn profits for the company founded by the count for whom it was named, but also to demonstrate the sustainability of commercial air travel. To achieve this, Eckener had appealed directly to the German people to raise funds for the airship's construction by giving lectures the length and breadth of Germany to stimulate interest in this great national undertaking. His background as a journalist and publicist stood him in good stead as the German economy slowly began to revive, and people opened their wallets to further a dream.

The *Graf* (German for "count") was not only the largest zeppelin built up to that time, it was also the most technologically advanced and elegantly appointed airship in history until the construction of its sister ship, the *Hindenburg*, in 1936. Everything that had been learned since the zeppelin project had begun thirty years before was now brought to bear in the construction of what Douglas Botting would call "Doctor Eckener's Dream Machine."* The new Zeppelin had a capacity of 3,707,550 cubic feet (exceeding that of the *Los Angeles*, with its capacity of 2,471,700 cubic feet, by a total of 1,235,850 cubic feet). From end to end it was 775 feet long (over two and a half football fields), and 100 feet in diameter at its thickest.[12] Five specially built Maybach engines producing 2,650 horsepower in total, generated a cruising speed of over 70 miles per hour. Borne aloft by its hydrogen gas cells, the *Graf* was powered by a special mixture of lightweight fuel that allowed it to cruise for 118 hours (approximately 8,400 miles) without landing to take on more fuel.[13] In addition, a gyrocompass replaced the outdated magnetic compass, making the all-important navigation in transoceanic travel far more precise. But the new airship also needed to accommodate, feed, distract, and make comfortable the passengers who would be paying richly for the pleasure of zeppelin flight. This required not only additional space in gondolas attached to the ship's underbelly for the passengers, but also for additional crew (stewards, chefs, and such) that would be serving them in flight.

In an article written a number of years later by Wolfgang Lambrecht, the chief aeronautical officer of the Hamburg-American Line, and in an official brochure produced by the same concern advertising trans-Atlantic zeppelin passenger service at about the same time, one can get a sense of the experience the *Graf* provided its paying customers. Lambrecht's description of "voyaging" aboard the airship is incomparable:

> The comforts of traveling by airship are hard to describe to persons who have not experienced this new mode of travel. The most striking sensation is one of smoothness. There is no throbbing of engines, no sudden pitching or rolling of the craft, no dust and dirt; everything is peaceful and quiet. The motors are located aft of the passenger quarters and might as well be absent as far as harsh noises are concerned. Odors from fuel and cooking are completely absent. Large smoking and lounging rooms, together with spacious promenades, give plenty of room for all. Comfortable cabins are provided with hot and cold water, with real beds in which to sleep in a restful atmosphere. The accommodations have most of the luxuries of steamships, with the redeeming feature that one need not put up with seasickness to enjoy them.[14]

The Hamburg-American Line's brochure emphasized the social and culinary aspects of voyaging aboard the *Graf*:

---

* The title of his excellent biography of Eckener.

All meals are taken in the large public room . . . which is also used as a social room generally. Passengers while away the time by friendly chats with their fellow passengers, by writing, reading, taking snapshots or playing games. . . . The meals served on board the Zeppelin and the choice of wines are in every respect up to the standard of a first-class restaurant. The few specimen menus here re-printed give some idea of the variety of the food.* The wine is sold at moderate charges; and as no other possibilities of spending money are open to passengers, there is no need for them to be unduly economical in gratifying their desires in this respect.[15]

No need to be unduly economical, indeed! The service that the Zeppelin Company and its partner, the Hamburg-American Line, was offering was unprecedented in air travel certainly, and the equal in many respects of first-class travel on the great trans-Atlantic steamers of the day. But in the end, it was an aeronautical proposition. Could it be done consistently and safely? The only way to know for sure was to put the *Graf Zeppelin* to the test in the very sort of conditions it might experience over the Atlantic.

Eckener's first journey to America in the *Graf Zeppelin* proved to be one of the most challenging airship voyages he would ever undertake. Following a successful thirty-six-hour trial flight in Europe, the date was set for the first trans-Atlantic crossing of the new craft. In the event, the departure from Friedrichshafen was delayed due to reports of heavy winds blowing directly into the intended flight path of the *Graf.* Eckener later admitted that he felt pressure to prove the viability of a transoceanic zeppelin service by flying the most direct route to its destination. Setting a course to the south of the broad swath of foul weather would add miles and additional time to the journey, which would be food for the critics claiming the scheme was unviable. Traveling north in what was called the "circle route" was shorter, but notoriously foggy and prone to autumn gales. On October 11, 1928, the *Graf Zeppelin* began its first great test. Eckener had chosen the southern route. Risking people's lives unnecessarily was not part of his modus operandi, critics be damned. The beginning of the journey was more idyll than trial. As Eckener described it:

At top speed we flew down the Rhine, over castles and medieval towns, along the south side of the Black Forest to Basle . . . shortly after noon, we arrived at the Mediterranean, and unforgettable attractions of a new kind again stimulated our senses. It was as if we were softly gliding through an infinity of surrounding misty blue.

---

* Items mentioned include "Poached Eggs with Bacon, Ragout of Veal, Fruit."

Air and sea merged imperceptibly with each other. We flew on, as if set free from hard, rough, material things, in a world of fragrance and soft light. As in a dream, the passengers sat at prettily decorated coffee-tables and, in a mood of wordles ecstasy, enjoyed good Friedrichshafen pastry together with the panorama of the sea.[16]

Alas, the idyll didn't last. South of the Azores, the *Graf* received disturbing radio reports of a terrific thunderstorm to the north. Unexpectedly, an influx of cold air had extended further south than anticipated, creating conditions for severe weather. At 6:00 the next morning, Eckener looked out from the flight deck to see "a blue-black wall of cloud of very threatening aspect"[17] advancing at great speed toward his airship, which itself was traveling at full speed. The combination of the storm and the Zeppelin meeting with such swiftness and, as luck would have it, a less experienced man at the controls of the airship's elevators as they collided, nearly led to catastrophe. The nose of the *Graf* turned suddenly and drastically downward, only to rise too far upward a moment later: "breakfast tables slid off with a crash. . . . Amidst the noise, which was increased by the crash of thunder, it was impossible to tell if the hull structure was breaking up."[18] And then came the rain—torrents of it for one hour. The relief felt by Eckener and his crew over the *Graf*'s ability to successfully weather an Atlantic squall of the first order was tempered by news that the fabric covering the left stabilizing fin had torn. If the tear spread, it would jeopardize the ability of the crew to control the airship. All could be lost.

Director Robert Wise, in his 1975 film, *The Hindenburg*, included a scene where the same damage happens to a stabilizing fin on the *Graf*'s larger sister. In a film with a somewhat weak plot, this scene stands out for its heightened sense of drama. Not only would crewmen need to go out onto the fin in mid-air, replace the torn fabric, and sew it on—they also had to avoid being blown away by the slipstream created by the airship's forward momentum. Engines needed to be cut back while they worked, but this had the effect of the airship dangerously losing altitude. The pressure on those on the flight deck, and the fortitude and skill of those out on the fin, is clear. In real life, it was even more agonizing for Eckener, as one of the volunteers out on the fin was his son, Knut. The rainwater that had fallen so heavily after the squall had hit was weighing down the *Graf*. This was why the engines needed to be engaged: to keep the Zeppelin from falling into the sea. But if he did so, his own son might be swept away. Ultimately, the volunteers succeeded in making the necessary repairs and the *Graf* continued on its journey. But would the repairs hold up under another severe stress on the fin?

For their part, the *Graf*'s first passengers—a mix of experts, potentates, and reporters—had received quite a shock. A number of them had come apart emotionally, fearing the day might be their last. Others had demonstrated a degree of poise that had impressed Eckener; none more so than the Hearst Papers' reporter, Lady Grace Drummond-Hay:

> She greeted me with a gay smile and remarked, looking at the broken china on the floor, "The Good Count has been in a surprising and expensive mood! Well, if we have to, we can get along without cups and saucers." Later, I heard at the moment the crockery tumbled she calmly called out to her friend and colleague, Mr. von Wiegand, "Karl, run quickly to my cabin and see that my typewriter doesn't fall on the floor"! Such coolness, particularly in a woman, could well have prevented the development of a spreading panic.[19]

Off Bermuda, another squall front blocked the *Graf*'s westward progress. Eckener later confided that his decision to enter the squall front with a patched stabilizing fin was the most difficult of a difficult journey. For an hour the *Graf* was battered by wind, rain, and hail, but then calmer skies greeted the giant airship as it approached the American coast. The patch had held. As darkness fell, Lakehurst Naval Station welcomed the weary travelers back to earth.

⁂

The *Graf* had passed its test. It had withstood the worst the Atlantic could dish out, and had safely reached its destination. The return journey to Europe provided more hard-earned lessons regarding the weather patterns of the Atlantic Ocean. But in the end, Hugo Eckener was well satisfied. One could only truly know if one's creation was up to the task if it had been truly pushed to its limits.* It had. And it was ready for something even more daring in conception, to capture the public's attention and stimulate its imagination.

With Charles Lindbergh having piloted his plane solo across the Atlantic the year before, Eckener's idea of establishing regular passenger service from Friedrichshafen to Lakehurst, New Jersey, no longer seemed fanciful. The

---

* Hans-Paul Stroehle of the present-day Zeppelin Company was one of the first instructors and examiners of pilots flying modern zeppelins. He has flown airships on four different continents, twelve countries, and has crossed the United States and Europe several times in an airship. He also was the former deputy director for the Zeppelin Company's flight operations. He expressed great admiration for Hugo Eckener as an airship pilot and as a visionary, but when asked why Eckener succeeded in coming through such harrowing confrontations with the weather, Stroehle said, "He was lucky . . . zeppelins should be not be put under that kind of strain."

following year (1929), with great public fanfare, Eckener piloted the *Graf Zeppelin* on an around-the-world trip to further promote airship travel. The well-heeled passengers in their luxuriously appointed lounge and handsome cabins bestowed a degree of glamour on the enterprise that suited the age. Alone amid the dozens of male passengers and crew on this voyage was a single returning female passenger: Lady Grace Drummond-Hay. This intrepid journalist-flapper-socialite-aristocrat would become Hugo Eckener's most ardent supporter. Their relationship, though it remained platonic, was nonetheless romantic in spirit. He admired her moxie—which she exhibited on more than one occasion—and she admired his consummate skill sailing his airship, and the not inconsiderable reservoir of sangfroid he was able to draw on in dangerous circumstances. He was a man pushing the envelope of the possible while making it appear not only plausible, but perfectly natural.

Lady Grace Drummond-Hay. *Courtesy of Lilo Peter, Harwood Watch Company Ltd.*

Hay's notoriety as a bold aviatrix of sorts was capitalized on by the Harwood Watch Company of Switzerland when they provided her with a new self-winding watch to wear aboard the *Graf*: "By its novel method of providing power the watch has aroused considerable interest, and the curiosity of the public is held by wonder of how it is done."[20]

The *Graf*'s circumnavigation of the globe began on August 7, 1929, at Lakehurst. Press magnate William Randolph Hearst had put up $100,000 for the exclusive story rights in the American and British press. This figure went a long way toward paying the costs of such an ambitious enterprise. Eckener had also begun to tap into the surprisingly lucrative world of stamp collecting to offset costs as well. Philatelists were eager to send and receive mail bearing the *Graf*'s postmark, and the amount of mail carried in its hold increased exponentially with time. The route chosen for circumnavigation would take the zeppelin back across the Atlantic to its base at Friedrichshafen; then across eastern Europe into Soviet Russia. As he had earlier during Italo Balbo's seaplane squadron flight to Odessa, Joseph Stalin seemed to appreciate the attraction that aviation held in the popular mind. Permitting the *Graf* to cross the Soviet Union from west to east—flying above Russia's ancient capital, Moscow; the Ural Mountains; and the seemingly limitless vastness of Siberia—was a generous concession on the part of the mysterious country's suspicious ruler. In the event, unfavorable weather reports forced Eckener's hand, and Muscovites (Stalin included) were left feeling snubbed when the airship failed to keep its rendezvous above the Kremlin.

Siberia proved to have an unsettling effect on many of the passengers and crew. Eckener himself was not entirely immune to these feelings either. The extent of the monotonous, trackless wastes going by beneath them were psychologically disturbing, leading to feelings of isolation. Even the elegant, modern surroundings of the *Graf* failed to dull the somber, reflective mood that many felt. But not all passengers succumbed to the general gloom. As the Zeppelin flew on above eastern Siberia near the Arctic Circle,* Eckener shared a memorable evening with an American:

> During the brief night hours a full moon rose, or at least attempted to rise, for it remained low above the horizon to the south, where it rolled slowly along on its brief course like a huge yellow ball. In the north the brightly glowing sky showed that the sun was only a few degrees below the horizon. An American passenger was so fascinated by these theatrical effects that towards 11 p.m., when everyone else had gone to bed for a brief rest, he called for two bottles of wine and

---

* Summer nights are quite short at these latitudes.

spent the night watching the moon and the twilit heavens. I kept him company for a while, for the wine we were carrying on board was not bad at all, and the celestial spectacle was quite extraordinary.[21]

Finally, the *Graf* reached the Pacific coast, but first the crew had to find their way through a narrow pass in the menacing Stanovoy Mountain range. As Douglas Botting later related, "They had never been charted, and their height was not precisely known." It was a dangerous business:

> On the bridge Eckener and his officers looked tensely ahead as the crest of the pass drew closer. An error now, any unforeseen trick of wind or weather, and a catastrophe could take place from which the chances of survival were almost certainly zero. . . . Transfixed, passengers and crew alike watched as the ground slid by barely 250 feet beneath them. . . . And then a great shout went up in the saloon as well as on the bridge. Stretching away almost directly beneath lay the vivid blue of the Pacific. They were through. "Now that," Eckener cried out, raising his arms in triumph and glee, "is what you call airship flying!" "Thalassa, Thalassa!"* cried those who knew their classical history.[22]

From the Sea of Okhotsk the *Graf* flew south over the Sea of Japan to the lighthouse at the port of Hakodate on the island of Hokkaido; and then south to the burgeoning Asian metropolis of Tokyo. For the residents of Tokyo and nearby Yokohama, the visit of this otherworldly craft in the skies proved to be a defining moment in the interwar period before Japan descended into the dark valley of fascism. Just six years before, the entire Kanto Plain, on which Tokyo is located, was convulsed by a massive, and massively destructive, earthquake. As in the earlier 1906 San Francisco Earthquake, it wasn't the quake itself but the fires that it triggered that made the great Kanto Earthquake as devastating as it was. Large swaths of Tokyo and surrounding areas were flattened, and the fires burned for days. Yet—against all the odds—Tokyo had been rebuilt and revitalized amid the ruins, and this visitor from the other side of the globe seemed to bestow international recognition of this great achievement. What could only be described as Zeppelin hysteria gripped the city.

During World War I, Germany and Japan had been on opposing sides in the struggle. In fact, Japan had attacked and seized the German concession in the Shandong Peninsula in China. However, by the late 1920s, the two countries had begun to recognize that they might share a common strategic

---

* Thalassa, in Greek mythology, is the spirit of the sea.

interest. Both were convinced that the Versailles Treaty, and U.S. President Woodrow Wilson in particular, had double-crossed them. Germans continued to entertain the fantasy that they had not, in fact, lost World War I, yet had been treated as a defeated country after the armistice of November 11, 1918. Japan, a victor nation, felt like a defeated power. They would find common cause.

Meanwhile, Eckener and his fellow globetrotters enjoyed six full days of entertainment and receptions in the Japanese capital. A typhoon had crossed Japan while they were there, and Eckener, always with an eye on the weather, determined that a departure on August 23 might allow the *Graf* to make use of favorable winds in the tail of the storm to propel them across the vast Pacific. His intuition proved correct, and the giant airship rode the tail deep out over the largest ocean on earth. Their course then took them into a vast area covered in fog and clouds. They made very good time crossing the Pacific, but could see little, and this tended to have a depressing effect on those aboard. But then at approximately 4:00 p.m. on August 25, the west coast of the United States came into view. By 5:00 p.m. they were above the "Golden Gate" and entering San Francisco Bay. The famous red-painted bridge that now spans the Golden Gate did not yet exist in 1929 (construction would begin in 1933), but the loveliest city on the North American continent certainly did. Hugo Eckener, like so many before and after him, was smitten by the man-made beauty of the city within the natural setting in which it was situated. As many have noted, the light of San Francisco Bay has a certain quality that is unique. It brought out the poet in Hugo Eckener:

> The beauties of San Francisco Bay have been sung in all languages. The "Golden Gate" has not been given the name without reason. As we steered inland at 1,600 feet and viewed the fabulous scene, we were deeply affected and even moved to tears. The setting sun flooded the sea and land and the surrounding mountains with warm, golden light and painted an extraordinary picture. And the reception which this beautiful city had prepared for us was no less magnificent. Squadrons of planes flew out to meet us and escorted us past the entrance. The vessels lying in the harbour and at the docks had dressed ship, their whistles sounded a greeting, accompanied by the tooting of thousands of motor car horns on the streets. We needed both eyes and ears to appreciate the enthusiasm of our welcome. Many times had we experienced such receptions, but this one, after our long and monotonous flight above clouds and fog, has remained unforgettable in my mind for its warmth and beauty.[23]

The *Graf*'s visit to the City by the Bay was relatively brief, if unforgettable. The trip's sponsor, William Randolph Hearst, was expecting them the following day in Los Angeles. So, they journeyed through the night down the coast. Above Hearst's legendary castle retreat, San Simeon, all of the lights of the magnate's private Xanadu switched on all at once in a passing greeting. A full day was spent in Los Angeles before the final leg of the circumnavigation commenced. It almost ended in disaster when the *Graf* barely cleared undetected electrical wires on takeoff. The deserts of Arizona and Texas provided another scare for the *Graf* when bursts of superheated air rose above the desert floor and suddenly lifted the Zeppelin like a toy balloon 600–1,000 feet in the sky.[24] But after reaching El Paso, and heading northeast into the vast Mississippi River Valley, the cruise evolved into a giant victory lap of sorts above some of the great cities of the interior of the United States—none more so than Chicago, whose flyover gave the Windy City a taste of what was to come four years later at the 1933 Chicago World's Fair.

When the *Graf* landed safely at Lakehurst on August 29, the city, the country, and the world toasted Doctor Hugo Eckener and his intrepid voyagers as only the Roaring Twenties could. New York City's mayor, the dapper Jimmy Walker, personally congratulated the German hero after a parade

Zeppelin fever (Berlin, 1929). *Alamy Images.*

down Broadway. Newly elected U.S. President Herbert Hoover, who had inherited an economy flush with capital and prosperity, invited Eckener to the White House. *Time* magazine featured the indomitable zeppelin commander on the cover of its September 16, 1929, issue. He was the man of the hour—no question about it. Some have speculated that if Hugo Eckener had entered politics at this point, he might have been able to carry the momentum from his aerial circumnavigation to victory in the 1932 German presidential election. This, of course, is counterfactual history. But that this thesis is even given serious consideration speaks volumes about his standing in Germany and the world as the decade of the 1930s dawned.

But Hugo Eckener wasn't interested in politics. He was interested in zeppelins. With the success of the *Graf*'s around-the-world journey behind him, he now set out to make the world's first transoceanic passenger air service a reality.

In the early 1920s, Eckener had made a scouting trip to South America to gauge interest in the potential for an airship route to and from Europe. A Spanish entrepreneur, with a similar vision, had reached out to Eckener and proposed Seville as a base for trips across the South Atlantic to Buenos Aires. However, it was Brazil that first pioneered this service. Recife, in the country's northeast, eagerly offered to construct a mooring mast and a refueling depot for the zeppelins arriving from across the sea. Over time, this service was extended southward to Rio and (as originally intended) Buenos Aires. It was by far the most successful, if not the most famous, zeppelin air service in history. Hundreds of intercontinental, transoceanic journeys were made between 1930 and 1937 in which thousands of paying passengers were safely transported over hundreds of thousands of miles. Hugo Eckener had realized his dream. In the inaugural voyage, he was moved much as his Italian counterpart, Italo Balbo, would be less than a year later, by the natural beauty of Rio and Guanabara Bay:

> when the sun rose towards 6 a.m. it flooded with its golden-red rays a landscape of such unprecedented beauty that we were silent with wonder.
>
> Rio Bay and its surroundings are famous, and have already charmed millions, but anyone who has not seen the picturesque view from an altitude of 1,000–1,300 feet has not become acquainted with its beauty. Certain landscapes . . . are fascinating and grand, but a bay with blue water, which is part of the scenery here, doubles its charm. And the mighty, beautifully laid-out city of Rio, stretching its arms out into the valleys and estuaries, produces a comforting impression of industriousness and successful human effort.[25]

He would return many times to *Cidade Maravilhosa*. Hugo Eckener had succeeded in bringing two worlds together. If nothing else, he should be remembered for this.

Alberto Santos-Dumont, once the toast of Paris, was now living the life of a recluse (a veritable Brazilian Howard Hughes). According to Hugo Eckener's memoir, published after World War II, he and his crew on this first successful journey to South America had assumed the great aviation pioneer was already dead. After departing from Recife, they flew above Natal before leaving Brazil, and dropped a bouquet of flowers in the great aviation pioneer's honor. To be dead (though not forgotten) while one is still very much alive . . . it says mountains about how fast, and dramatically, the world had moved on since Santos-Dumont's aerial feats in Belle Époque Paris. But the two men were linked in spirit. They viewed aviation as a means to both liberate and unite mankind. And in these years before the dark shadows of fascism and war crowded out the light, it still looked like they might be right.

The next few years were busy ones for Hugo Eckener and the zeppelin project he had inherited from the "mad" count. His aim was to build a larger, more opulent version of the *Graf*, with an eye toward establishing a regular airship service between Europe and North America, as well as South America. But the worldwide Depression that struck in late 1929 forced a degree of unanticipated austerity-minded belt-tightening that set back these plans a number of years. In the interim, Eckener cultivated the world press, governments, and public opinion in a series of interviews, statements, and attention-grabbing scientific and geographical expeditions above the polar seas.

Along with Italo Balbo and Charles Lindbergh, Hugo Eckener had become the international face of aviation. Bearing this out, the *New York Times* devoted a full-page feature article on Eckener's vision (with illustrations) in its March 8, 1930, edition to make his case for the zeppelin, then gave him equal billing with Lindbergh and Glenn Curtiss, a motorcycle racer turned aircraft designer, in another full-page feature later in the spring extolling the benefits of civilian air transport. In July, Eckener joined Lindbergh and Italo Balbo in issuing statements to be read before a special meeting on air transit at the headquarters of the League of Nations in Geneva, Switzerland. It's interesting comparing the remarks made by the three high priests of aviation's golden age, in 1930, before the rise of Adolf Hitler:

> **Lindbergh:** The air has no boundaries. International borders become imaginary lines and every city a port of entry. Civilization has always progressed hand in hand with its facilities for transportation. As distances have been reduced in time, commerce has made nations more

and more dependent upon one another. . . . Closer international
relations become unavoidable as the vague distances of an old era are
measured on a new scale of relativity.[26]

Eckener: As a result of the success of the world flights recently undertaken, we think it can be regarded as proved that air navigation is
destined to render valuable services in the sphere of passenger traffic
and mail carrying, especially when great distances have to be covered.
The enthusiasm with which airships have been greeted everywhere in
foreign countries, both when flying and landing, emphatically demonstrates that air traffic is likely to bring peoples nearer together. . . .
But this will only be possible if air traffic develops in an atmosphere
of good-will and not one of mistrust.[27]

Balbo: Air traffic has made enormous strides during the past five
years. A network of air lines connecting all the large centers has now
been marked out in the skies of Europe and forms an ideal link between all the nations regardless of frontiers. . . . For the development
of commercial aviation on internal lines, I consider that all nations
should adopt the principle of effective cooperation in air navigation.[28]

Together these statements are convincing evidence that the 1930s offered
an opportunity for cooperation over competition and peaceful collaboration
over aggression, with aviation leading mankind to a better world. Given the
platforms these men were given at the time, one can't just easily dismiss
them as naïve dreamers. People listened to what they had to say. It's one of
history's great tragedies that other, louder, shrill voices drowned them out as
the 1930s wore on.

Between 1930 and 1933, perhaps the most captivating exploits undertaken by Hugo Eckener and the officers and crew of the *Graf Zeppelin* were
the air voyages above the Arctic Circle to the forbidding island of Spitzber-
gen in 1930; and then to the Barents Sea and Franz Josef Land in 1931.
These were accentuated in the public's mind by the doomed Italian polar
airship expedition under Umberto Nobile in 1928, which led to gloomy
prognostications from "experts." Eckener was, frankly, dismissive of these
concerns, arguing that the polar skies were generally more clear and stable
(in terms of temperature) than those in lower latitudes, and that Nobile had
been temperamentally unsuited to command such an expedition.[29] In point
of fact, Eckener's remarks in his memoir on Nobile are perhaps the least
generous things he had to say about anyone (other than Nazis). They seem
out of character. But Eckener was not one to suffer fools lightly, particularly
if it involved unnecessarily putting other people's lives at risk.

In all of his travels, among all of the beautiful things he had seen in the sky, or cruising above the earth, the beauty of the polar seas in summer made the deepest impression on him. He later described what he saw as something akin to a Rockwell Kent painting infused with translucent Technicolor:

> What now began to sparkle in light and colour was so overwhelmingly beautiful and extraordinary, so unforgettable in comparison to anything I had ever seen before, that later, recalling it I made bold to remark, "Whoever has not seen a Polar landscape like Franz Josef Land, with its gleaming and transparent glaciers, in the fairy-like delicate tones, and the endless symphony of colour of its ice masses—its colourful beaches and blue inlets between the fantastically shaped islands and foothills—has not known anything of the most beautiful thing which this earth has to offer to our eyes and our souls."[30]

Considering the source, this is quite an extraordinary observation. Eckener's "Viking passion for voyaging and adventure"[31] continued to enlist more converts for the zeppelin project, which—as it went global—became more of an ideal than simply an enterprise. Most of the people reading about the *Graf* and its commander, their journeys to far-off lands of icebergs and palm trees, would never travel in a zeppelin. At most, if they were lucky, they might be able to catch a glimpse of one flying gracefully overhead. But these millions that Hugo Eckener was making his mission to enlist in the zeppelin cause were part of something larger than themselves. The "mad" count's invention had come to symbolize something more, far more: a better world.

CHAPTER 5

Up!

They met in Chicago. Jean Piccard was a highly esteemed professor of chemistry at the University of Chicago. Graduate student Jeannette Ridlon was a chemistry major. Their love of science brought them together. Their love for each other changed history.

Jean was the twin brother of physicist Auguste Piccard. They had been born just across the border from Germany, in Basel, Switzerland, in 1884, in the middle of the Belle Époque. This was a time of dizzying advances in both physics and chemistry, and the Piccard brothers entered their chosen fields at the same time that Albert Einstein, Max Planck, and Pierre and Marie Curie were introducing groundbreaking theories and processes. If science was the new religion, then Auguste and Jean qualified as members of the new priesthood. Yet the twins had another passion they indulged.

L. Frank Baum's fanciful novel had introduced to the world the mighty wizard who had ascended to a land of witches and Emerald cities, and exerted his power through a clever manipulation of propaganda and technology. But his origins were far more true-to-life than that of a balloonist blown off course by a Kansas twister. At least since the mythical Daedalus and his willful son, Icarus, had tried to escape Crete on wings of wax and feathers, man had dreamed of breaking free of the Earth. However, it was not until 1783, when Pilatre de Rozier and the Marquis d'Arlandes successfully flew in the Montgolfier brothers' hot air balloon above France that the dream had become reality. In the century since, man had associated flight with these majestically shaped inflatables carrying fragile baskets suspended from ropes. For travel between specific locations, they were decidedly unreliable. But attached to the ground, they made wonderful observation platforms (as in the American Civil War and the Franco-Prussian War). And, of course, if one's goal was simply to go "up," then the possibilities were apparently limitless. The first serious attempt was conducted in 1875 by three intrepid Frenchmen, Henri Sivel, Croce-Spinelli, and Gaston Tissandier, only one of whom survived to tell the tale. The freezing temperatures and the lack of oxygen put these first aeronauts in a hellish situation. Conditions well known today had yet to be discovered. It was their misfortune, and their glory, to be the first. Manned balloons had been in existence since the latter half of the eighteenth century, but they were frustratingly fickle. They went wherever the wind took them. Controlled flight in a horizontal direction eluded the best minds in aviation for decades. Over time, ballooning "aeronauts" ascended higher and higher into the sky. With the advent of the altimeter, these pioneers were able to confirm and document the heights they had reached. But one thing soon became evident. There was a ceiling on what the human body could withstand in terms of temperature and the thinness of the air. Oxygen deprivation* makes the mind do strange things. To ascend further than five miles would require a new approach. This intrigued the young brothers from Switzerland. For them, science was not merely proofs written in chalk on blackboards or test tubes filled with liquid substances in laboratories; it involved interacting with the physical world and taking personal risks. Over time, their quest would absorb more and more of their time and thinking.

It all began in the pristine Alpine world of their childhood, a time and a place of wonder and discovery that their parents urged them to explore and understand. This approach to life and learning, first developed in mountain meadows and lakes, would ultimately take them into outer space.

———————

Auguste and Jean Piccard were born identical twins. It's a curious relationship, one that only identical twins themselves truly understand. They have a bond that transcends the physical—the shared DNA—and speaks to the soul. At its most extreme, it's as if two persons are, in fact, one. And rather than seeing them as "half" of something, it might be more accurate to say it doubles the potency. All of their lives, Auguste and Jean would support each other. Petty sibling rivalries didn't mar their relationship, their work, or their collaboration. This is a crucial point when considering their separate attempts to reach the stratosphere in the 1930s. They were not competitors; they had each other's backs.[1]

As youths, the twins' education included an immersion in the natural world. For their parents, Jules and Hélène Piccard, science was not divorced

---

* Low air pressure makes it more difficult for the body to absorb oxygen.

from an appreciation for beauty, or moral and ethical considerations. Once, on a hike with their sister Marie, older brother Paul, and their parents, lugging their father's cumbersome photographic equipment, they encountered a mountain meadow full of wildflowers:

> The field in front of them slanted upward. It was a flaming carpet of rich gold, touched with flashes of white and deep, brilliant blue. They all stood silent before its beauty . . . "Remember to pick only one of each kind," said their mother. "We must leave such beauty for others to enjoy too."[2]

Like Hugo Eckener, out alone on the Baltic in his sailboat, the Piccard boys were encouraged to take risks and practice self-reliance. On holiday in the Italian-speaking canton of Ticino as adolescents, Auguste and Jean had taken a rowboat, painted blue, out on Lake Maggiore to visit the ruins of an infamous pirates' castle. This picturesque Alpine lake is quite large, and taking a small boat out on its waters to row eleven miles across the Italian border to the "island" took stamina and nerve. The ruins didn't disappoint. One of the outstanding characteristics of the Piccards was that as much as they would become men of science, they were also men of adventure. Seeing the tumbled stones of the bandits' lair from which they had spread terror among the good citizens living along the shores of Lake Maggiore, generated a thrill in the boys along with quiet thoughts of a time many centuries past.

The scent of adventure resulted in the boys crossing from the lake's western shore to an Italian village on its eastern shore. But once they had reached the midway point, the Alpine wind began to churn the lake from placid calm to turbulent and wave-filled. They pulled for the far side, but within sight of land, they realized there were only jagged rocks to welcome them. As the next wave crested, Jean caught a glimpse of a narrow shingle of sand. He told his brother to pull hard right; "Auguste heard and obeyed. He knew there must be some reason for Jean's directions. Both boys pulled with all their might against the heavy waves. . . . It was going to take very careful calculations indeed to bring the boat into shore at just the right moment."[3] This combination of physical hardiness, courage, and cool-headedness under pressure would become a defining characteristic of the two brothers in the years and decades to come.

They made it through the rocks. The local villagers, unbeknownst to the boys, had witnessed the suspense-filled final act of their crossing of the lake. They rushed to see if they'd come through safe, unbelieving when the Piccards told them they had crossed all the way from the other side in waters that rough. They insisted that the boys stay the night as guests of the entire village. But Auguste and Jean had a dinner date with their family back up the lake in Locarno. When the winds died down and the lake's surface returned to its previous calm, they put their blue boat back into the water and, over the protestations of the villagers, rowed north. Their close call with danger in no way diminished their confidence in their ability to reach their family, as long as the weather held. It did.

As a man of science, Jules Piccard encouraged Auguste and Jean to conduct experiments and take ownership of their learning. The only way to truly learn was to do it for oneself. This ad hoc process involved dead ends and messes, as well as occasional gratifying proof of success. And there was their common fascination with ballooning. It was a barnstorming Swiss aeronaut that first lit the spark that would inspire the twins to marry their love of science (physics, chemistry) with their imaginations.

Eduard Spelterini* must have seemed a veritable Wizard of Oz to the two young boys the first time their father took them to see him "ascend" into the skies over Basel. He returned a few years later and his feats inspired Auguste and Jean to create their own first crude gas balloons for themselves.

The Piccards were certainly not alone in their fascination with flight. The Swiss, in general, were keen on aviation. In fact, in 1905, the Fédération Aéronautique Internationale was formed with its headquarters in nearby Lausanne, Switzerland. The FAI would become the foremost aviation/aeronautical organization in the world—the arbiter of world records and the standards by which they were measured. Like their Italian contemporary, Italo Balbo, the Piccards came of age in a time when aviation was constantly being pushed ever onward and upward. But at that time, it was in no way clear that the twin brothers would one day achieve aeronautical feats worthy of notice by the FAI. They had to earn a living, for one thing. A career in the classroom, or in the laboratory, seemed natural enough paths. But the sky was never far from their minds. They had "the bug." There is no doubt about it. Whether they would ever be able to act on it in a serious manner was the question.

Ultimately, Auguste and Jean would attend university together at the Swiss Federal Institute of Technology in Zurich and pursue their individual scientific interests in physics and chemistry, respectively. But as rigorous as their studies were, the twins couldn't help playing pranks on unsuspecting residents in, what was for them, a new city. Years later, one prank in particular could still elicit side-splitting bouts of laughter.

---

* Eduard Schweizer was his real name; "Spelterini" was his stage name.

Auguste and Jean had let their hair grow quite long and it was clearly time to pay the barber a visit. But Jean had an idea, a very funny idea. He went by himself, and after striking up a conversation with the barber, he explained how his hair grew incredibly fast. The barber assured him that when he was done, Jean would like the results. To this Jean replied, "It looks all right *now*."[4] The next day, of course, Auguste walked in with a mass of hair on his head, to the jaw-dropping astonishment of the barber!

Jean stood out at the Institute. In 1909 he received his doctoral degree, and was also recognized with a special silver medal for his work in chemical compounds. His work on their color and composition, and his observation that "certain types of molecules split apart in solution,"[5] led to his thesis being commonly referred to as the "Piccard effect" in chemistry textbooks. Offered a teaching post in Munich, Jean Piccard left his Swiss home and parted ways with his twin brother. In Munich, Jean worked with Nobel Laureate Alfred von Baeyer. The outbreak of World War I in the summer of 1914, however, forced Jean to return to Switzerland to avoid being called to serve in the Kaiser's army. As a member of the faculty in Munich he had been required to take an oath to Imperial Germany, and what had once seemed *pro forma* now carried the potential for quite serious consequences. An opportunity to teach in Lausanne, not far from home, decided the issue. Beyond his homeland's borders, World War I raged. The Piccard brothers adhered to their mountain country's policy of strict neutrality. When one considers the slaughter of the trenches on the nearby Western Front—the senseless attacks ordered by distant commanders—they probably did well to steer clear of it.

The seeds planted by Eduard Spelterini also began to bear fruit in the years just before, and during, the war. Auguste Piccard had visited Paris in 1912 to assist with the start of the Gordon Bennett Cup (a distance competition, and one that often proved deadly). The competition itself interested him very little, but the magnificent balloons themselves, straining at their tethers, interested him a great deal. By September of that year, he had made his first solo ascent. The following year (1913) he was joined by Jean in a sixteen-hour flight from Zurich over Germany and France. It must have been a realization of all of their boyhood hopes: "Just like Spelterini!"[6] During the war years, both Auguste and Jean served in the Swiss Army's "lighter-than-air" service but were officially barred from active service in balloons, instead being assigned the role of "civilian advisors." Their prodigious height was deemed too tall for a gondola! Considering future events, this determination was rich in irony.

And then a new opportunity unexpectedly presented itself. Jean had been invited to visit the United States and teach in Chicago. To leave a continent locked in its death throes, cross an ocean, and visit a giant new land called America—well, this must have been quite something. He had his doubts—which he confided to Auguste—but in the end he chose the bold course. It would change his life forever.

Arriving in the United States (then still at peace with the warring powers in Europe) in 1916, Jean Piccard was presented with a whole new world. Nothing in his experience had prepared him for the frantic pace and intimidating size and scope of cities such as New York and Chicago. But he took to it.

Swiss "aeronauts": Jean Piccard (left) with his brother Auguste (right) during World War I. Note how tall each of them are—six feet, six inches, in fact.

The scale of the country also made a deep impression on him (as it would on Italo Balbo later on). Traveling from the Eastern Seaboard to the West Coast, Jean Piccard absorbed America in a way now lost to most Americans themselves in the age of jet travel: the freedom, its raw beauty, the flora and fauna (he delighted in the natural wonders of Yosemite National Park, for instance). Back in Chicago, he gained an intimidating reputation as a brilliant but somewhat impatient professor. The University of Chicago was fast becoming one of the most prestigious research universities in the United States. Teaching on Chicago's South Side, at a university generously primed with Rockefeller money, was a plum position for the young Swiss professor. If one could drown out the grim news of the war in France (the United States had entered the conflict in April 1917) and avoid the deadly hand of the influenza pandemic sweeping the land, life was good. His graduate students were co-ed and eager, if a little scared of him. One of them was named Jeannette Ridlon.

———— ∞ ————

Jeannette Ridlon was born in Chicago (two years after the first great Chicago World's Fair) in 1895 to a well-to-do family. Her father was a respected medical doctor. Like Jean and his brother Auguste, Jeannette and her sister Beatrice were identical twins. It's remarkable if one stops and considers for a moment this fact. But the story had a different arc. Unlike the Piccard boys who grew up inseparable, sharing adventures near their home in the foothills of the Swiss Alps, conducting ad hoc experiments, and, predictably, playing pranks, Jeannette and Beatrice would have less time together. Tragedy intervened when the young sisters were growing up in Chicago. At the age of three, Beatrice suffered severe burns while playing with a toy stove, and died. Jeannette witnessed the horrible accident, and would be haunted by it for the rest of her life.[7] Even after Beatrice was buried, Jeannette said, "She never felt alone."[8] The loss of a twin is different than the loss of a brother or a sister born separately. Part of one's self, one's soul, is amputated. Beatrice's ghost was tangible in a way that few could understand. Jean, however, was better equipped to understand.

It was the fathers in both Jean's and Jeannette's lives that would shape their course and their characters. Jean's father was a man of science; Jeannette's father was a man of medicine. Both men actively encouraged their children to learn for themselves, question everything, push limits (whether personal or societal), and be brave. In Jeannette's case, growing up in the shadow of the Victorian Age, there was the added burden of her gender, which her father refused to impose as a restraint on her ambitions. At the age of eleven Jeannette announced to her mother that she wanted to become an Episcopal priest. Aghast, her mother fled the room. But her father took her seriously. This same seriousness of purpose was exercised by the Piccard twins' father. If his youthful sons were to undertake an endeavor, he treated them as persons worthy of sober discussion and careful scrutiny. This base, laid down by these two progressive-minded men, empowered their children to move forward when others might dismiss them. It was a gift that led to greatness.

Jeannette grew up at a time when the expectations American women had for their lives were changing. The opportunity to attend college, pursue a profession, and, ultimately, to vote and take part fully in public life, were her lived experience.

She pursued her bachelor of arts degree at the exclusive Bryn Mawr College outside Philadelphia during the war, with a double major in philosophy and psychology. Unsurprisingly, in 1916 she wrote a paper entitled, "Should Women Be Admitted to the Anglican Church?" Her answer was a decided "Yes." Upon graduating in 1918, Jeannette returned to her native Chicago and enrolled at the University of Chicago. Demonstrating the breadth of her interests and the intellectual versatility of a true Renaissance woman, she began her pursuit of a master of science degree in chemistry. It was this love of learning, inculcated by her father, that ultimately placed her in a classroom where a tall, distracted, and eccentrically handsome Swiss professor, whose father had also inculcated a love of learning, was lecturing.

Years later, Jeannette Ridlon Piccard shared with her granddaughter, Mary Louise, what her first encounter with Jean Piccard had been like: "I was walking up a flight of stairs, and stopped on a landing—I looked up and saw the most beautiful man I had ever seen in my life."[9]

One can well imagine her shock—and her delight—when the object of her appreciation turned out to be one of her new professors. His reputation preceded him, and Jeannette did all she could to avoid a one-on-one discussion with this brilliant, "beautiful," but intimidating man. She made a point of staying out of his line of sight. Later she confided to him: "When the big double doors to the graduate lab opened and you rushed in, I would watch. If you went to the left, I would go to the right and slip quietly out the door. If you went to the right, I would go to the left behind the desks and slip out that way."[10] Finally, on November 11, 1918, something remarkable happened that finally broke the ice between Jeannette and Jean. The war was over! Professor Piccard, grasping the significance of the moment, told his students working in the laboratory to drop whatever they were doing. He

Jeannette Ridlon, Bryn Mawr, Pennsylvania (1914). *Courtesy of the Shipley School.*

was still youthful enough himself to organize the occasional social outing. And this occasion certainly called for one. A favorite activity was to picnic on the dunes along Lake Michigan. They stopped at a deli for sandwiches and something to drink. Jeannette Ridlon came along too, to celebrate the end of the war and the Allied victory. Somewhere between the chalkboard and the sand, a romance blossomed. Seven months later, on August 19, 1919, Jeannette Ridlon and Jean Piccard were married, and immediately set off for his native Switzerland to start their new life together.

As their ship left the harbor, heading toward the Atlantic, the two new-lyweds reminisced about the fall of 1918 when Jeannette was too intimidated to face Jean one on one. She recalled the first time she decided to face him. He recalled how she held the desk tightly with both hands, refusing to be intimidated . . . being brave. He reflected, "I'm glad you were. I hope from now on you will always be brave enough to stand your ground and keep from running away. I hope you will be brave enough to come *with* me anywhere."[11]

These years were fruitful ones for Jean and Jeannette. Both taught at the University of Lausanne until Jeannette became pregnant with the first of their three sons. Motherhood was a full-time occupation in that period of her life. Meanwhile, Jean pursued a successful career as a world-renowned chemist: first in Lausanne, then at the Massachusetts Institute of Technology. He encouraged the same combination of physicality and intellectual vigor in his sons that his father had instilled in him. Visitors remarked how he glowed in the rough but affectionate play of his boys (even as they at one point poured a box of cornflakes on his head). But he also was keenly following developments in balloon technology that promised to lead one day to an attempt to reach the stratosphere. And it was his twin brother, Auguste Piccard, that would take the lead in going where no man had gone before.

—— ✦ ——

Auguste Piccard had also left Switzerland, in 1922, to teach at the Université libre de Bruxelles (Free University of Brussels, Belgium). In 1920, he had married the daughter of a French professor of history who taught at the Sorbonne in Paris. Her name was Marianne. They would have four daughters and a son. Like his brother, Jean, Auguste Piccard inspired in his students a respect for his genius. But he also became a popular figure on campus, someone who enjoyed the interplay between subject, professor, and student. His lectures were well attended.* But he was no prima donna. Auguste Piccard was genuine,

---

* Among the attendees was a young German student named Wernher von Braun.

and this was largely the secret of his great appeal among students. Students can sense when a professor or teacher isn't genuine. With Piccard it was never about *him*; it was about the subject—and on an even deeper level, it was about a profound faith in science. As Tom Cheshire, in his excellent three-part biography of the Piccard family, explained:

> Piccard was always calculating, secure in the belief, common to the age, in the supremacy of scientific technique: everything, if you worked through it well enough, could be explained. His response to any problem was to start inscribing calculations in his notebook, earning him the nickname of the "extra decimal point."[12]

Auguste unwittingly became the model for the character Professor Calculus in the popular "Tintin" books by Hergé. Tall, wearing high, old-fashioned collars, outwardly seemingly distracted but in fact intently focused on how best to achieve solutions to seemingly intractable problems, "the Professor" cut quite a figure.

Comic books aside, Auguste Piccard's contributions to physics were not inconsiderable. Albert Einstein had been one of his examiners when he successfully presented his doctoral thesis in 1914. His work on the magnetocaloric effect "opened the way into research on superconductors,"[13] and his hypothesis on a third radioactive body ultimately led to the isolation of U-235, used in the creation of the first nuclear weapons. In 1926, Auguste again went aloft in a balloon christened the *Helvetia* (after his native land) in order to take measurements on the speed of light at higher altitudes. This was crucial in proving that Einstein's theory of relativity—according to which the speed of light was constant—was in fact correct. He was among those invited to attend the now famous Solvay Conference in 1927, which was particularly influential in the development of quantum theory and notable for the arguments between Albert Einstein on the one hand, and Niels Bohr and Werner Heisenberg on the other. Einstein's theories, of course, had posited that there should be evidence of cosmic radiation (or "rays") beyond the Earth's atmosphere. But as yet no human being had reached the stratosphere to measure this in person. It's fairly clear that during this time, Auguste Piccard began to see how his passion (ballooning) might be married to his profession (physics) to potentially important effect.

In 1930, Auguste Piccard had built a pressurized spherical gondola or "capsule" made of aluminum. Piccard didn't drink, but it was partly the new pressurized vats for making beer that inspired the capsule design.[14] Small windows would enable the capsule's inhabitants to observe the stratosphere,

The 1927 Solvay Conference (note Einstein seated center front; Auguste Piccard standing at top left).

the Earth below, and the stars embedded in the inky black void above. This spherical capsule would need to protect those inside from the thin air and cold temperatures of "outer space" as Auguste intended to ascend to the stratosphere and obtain definitive evidence that cosmic rays did indeed exist. The king of Belgium had created a fund for scientific research, the Fonds National de la Recherche Scientifique, and Piccard secured 500,000 Belgian francs from it toward construction of a hydrogen-filled balloon and the spherical gondola. The latter would be the first of its kind—essentially, a "space capsule." As Tom Cheshire explained, the logic of the sphere—over an oblong gondola, for instance—is that it "offered the maximum volume for the smallest surface area."[15] Again, it was the math.

Of course, at the altitudes Piccard intended to reach, any leak in the gondola could prove fatal. The usual sand or water ballast taken on by a conventional balloonist wouldn't work in the sphere either (there simply wasn't room), so more dense lead pellets, as fine as grains of sand, were substituted. Poured through a tap inside the capsule, these were then sealed in a separate airtight intermediate compartment before being jettisoned by a second tap on the outside of the sphere. The gigantic balloon (with a volume of 14,130 cubic meters*) would expand as it ascended due to the decrease in atmo-

---

* As Tom Cheshire astutely points out, this compares to the average volume of 2,800 cubic meters of most modern-day hot-air balloons (i.e., Auguste Piccard's balloon to the stratosphere was enormous).

spheric pressure—thus, not reaching its full awe-inspiring size until it was in the stratosphere itself. It would be a giant gas-filled sphere holding aloft a tiny aluminum sphere under its belly. With an eye for promotion, Piccard christened the gas bag and the capsule the *FNRS*, the acronym of his sponsor.

On May 27, 1931 (two years to the day before the opening of the 1933 Chicago World's Fair), Auguste Piccard and his fellow aeronaut, Paul Kipfer, took off from Augsburg, Germany and ascended 51,775 feet (nearly ten miles) into the sky. The ground crew (always crucial in any aeronautical endeavor) had made what turned out to be a crucial error: attaching an additional rope securing the sphere to the balloon, which in turn blocked the valve that allowed those within the sphere to release hydrogen gas to descend. In addition, a strong gust of wind had knocked the gondola around just before takeoff, damaging it sufficiently to create a small, slow leak. Neither of these dangers was readily apparent when Piccard and Kipfer began their ascent . . . but the seriousness of the low whistling sound that reached their ears became apparent soon after. Rather than abort the mission—which, unbeknownst to them, was not possible due to the blocked valve—Piccard had the presence of mind to stop up the leak with a mixture of Vaseline and tow. It worked, temporarily. On they shot upward. In less than half an hour they had reached the bottom of the stratosphere, and continued to ascend. They were now higher than any human beings had ever been.

The press was keen on following the spectacle, both from the ground and in hired aircraft following the course of the *FNRS* as it was carried first west, then southeast toward the Austrian Alps. This interest resulted from a mix of equal parts genuine interest in science/exploration and grim fascination with the grisly fate that might await the hero-aeronauts. A few years earlier, a U.S. Army officer named Hawthorne Gray had ascended to what was then a record height of 42,470 feet in a balloon with an open gondola. The instruments that the vessel was carrying confirmed his achievement, but the gondola returned to earth with a corpse aboard, as the elements and the altitude had done their work on the pilot. Albert Einstein had urged Auguste Piccard to think of his wife and children. What would they do if he didn't return alive?

At 51,775 feet, the two aeronauts allowed themselves a momentary pause to observe the Earth and outer space from their tiny windows. It must have been an awe-inspiring moment. They were the first humans to see the curvature of our planet. What they witnessed stunned them. Piccard later described how "It (the Earth) seemed a flat disk with an upturned edge."[16] He later admitted his attempt to describe the color of the stratosphere eluded his limited ability to convey the qualities of color. But then there was the business at hand: taking measurements (the whole raison d'être for ascending in the first place, mind you), thinking about the descent (how and where to land safely), and rationing the supply of precious oxygen they had brought aboard until they could open the hatches and breathe fresh air at lower altitudes. Meanwhile, the sun's rays on one end of the sphere raised the temperature to uncomfortably hot while on the other end it was freezing cold. And the ground crew had thoughtlessly left them with an insufficient supply of fresh water. Before long they were collecting condensation from inside the walls of the sphere's frozen side to supplement what little they had to drink. Then it was time to begin their descent. They tried to open the valve that released the gas from the balloon, but it wouldn't budge.

As evening began to descend across Europe, cooler air would contract the hydrogen gas inside the balloon, and it would eventually return to Earth on its own. But how long would this take? Could Piccard and Kipfer hold out long enough to avert death through lack of oxygen, thirst, cold? Piccard's initial calculations inside the capsule estimated it would take fifteen days for the balloon to land—and fortunately, in this instance, his calculations were incorrect. The rate of descent from the stratosphere did not remain steady but accelerated as the balloon descended further toward the Earth's surface. Soon they crossed 33,700 feet in altitude, leaving the stratosphere above them. At 15,000 feet Piccard deemed it safe enough to open the small hatches in the capsule and to stick their heads out to gulp lungfuls of fresh air. But the view rapidly coming to meet them from below was, though breathtakingly beautiful, decidedly ominous. The magnificent, jagged Austrian Alps could be the end of them, and they knew it.

As the *FNRS* descended, it was being closely followed by those on the ground, most of whom suspected the aeronauts within were dead. The initial plan had called for a midday landing, but now darkness was setting in and God only knew on what rock the capsule would finally come to rest. In the Inn River Valley, locals spotted an object in the sky. Tom Cheshire's description of the object captures the wonder inherent in that moment: "a little moon, a tiny crescent, which had a halo: the F.N.R.S., still reflecting the sun's rays, was brilliantly illuminated against the dark sky, the celestial chariot hitched to a falling star."[17]

But this was no falling star. The aeronauts' descent proved perilous. As they reconnoitered the unpromising terrain below, they noted a giant field of ice that might do. Piccard pulled the rip cord, immediately emptying the balloon of all of its remaining hydrogen gas. This was it! Their capsule rolled, skidded, and bounced to a halt in the middle of the night atop a glacier. Trying to make it down off the glacier at night was a non-starter. So the two hungry, shivering men huddled together for warmth under the deflated balloon fabric and waited for morning. Unbeknownst to them, a team of crack Austrian alpine troops had been sent to retrieve them (or their bodies). In the morning, as Piccard and Kipfer descended the glacier toward civilization, the mountaineers passed them on the way to the empty capsule!

A Pathé film of Piccard in the Austrian village that he and Kipfer reached later that morning shows a vigorous, self-possessed man at the height of his powers and the summit of personal fame. He looks comfortable with it.[18]

The outside world wanted to know what this Columbus/Lazarus of the stratosphere had to say. His first thought was for his wife, Marianne, to let her know he was well and had reached his destination. The world press was ravenous for details of the flight—the extent to which Piccard and Kipfer had been in dire peril. What had it looked like up there? What had been learned? Then, and now, aviation and science writers have debated the merits of Piccard's achievement. Detractors claim that the measurements he had taken could have been obtained using unmanned balloons; that he was lucky not to have died, and taken Kipfer with him; that it was more about the personal satisfaction he took from going higher than any human had gone before—and doing it in a craft he had designed himself. These are fair criticisms. On the other hand, the observations Piccard and Kipfer made could not have been made by an unmanned balloon. The aeronaut was also pushing the limits of what humans and human technology could do. This last point is vital. Piccard was going where no man had gone before, and showing the way for others to follow. This has been our path since the days we danced around fires and barked at the moon. Progress has taken us from primitive existence to civilization—but it didn't simply happen as some sort of inevitable, natural process. Auguste Piccard was, and is, a model of someone who was curious about the universe, talented enough to devise solutions to satisfy that curiosity, and bold enough to do it himself at great personal risk. This is why he matters.

When Auguste returned to Belgium, he found himself a celebrity. But as previously mentioned, not all of the notoriety was welcome, or kind. Albert Einstein congratulated him on his achievement, but tried to extract (successfully, or so he thought) a pledge from Piccard not to repeat his stratospheric ascent. He initially consented, but the critical characterization of Piccard as some sort of madcap daredevil scientist whose accomplishment was a lucky anomaly rankled. The following year, on August 18, 1932, Auguste Piccard entered the *FNRS* capsule for a second ascent to the stratosphere. It's now clear that Piccard wanted to demonstrate that what he was doing—or something like it—would seem normal in a short time to come. The madcap daredevil characterization needed to be dispelled once and for all. He was a man of science, and science would lead to innovations that would improve travel to outer space. This second attempt, with fellow aeronaut Max Cosyns, would do much to achieve this end. For one thing, the ground crew was more thorough and more thoroughly coordinated with the aeronauts inside the capsule. Compared to the first danger-filled ascent in 1931, the 1932 ascent was a "cakewalk." This was exactly what Piccard had intended—to make it look easy—which it most certainly was not. He broke his own altitude record, ascending to 55,152 feet. The *FNRS* was equipped this time with a transmitter, allowing Piccard to broadcast a brief radio message back to Earth.*

The balloon ultimately came down in much the same rather rough-and-tumble manner as in 1931, this time near Lake Garda in Italy. Piccard and Cosyns collected themselves and set to on a can of peaches they had brought along. This was supplemented by villagers from nearby Desenzano, who brought the aeronauts some bananas.[19] Air Marshal Italo Balbo was waiting for Piccard. Upon hearing the news, Balbo drove to the village to personally invite Piccard to attend a fête in his honor in Venice. The professor begged off, claiming he had no evening clothes with him. In a comradely, if obviously disingenuous manner, Balbo said he didn't either. Decades later, Auguste Piccard's grandson, Bertrand, shared a family story about that night. The dapper Balbo simply decided that if Monsieur Piccard had only his "flight suit" to wear, he would reciprocate by donning one of his own.[20] One can only imagine the astonished looks on the guests' faces as Balbo and Piccard entered the ballroom looking like they had stepped out of one of the newsreels that had made them famous and instantly recognizable the world over. The two enjoyed an evening together on the Lido in one of Europe's most stylish cities. There was no doubt—Piccard's feat captured the world's imagination. But it also begged the question: How much higher could humans go? And what might they find there?

No one was as excited for Auguste Piccard than his twin brother, Jean. No one better understood what motivated him, and what he hoped to achieve. By 1931 Jean Piccard, the husband of an American and father of three Americans, had himself become an American citizen. This was home now. When Auguste was invited to the United States to meet with American aviation's aristocracy, Jean was there to greet him at the pier in New York. In a nutshell, the tour wasn't quite the success one might have hoped. Auguste Piccard didn't translate to Americans the way that Hugo Eckener,

---

* "All is going well. Observation good."

for instance, did. He was too honest. When asked what he thought of New York's magnificent Art Deco skyline, he remarked that it had nothing on the Alps. Perhaps.

The Chicago World's Fair committee had an eye on Professor Calculus as a potential interest-generating, ticket-selling attraction. Another record-breaking ascent, originating in Chicago, held great appeal and could count on generous sponsorship. But Auguste Piccard had other ideas. He returned to Europe and offered his brother Jean as a worthy substitute. The baton

Members of a very elite club: Italo Balbo and Auguste Piccard talk in the park of the Villa Pellegrini Malfatti in Desenzano (1932). *Getty Images.*

was being passed. Jean Piccard was about to be swept into the maelstrom of a media frenzy ultimately weighted with nationalistic, sexist, and ideological overtones.

———— ∞ ————

The professor and the graduate student had married, started a family, and moved to the groom's home country to teach together at the University of Lausanne; then returned to the bride's home country to make a life in the New World. Theirs was a true partnership of equals: raising their three sons, discussing advances in the field of chemistry and, inevitably, ballooning. At a certain point they reached a similar conclusion: Why not go "up" together? This represented the seed of an idea that would germinate in the months ahead. They then had no idea of the resistance they would encounter. But greatness often demands this. Meanwhile, the world fell down . . .

CHAPTER 6

Crash

As Italo Balbo, Hugo Eckener, and the Piccards pushed the envelope of what was possible in the 1920s and early 1930s, the wider world experienced an unparalleled boom, and then a crushing bust. The giddy party on Wall Street came to a shuddering halt on "Black Tuesday," October 29, 1929. The gigantic American economic engine had become detached from the speculative bubble on the stock market, which had soared ever upward, and the crisp air of autumn had finally awakened those with the foresight to get out first. Then everyone tried to get out. Bank failures on both sides of the Atlantic created a downward spiral. Businesses were shuttered; homes and farms were foreclosed on; the lines of the unemployed stretched ever farther; and suspicion, mistrust, and despondency infected the populace.

The historical context for this period, which would come to be known as the Roaring Twenties, was World War I. So much of what ultimately defined the boom and bust, and the society it produced, came out of that terrible conflict. Europe in 1914 stood unchallenged in a way no other part of the world ever has. Economically, culturally, technologically, ideologically— it dominated the rest of the world. But of course, Europe was not unified politically. Its various component parts competed with each other to share a bigger, more prestigious slice of the global cake. They told their people that their claims were just, and those of their competitors were not. Finally, in the summer of 1914, a series of unfortunate—albeit often willful— acts brought on a gigantic war; a war that more recent historians have characterized as Europe's "suicide attempt." Italo Balbo and Hugo Eckener had been swept into the struggle; the Piccards had fortunately managed to avoid it to the degree that it could be avoided in 1914–1918 Europe. The leaders of what would later become the first two Fascist states had also been swept up in the war. Mussolini had posed as a patriot-soldier for political effect. Adolf Hitler's wartime service was of a more serious nature. This failed painter had left Vienna and found his life's purpose as a volunteer across the border in the kaiser's army. He was noted by his comrades and officers as being very quiet, fanatically devoted to Germany's cause, personally brave, and completely lacking in leadership skills. Germany's best chance to win the war was in August and September, 1914. Once this quick victory had eluded them, the war became a long, ugly, drawn-out struggle between the Germans dug in on French and Belgian soil and the Allies trying to force them out. *Attrition*: this word took on a new, modern, and particularly sinister meaning in World War I. As these large, wealthy, technologically advanced sister countries butchered each other, they found that the industrial methods that had allowed them to rise to global dominance now needed to be applied to war. The efficiency and scale of Henry Ford's assembly line had to be adapted to mass murder to achieve victory. The treasure and blood of a whole generation was thrown into the fray. The result was stalemate.

America, generally in step with President Wilson, managed to stay out of the war until 1917. Wilson, who had once decried the militarism of the Old World, now harnessed America's vast industrial potential and large population to play a decisive role in ending the stalemate and winning the war. The U.S. government intervened on a hitherto unimaginable scale in the American economy, and "efficiency" became the watchword, as important as courage, skill, or morale. "Taylorism," based on the efficiency model created in the early twentieth century by Frederick W. Taylor, was instituted at all levels to ensure an Allied (American) victory. Charles Dawes, the scion of one of Chicago's oldest and wealthiest families, with the ear of presidents and powerful bankers, was ultimately put in charge of the wartime General Purchasing Board of the American Expeditionary Forces.[1] John J. Pershing, the AEF commander, placed absolute faith in Dawes's ability to get the troops what they needed to win—without wasting taxpayers' money. It would be Dawes and his younger brother, Rufus, who would be the main movers behind the 1933 Chicago World's Fair. Charles (who would serve as Calvin Coolidge's vice president from 1925 to 1929) would become known in the Chicago press for his ubiquitous poker pipe, while Rufus acquired a well-earned reputation as an exceptionally natty dresser. They were quite a pair.

Another figure whose wartime experiences shaped his understanding of organization on a large scale was U.S. Army engineer, Lenox Lohr. Lohr's expertise ultimately caught the attention of the Dawes brothers and they hired him to manage the great fair that they were planning to open in 1933. Lohr's disinterested and professional manner, combined with his confidence in his ability to take wartime Taylorism and apply it successfully to any endeavor, made him the ideal choice. As historian Cheryl Ganz explained, Lohr "determined that with careful organization and planning, the fair would be both economically and educationally effective."[2] He was a "can do" guy, and he spoke the Dawes brothers' language. He also would bring with him a very able lieutenant in Martha Steele McGrew. They would work like slaves for years to make the Dawes brothers' vision into a reality. But it's important to keep in mind how World War I shaped that vision, and Lohr's understanding of how to implement it.

The Dawes brothers made a killing in the stock market's boom years while at the same time staying involved in civic undertakings. Charles would eventually administer the committee tasked with restructuring Germany's economy following its defeat in the war. Its solution—a predecessor of sorts to the later Marshall Plan after World War II—is known to history as the "Dawes Plan." The scheme whereby the United States would loan Germany money in order to help rebuild its economy, shattered since 1918, was spectacularly successful. Charles Dawes also helped rework the sticky issue of reparation payments owed by Germany to her wartime foes, to which she had agreed by signing the 1919 Versailles Treaty. By 1929, Germany was a fully rehabilitated member of the international community with a thriving economy and a vibrant arts scene. Adolf Hitler, convinced that 1. The German Army had not lost the war, and 2. The Treaty of Versailles was a violation of the terms that the armistice was signed under, had gone into politics after the war. Closely following the political progress and copying the methods of Mussolini, Hitler built up a political organization around himself that existed solely as an expression of his Nietzschean will to power. As Germany's economy was brought to its knees in the early 1920s, this political neophyte was able to gain national notoriety for a failed putsch in 1923. In prison (for a surprisingly short time) he drafted his personal political manifesto, *Mein Kampf* ("My Struggle"). The book was little more than a rant against Leftists, Jews, the Weimar Republic, the League of Nations, and anyone else who stood in the way of the national and racial destiny of the German "volk," as he saw it. But then (largely due to the American money Charles Dawes had freed up) times changed. Hitler continued to rant, but few were listening.

Then on October 29, 1929—"Black Tuesday"—the Wall Street crash occurred and history moved back in Hitler's direction. Germany was hit particularly hard. What made it even more psychologically devastating was that the German people had thought they'd left this economic and social uncertainty behind them. And now? With the ground seemingly caving way beneath them, Germans were far more willing to listen to angry orators such as Adolf Hitler. Seemingly overnight, the ex-corporal and watercolorist went from being dismissed as a political crank to being taken seriously as a potential national savior.

For his part, Benito Mussolini saw the large-scale failure of capitalism as partly a result of its liberal democratic underpinnings. The State should intervene by forming a corporatist relationship between management and labor for the benefit of the nation, rather than any one individual. It went without saying that he represented the nation. By 1931, with the economic maelstrom sucking all of the industrialized economies into its maw, socialism also seemed to offer an alternative. In the secretive Soviet Union, its new master, Joseph Stalin, had already launched the massive "Five Year Plan" before the crash; many idealized this red star in the east, not remotely comprehending the human cost this "plan" would extract. Totalitarianism, whether of the leftist or rightist variety, seemed to own the future. One could choose to be terrorized by ideologues or bullies, it seemed. America licked its wounds, and Hollywood pretended the party was still going on. But there were some who woke clear-eyed to these increasingly ugly or delusional realities, and acted.

Lauro de Bosis was an Italian conservative, the son of an Italian poet, Adolfo de Bosis, and a New Englander mother, Lillian Vernon. De Bosis believed in the democratic system and hated Mussolini for what he had done to his country. He felt a single decent act might awaken the nobler soul that he felt lay sleeping in his fellow Italians—so many of them seemingly mesmerized by the glorious laurels Italo Balbo had won for Italian aviation on his just-completed air voyage to Brazil. De Bosis was under no illusions about what Balbo's successes symbolized. His master, Benito Mussolini, exploited these like a narcotic peddled to the Italian people to keep them artificially sated with nationalistic triumphalism. If Balbo could win hearts in the sky, why not someone else, with a different message? In a farewell letter published in newspapers throughout the world, de Bosis argued—from exile in France—that the sky still belonged to free men.[3] He wrote that if "my friend Balbo has done his duty,"[4] he'd likely be shot down in flames before he could complete his mission. In a daring "raid" reminiscent of D'Annunzio's wartime exploit to drop leaflets on Vienna demanding Austria's surrender, de Bosis flew his airplane from the island of Corsica, violated Italian air space, and headed for Rome. The eminent historian Piers Brendon best described what happened next:

> With only seven and half hours of solo flying experience to his credit
> he set off . . . in his russet-colored, white-winged Pegasus and glided

like a phantom over the Eternal City. He flung out a shower of leaflets denouncing Mussolini's corrupt and tyrannical government, appealing to the King and urging a boycott of every Fascist enterprise and ceremony. They floated onto the green lawns of the Quirinal Gardens and the outdoor cafés in the Villa Borghese. They landed like snowflakes on the Piazza di Spagna and the Piazza Venezia. De Bosis was not shot down but on his return journey he apparently ran out of fuel and crashed into the Mediterranean. No trace of him or of the Pegasus was ever found. Commenting on this act of self-immolation, The Times said: "So long as there are men like Lauro de Bosis, the safeguarding of freedom is assured."[5]

Before he set off, de Bosis wrote a poem entitled "Icarus." In it, he emphasized the nobler aspect of man, which he saw being degraded in Mussolini's Italy. Reading the poem, one can't help but feel that Italo Balbo would have felt an instinctive kinship with the young poet-pilot. The difference was that one had all, but sold his soul to the devil, while the other had never made that compromise with eternity:

> a noble goal
> Son, child of mine, thou art not dead.
> Mine eyes have seen thee like a god illuminated by the sun.[6]

Thus, the 1930s dawned quite bleak from the perspective of the liberal, democratic, capitalist order that had appeared to have emerged victorious from the 1914–1918 war. The new U.S. President Herbert Hoover certainly didn't help lighten the atmosphere either. He had received the presidential baton from the equally buttoned-up Calvin Coolidge in March 1929 when the good times looked like they would go on forever. But, of course, they didn't. And Herbert Hoover just did not seem up to the task. On top of the bread lines, soup kitchens, and shanty towns, the failed and hypocritical experiment in social engineering known as Prohibition was still the law of the land. No one seemed to take it particularly seriously, not even the Bible-thumping bourgeoisie of Middle America who had done so much to initiate it in the first place. Or, rather, they didn't take it particularly seriously where they themselves were concerned—it was only when the "other guy" wanted a drink, particularly if they were of immigrant stock, that they took it seriously. The hypocrisy reached all the way up to the corridors of power in Washington. Inevitably, Prohibition had a corrosive effect on the social mores the Bible Belt claimed it was trying to protect. That is, a law that would be difficult to enforce even if it was taken seriously, let alone applied sporadically and hypocritically, wound up undermining respect for all law, and to a certain degree social convention in general. Thus, the irony of the most libertine period in American history taking place under the auspices of multiple conservative administrations. Hemlines rose, pre- and extramarital sex became, if not the norm, at least far more common, and the recreational consumption of alcohol and drugs increased. The generation of women who had struggled for the right to vote now disapprovingly saw their increasingly scantily clad daughters and nieces going places and doing things they felt demeaned women. This was *not* what they had struggled for. But the younger generation of women, with their bobbed hair and exposed legs free to dance the "Charleston," disagreed. They felt empowered. Times were indeed changing.

The Roaring Twenties indeed roared. The "lost generation" that had come of age during the war (whether on the winning or losing side) seemed to want nothing to do with idealism, instead embracing hedonism as their modus operandi. Social critics, such as the young author F. Scott Fitzgerald, decried this loss of idealism in his timeless novel of the age, *The Great Gatsby*. What made the self-invented, quasi-fraud Jay Gatsby "great" was that, unlike everyone else around him in the Twenties, he had *not* lost his idealism. He held tight to it, and stayed pure, despite his half-truths and criminality. However, this contextual understanding of the period, one could argue, is flawed. First, the Roaring Twenties implies that the period is confined to that decade only when in fact as a recognizable historical and cultural period it really can be traced back to the enactment of Prohibition on January 17, 1920 through its official termination on December 5, 1933. In other words, the Roaring Twenties were really the Roaring Twenties *and* early Thirties. What of the stock market crash, and the subsequent depression? Though the crash would come to define the beginning of the Great Depression in the public mind, at the time this was not necessarily the case. For one thing, economic depression had already inflicted serious damage in the agricultural countryside. It was news to farmers that the Great Depression started on October 29, 1929. And it was not altogether clear at the time whether the crash was a momentary corrective—that while inflicting some real pain (like the 1893–1894 economic downturn), it would eventually turn out to be relatively short in duration. Those involved directly, and heavily, in the stock market often did take a disastrous hit because of the crash (for their part, the Dawes brothers had had the foresight to get out before Black Tuesday). But not everyone was broke. The grim, grinding poverty that we have rightly come to associate with the Great Depression wasn't being documented yet to the same extent as it would be under the progressive-minded Roosevelt administration later in the 1930s. The good times rolled on, where they could (such as in Hollywood), and the Zeitgeist remained more firmly linked to the pre-Depression Twenties than to the later post-Prohibition era. This is important when looking at the genesis of the 1933 Chicago World's Fair—yes, real economic loss and social disruption was happening, but it took some time for the psychology of the times to catch up to the evident historical realities. Thus, the 1933 Fair, planned in one era of plenty and carried out in another of austerity, in fact was part of the same era, the same mindset. It was the end of Prohibition that signaled the end of this era, not the crash.

———— ∞ ————

This was the context for the great Chicago World's Fair of 1933. The origins for the idea of *a* fair began with a local booster named Myron Adams. He initially suggested making the lakefront south of the "Loop" into a grand triumphal arcade for the victorious Allies of World War I. But this then evolved into a more ambitious proposal to have Chicago host its second World's Fair—this time to commemorate the centennial of its incorporation as a town in 1833 (thus, the fair's eventual title: "A Century of Progress"). In 1923, Adams formally proposed his idea to the city's mayor and received an enthusiastic reception. However, with a change in administration in City Hall, the idea was greeted with greater skepticism; the most important being: "Who is going to pay for it?" There had been World's Fairs since the first in London in 1851, and certainly there were plenty of Chicagoans who recalled quite well the remarkable Columbian Exposition of 1893. But for all the fairs that had successful runs, there were plenty of other examples that demonstrated they were anything but guaranteed. The city's treasurer, Charles Simeon Peterson, ultimately took up Adams's idea and on a fact-finding trip to Europe viewed smaller international expositions to learn. After returning to the United States, Peterson reached out to the city's most prominent men, and at a meeting on December 13, 1927, the die was cast. Two major decisions made that day would shape the 1933 Chicago World's Fair—the first, a recommendation from the president of the National Bank of the Republic, George Woodruff, urged that this new fair look forward, not backward, as its predecessors (most famously the 1893 Columbian Exposition) had done. The second major decision was the selection of the dapper, tightfisted, Rufus Dawes as the president of the Fair Committee. It now had a vision, and a leader capable of realizing it.[7]

Chicago's corrupt mayor—a puppet of Al Capone—gave his tepid endorsement, but pledged no funds. Charles Dawes and his brother Rufus, with connections at the highest levels of American business and finance, would have had it no other way. Their vision was for a privately funded fair that would not only pay for itself, but turn a profit. Efficiency, the god of the progressive era that formed these men, would work seamlessly with science and innovation to triumph over corruption and waste. The new age that dawned so unpromisingly on the horizon was not one to be feared, if one had the nerve and the brains to meet it.

CHAPTER 7

A Single Beam of Starlight

May 27, 1933, was a lovely spring day along the shores of Lake Michigan. The combined efforts and hopes of the 1933 Chicago World Fair's planners, designers, lighting experts, carpenters, plasterers, landscapers, concessionaires, and publicists were finally ready to be put on display for an eager public, clamorous for both diversion and inspiration. On that first day, over 120,000 visitors passed through the fair's gates. But it was that evening, at sunset, that the true spectacle of the day's events transpired.

The 1933 Fair's organizers had hoped to capture the scientific, futuristic element of the event in an unmistakable manner. In the months leading up to the grand opening, leading scientists and university astronomers had been teamed with the best and brightest from General Electric, Westinghouse, and AT&T to develop a scheme whereby the light of a distant star would be used to power the "on" switch for the fair's glorious Technicolor light show. This "single beam of starlight" came from the star Arcturus, thousands of light years away. In fact, it was calculated that the light, traveling at the nearly immeasurable speed of 186,000 miles per second through space, took forty years to reach Earth. Thus, the light used to power the switch had been generated in 1893, the year of the original Chicago World's Fair.[1]

This clever way of generating public interest in the fair's official opening displayed the wonders of science while at the same time reminding everyone that Chicago had previously (and quite successfully) hosted a World's Fair. The earlier fair had been staged further south along the lakefront, while this newest incarnation was set closer to the city's downtown, on Northerly Island and the adjacent lakefront near the city's major public venues such as the Field Museum of Natural History and Soldier Field. Another of these institutions, Adler Planetarium, was located within the fairgrounds and was a physical example of the importance the city of Chicago itself placed on astronomy. It was telling, however, that the Arcturus project was a product of private enterprise—not public largesse.

Lenox Lohr had been tasked with creating this futuristic wonderland in such a way that it would incorporate the most modern, cutting-edge methods and materials to inspire, educate, and uplift the hoped-for, admissions-paying masses, but in a manner that would pay for itself. The Dawes brothers could not have hired a more competent manager—his total commitment to the enterprise, perhaps more than any other single factor, is what made this fair, the "Fair." One of the key elements was his ability to organize the fair's major exhibits by technology, not by individual companies, and thus realize Rufus Dawes's vision of cooperation within industries. If GE and Westinghouse could join forces to produce such an awe-inspiring opening, then why not Ford and General Motors, and so on? Collaboration, not competition, produced the war-winning formula for the United States in 1917–1918, and could be employed again to make a roaring success of the fair. Eliminate redundancies, share costs, articulate a common message about the importance of a given industry, and make a greater impression on the public. Architects, electrical engineers, and set designers were eager to try new ideas and materials in what everyone understood was a temporary installation, its very impermanence making it more attractive to people who were thinking boldly. As Lisa Schrenk explained in her book on the fair's architecture:

> the event offered a rare design opportunity, as they were able to develop, and present their ideas without having to deal with the difficult clients, zoning rules, skeptical bankers, or restrictive programs that often dictated more permanent building projects. . . . A lack of a rigid building code allowed exposition architects to break away from conventional standards. The knowledge that the buildings were going to be short-lived and set outside the everyday world offered the designers the freedom to experiment.[2]

And they didn't disappoint. With rare exceptions, those architects, engineers, and designers who were lucky enough to have been selected by the Fair Committee to contribute gave Chicago and the world something extraordinary. From the perspective of the twenty-first century, it can be quite frustrating to realize that almost nothing is left of the 1933 World's Fair. But this was the plan all along. Even before the fair began, every structure (often covered with remarkable works of art) was designed on the understanding that it would be removed when it ended—its various component parts slated to be dismantled and used in other construction projects, or recycled as scrap. Before lamenting this loss, one also needs to keep in mind that this "temporary-ness" was the very reason why these structures with their various works of art were so extraordinary. It allowed artists and businessmen to take risks. It was the cost of greatness.

Exterior view of the Hall of Science, with relief sculptures depicting (from left): Fire, Light, Night, and Storm. *Courtesy of University of Illinois Chicago Special Collections.*

Of all of the structures at the 1933 Chicago World's Fair, the wondrous "Hall of Science" takes first prize for the daringness of its conception and for its realization of both the fair's vision and the times it inhabited. Located near the bridge that divided the north and south "lagoons,"* the Hall was constructed roughly in a U-shape, framing a Court of Honor in front of its main eastward-facing entrance. The Hall's giant white pylons broken up by bas-relief panels were unlike anything the world had ever seen. No Corinthian columns or graceful classical porticos here, but rather a powerful expression of the as-yet-unseen future. The various arms and sides of the "U" featured giant works of sculpture whose style mixed the ancient and the futuristic. Art Deco architecture was all the rage in the late 1920s and early 1930s (another example of the cultural continuity of the Prohibition era). It was at least partly inspired by the archaeological discoveries of the period, in particular Howard Carter's remarkable find in Egypt's Valley of the Kings of the tomb of Tutankhamun. The date of the find (1925) is important in that it coincided with the *Exposition internationale des arts décoratifs et industriels modernes* being held in Paris, which incorporated ancient forms and design into its cutting-edge, streamlined structures.[3] This was the style Charles Simeon Peterson had seen during his fact-finding tour of Europe years before. It was this congruence of unbroken straight, curved, and zig-zagged lines drawing the viewers' attention, combined with motifs from Sumerian ziggurats, Mayan temples, and Egyptian obelisks, that captured the age. A stylized lotus or lightning bolt explicitly connected design across millennia. Art Deco was sleek, elegant, modern, mysterious, and ancient. What it was *not*, was classical.

One of the finest examples of this style in sculpture was the giant depiction of "Knowledge Combating Ignorance" gracing the Hall's north-facing court. Sculptor John H. Storrs's "Knowledge" is depicted nude, in human form, vanquishing the stylized serpent representing "Ignorance." "Knowledge" possesses great power but, unlike Michelangelo's classically inspired David, there is an unnatural, angular, almost super-heroic element to the form: more god-like than merely human.

Inside the Hall's open-air rotunda was set the fair's main (and most lasting) artistic contribution. Louise Lentz Woodruff, the wife of banker George Woodruff, had been commissioned to create a work of art that would encapsulate the main ideas of the fair. Her brilliant "Fountain of Science" featured figures cast in lustrous white bronze. This moving three-part statue of a powerful but benign robot, head bowed, nudging figures of man and

---

* This was really just an inlet of the lake separating Northerly Island from the lakefront.

FOUNTAIN OF SCIENCE. CIRCULAR TERRACE, HALL OF SCIENCE. THE THEME OF THIS
FOUNTAIN IS SCIENCE ADVANCING MANKIND.
A CENTURY OF PROGRESS—CHICAGO'S 1933 WORLD'S FAIR.
(LOUISE LENTZ WOODRUFF, SCULPTOR)
7057-7:

Louise Lentz Woodruff's masterpiece, *Science Advancing Mankind*.

woman* into the future, welcomed visitors. Unlike the robots in filmmaker Fritz Lang's 1927 futuristic dystopia in *Metropolis*, this robot was not to be feared, but trusted.

Installed on the various panels at the statue's base above the fountain's eight pools, Lentz Woodruff created a series of bas reliefs in an even more explicitly Art Deco style. The panels represent stylized interpretations of the various sciences being featured at the fair,† driving humanity forward. The work itself was titled *Science Advancing Mankind*, epitomizing the fair's official motto: "Science Finds, Industry Applies, Man Conforms." This motto certainly possessed a certain totalitarian tone in its directives, which, in retrospect, frankly don't seem open to discussion. Fortunately, today one can still appreciate Lentz Woodruff's conception in its totality, in person (minus the elevated base and pools). When the fair ended, she donated her masterpiece to her alma mater, Joliet Central High, located a little less than an hour southwest by train from Chicago. It is magnificent.‡

---

* Both depicted nude from the waist up, wearing ancient Egyptian clothing and hairstyle.

† Botany, zoology, medicine, geology, astronomy, physics, mathematics, and chemistry.

‡ Before venturing to Joliet to see Lentz Woodruff's artwork, one should make arrangements with the school's administration.

In addition to its modernist, Art Deco exterior, the Hall of Science featured a 186-foot-high tower that was unlike anything in its time. Today, when one looks at a photograph of the "Carillon Tower," it still looks strikingly modern, a building that wouldn't be a bit out of place (if it was vertically stretched) in the skyline of twenty-first-century Miami Beach, Hong Kong, or Chicago itself. The interior of the building—as would be the case with a number of the more prominent structures at the fair—would feature very little natural lighting. Windows were apparently not modern. Giant towers with outer skins made entirely of glass, such as the present-day One World Trade Center in New York, were still beyond the conception, it seems, of most modern architects at the time.*

The Electricity Building, located across the south lagoon from the Hall of Science, was perhaps more impressive still. Laid out in a more shallow U-shape than the Hall of Science, its open courtyard faced the lagoon and featured two giant bas-relief sculptures flanking the top of the "U"—one female, one male, harnessing the wonder technology of the age. At the end of the U's northerly arm, two giant rectangular pylons reminiscent of Mayan temples faced the lagoon. The fronts of each of these pylons were covered with more works of sculpture of a similar theme and style to those at the top of the "U."

In 1893, Edison, Westinghouse, and Tesla had awed the world. Forty years later, electricity continued to have a powerful hold on the public. This was particularly true in rural areas. In 1933, large swaths of the United States had yet to be electrified. This was before the gigantic government-directed hydroelectric projects in the Tennessee Valley and at Grand Coulee. If fire had been Prometheus's great contribution to man, then electricity was the great contribution of modern Prometheuses. The fair made this clear.

Adjacent to the Electricity Building, facing the north lagoon, was the U.S. Government (or "Federal") Building. It was an odd cross between three white streamlined windowless towers reminiscent of a Le Corbusier design, and the Jefferson Memorial. It was the towers that got everyone's attention. Clustering three identical towers like that was also something new. Today one can recall the former twin towers at the World Trade Center, or the myriad public housing projects built in urban areas after World War II. But in 1933 it was strikingly modern. Thus, if one came to this new fair looking for "a century of progress," documenting Chicago's evolution from outpost to metropole,† one would have come away disappointed. Yes, there was a

---

* Le Corbusier, perhaps, being the notable exception.
† The area that today roughly constitutes what is popularly called "Chicagoland."

The Electricity Building pictured with the Goodyear blimp in the sky (these blimps were dwarfed by the much-larger zeppelins). *Courtesy of University of Illinois Chicago Special Collections.*

mock-up of the War of 1812–era Fort Dearborn, as well as du Sable's earlier trading post. But the unmistakable thrust of this fair was the *next* century, not the one being commemorated. This would have been immediately apparent to everyone paying their 50-cent price of admission. No one had ever seen anything quite like this, because nothing like this had ever been conceived before. The future had landed on the shores of Lake Michigan.

CHAPTER 8

Rainbow City

Following its spectacular opening in the spring of 1933, the public flooded the Chicago Fair's grounds and exhibits on a daily basis. Before it was over—Depression or no Depression—a then-record 48.5 million visitors passed through the turnstiles. And there would be no small irony in the fact that in the midst of the greatest economic depression in modern history, the 1933 Chicago Fair was the first World's Fair in history to turn a profit.[1] Similar to the earlier 1893 Columbian Exposition and World's Fair, the 1933 World's Fair featured a centrally located lagoon flanked by various "halls" representing the latest advances in various industries (electricity, transport, communication, etc.). Arching over all was the giant "Sky Ride" suspended between two steel towers 625 feet high.

A conscious effort was made to differentiate this new fair from the 1893 exhibition by not only scrupulously avoiding the application of Beaux-Arts architecture, but also to use color (both bright, durable paint and colored neon lighting) to contrast the monochromatic "whiteness" of the earlier fair with a rainbow of colors. Experts in psychology, art, and engineering collaborated with Broadway set designers such as Joseph Urban to magnificently realize this vision. Urban was an immigrant artist from Vienna who had been discovered by the legendary Broadway producer, Florenz Ziegfeld, after initially coming to the United States as art director for the Boston Opera. For twenty years, Urban had used his unrivaled skills as a set designer to bring Ziegfeld's famous "Follies" to life. Unlike painters such as Gustav Klimt, who had influenced his early work,[2] Urban used his remarkable talent to create work that was temporary in nature. This, of course, fit in well with the overall concept of the 1933 Fair. For Urban, color and light, when employed in an intelligent and creative manner, could in themselves constitute

93

architecture. Thus electricity, spray paint, and the new neon technology were as vital as construction materials in creating an overall effect.

It certainly was a real coup for the fair's organizers to bring Urban on as an advisor. He was in great demand, not only designing sets but also clubs, schools, office buildings, and hotels. In the late 1920s, in fact, he was hired as chief designer at the posh new Mar-a-Lago resort in West Palm Beach, Florida. In 1985 it was purchased by real estate developer Donald Trump, and has remained in his family to the present day.

Urban's genius was perhaps best on display at the Hall of Science. As Cheryl Ganz explained in her book on the fair, Urban "used two shades of orange, two shades of blue, white, and touch of red to create the building's arresting appearance."[3] For the evenings, Urban recommended using lamps filtered through colored glass, and the installation of thousands of feet of neon gas tubing. The building itself was then set off by "floodlights and motion searchlights" that "lit the building on all sides."[4] The effect was spectacular, and was repeated throughout the fairgrounds. Color photography was then still in its infancy in 1933 (George Eastman's Kodachrome film wasn't introduced until 1935), and hand-drawn color illustrations or clumsily hand-colored photos simply don't convey the overall effect of Urban's contribution. In the twenty-first century, with enhanced colorizing technology available, more photographs originally taken with black-and-white film are being given vivid new life. Some photos of the fair fall into this category. Hopefully in the future our understanding of, and appreciation for, Urban's work will be enhanced as well. Tragically, Urban was in very poor health when the fair opened, and he never saw his final creation in all its glory. He died soon after the fair's opening. In the *Chicago Tribune*, art critic Charles Collins eulogized this rare genius:

> The late Joseph Urban, who died while millions of people were admiring his latest masterpiece . . . was an artist whose work was too closely related to life to be imprisoned within the art museums.
>
> His style of decoration, Viennese of origin and formed at a time when modernism was not divorced from sanity, was for the masses in the mood of happy carnival. His influence was so far flung that I believe he deserves consideration as one of the greatest American artists of the period.
>
> His sketches of course, will find their way into the archives, but, being merely notes for the execution of large scale designs, they will be viewed with rapture only by technicians.[5]

Color was also employed by Joseph Urban for psychological, as well aesthetic, purposes. A common experience for all of the fair's visitors entering at the busy north entrance adjacent to the planetarium was the central pedestrian artery known as the "Avenue of Flags." This promenade ran straight from the north entrance to the north court of the Hall of Science, between Soldier Field and the north lagoon. Brightly colored banners were employed to send various messages to fairgoers strolling the grounds. On any given day the flags were all of one color—vibrant red or yellow or green, for instance— and were used to suggest a mood or feeling for the day, something hot for bright red, and so on. It was a remarkable attempt to use color as a form of social engineering, one that was subtle enough not to offend, but rather to suggest and uplift. The uniformity of the giant banners one after another was intended to have a soothing or stimulating effect on fairgoers depending on what the organizers were aiming to achieve. Looking at both black-and-white photographs and early colorized photographs of the Avenue, one can grasp something of the effect Urban was hoping to see realized.

———— ∞∞ ————

The "Avenue of Flags," social engineering through the application of color. *Courtesy of University of Illinois Chicago Special Collections.*

By 1930, Chicago's Municipal Airport was the busiest not only in the United States, but in the entire world. The Windy City had fully embraced the concept of aviation in all of its forms (including a robust embrace of commercial air travel), and the 1933 Fair featured this very prominently. Suspended from the interior dome of the Travel and Transport Building was the *non plus ultra* in heavier-than-air commercial aviation of that time, a new Boeing 247. The prestigious Gordon Bennett Balloon and Air Races were held in Chicago that summer, with cash prizes for distance (balloons) and speed (airplanes). World War I German air ace Ernst Udet was a leading attraction, though the speed record was broken by Texan Jimmy Wedell at 305 miles per hour. The Goodyear Tire and Rubber Company too contributed to the spirit of aviation, evident at the fair by regularly flying its fleet of "blimps" above the grounds. These blimps were similar to the original flying airships designed by Alberto Santos-Dumont in fin de siècle Paris—an inflated, fat, cigar-shaped balloon, powered by a motor. Zeppelins they were not. But they still were exciting for the crowds to see overhead. And of course, the grand "Sky Ride" was meant to simulate the sensation of flight.

The genesis for the Sky Ride was the desire to go George Ferris one better, and top his earlier, kindred, attraction: the Wheel. That desire to climb higher, to indeed be above all one surveys—our heritage from Icarus—was understood by those in charge of the 1933 Chicago Fair.

The basic concept for the Sky Ride was designed by the bridge construction firm, Robinson & Steinman, with significant contributions from the Otis Elevator Company and Goodyear-Zeppelin. Two towers, 625 feet high, were erected on either side of the lagoon below. Suspended from cables attached to the towers, passengers rode in sleek, if not necessarily fast (only six miles-per-hour), enclosed cars two hundred feet above the fairgrounds. The view represented a genuine thrill. One needs to keep in mind that most people in the 1930s had never flown before. Therefore, traveling suspended in the air at that height was the closest most of the fairgoers had been to the experience that most of us today take for granted. America's "public enemy number one," John Dillinger, reputedly was a repeat customer; melting into the relative anonymity afforded by the large crowds, purchasing a ticket, ascending in the lift to the top of the giant tower, leaving worldly cares behind, catching a glimpse of his native Indiana to the south beyond the dunes.

Another feature of the fair was the attempt to include the city's many ethnic groups in the celebration of the city and the century. Of course, Chicago's oldest ethnic group were African Americans. The city's black community was keenly aware of Jean-Baptiste du Sable's role as founding father of the settlement that became Chicago. However, the Fair Committee had to be grudgingly brought around to the idea of explicitly recognizing du Sable's legacy, and placing it in its proper historical context rather than trivializing it. The main mover in this effort, dating back to 1928, was Chicago native Annie Oliver. Ultimately her efforts were successful, and interested fairgoers were able to tour a mock-up of the first settlers' cabin and read historical literature on his place in Chicago's history. In addition, African Americans could take pride in the performance of composer Florence Price's Symphony no. 1 in E Minor. Price's story is surely one of the highlights of a great fair.

Like many of Chicago's black residents, Florence Price was originally from the south. She was part of the Great Migration of the 1910s to 1930s, one of the greatest internal migrations in American history. Her genteel background in musical composition originated in her native Fort Smith, Arkansas, but for both personal and professional reasons Chicago became her home. However, as a composer who was both black *and* a woman, it was very difficult to get her work taken seriously in the male-dominated world of classical music. Her break came with the attention given her work as a result of being awarded the Wanamaker Prize in 1932 for the Symphony no. 1 in E Minor. The Chicago Symphony Orchestra conducted by the German violist, Frederick Stock, chose to feature Price's symphony at a special concert being given in conjunction with the World's Fair.

It's important to keep in mind the racial and historical context of this moment. In 1933, all adult Chicagoans could recall the terrible race riots of 1919 that left nearly forty of their fellow citizens—black and white—dead. It had started when a black youth had swum near a segregated white beach on the lakeshore. Outraged whites then threw rocks at him, and he drowned. The explosion of rage among Chicago's black community over this senseless act of violence and bigotry was unprecedented up to that time in American history. For decades, race riots that featured white-on-black violence (often abetted by police forces) had been a recurring theme in urban areas. But this time, it was met with an equal measure of black-on-white violence.[6] To call what happened in the summer of 1919 "Chicago's civil war" would not be an exaggeration. The National Guard had to be called in to restore order. To a certain degree, the reaction by the black community can be explained within the context of the Great Migration. Many of the rioters were recent migrants. They had had their fill of white terrorism, often coming north to escape it. So, they had taken a stand. This traumatic event had seared itself into the memories of many who attended the fair in 1933. Race relations in Chicago were not good.

Frederick Stock was a German who had been persuaded to come to Chicago to build a symphony orchestra worthy of the lakeside metropolis.

Today, in the early twenty-first century, the CSO under its Italian director, Ricardo Muti, is considered one of the finest symphony orchestras in the United States—if not the world. But it was Stock who put it on the map in the first place, taking risks by featuring works by what were then considered fringe, modernist composers such as Mahler and Prokofiev. Therefore, it shouldn't have come as a surprise that he would place Price's work at the center of the CSO's performance on June 15, 1933, in the famous auditorium built by architect Louis Sullivan. He recognized talent when he heard it, and he was willing to take risks.

The Symphony no. 1 in E Minor is a powerful, expressive piece of music—at times playful, sometimes haunting. At just over thirty-eight minutes, it explores a number of themes in the African American experience: sorrow, joy, liberation, struggle. The "Juba Dance" component of the symphony evokes America and the African American experience, anticipating later, more well-known, works by Aaron Copland, for instance. The concert proved to be an unqualified success. After the performance, the next edition of the African American weekly, the *Chicago Defender*, gushed:

> First there was a feeling of awe as the Chicago Symphony Orchestra . . . swung into the beautiful, harmonious strains of a composition by a Race woman. And when, after the number was completed, the large auditorium, filled to the brim with music lovers of all races, rang out in applause for the composer and the orchestral rendition, it seemed that the evening could hold no greater thrills.[7]

For Florence Price, the concert was the highlight of her career. It did not open the doors that one might have expected, however. America was still very much a racist (and sexist) society in the 1930s. Price died in 1953, largely a forgotten figure. Not until the twenty-first century has her work finally begun to receive the acclaim it deserves. But for one night at the World's Fair in 1933, the city was hers.

———— ∞ ————

The Chicago Symphony Orchestra enjoyed a wide audience for its performances of classical music at the fair. Americans love music. Popular music of that time—the Prohibition era—has a lot to say about who music-loving Americans were. Recording certainly had improved by 1933, and the advent of radio in the 1920s provided a medium for artists to reach a wider, national audience. Jazz had reached the northern urban areas largely as a result of the Great Migration. Chicago's South Side and Harlem in New York were transmitters of this exciting new music. By 1933, jazz had begun to morph into a musical form known as "swing," and it was swing that defined the age. Some of what would later be called the "big bands" featured vocalists, others did not. What all of them had in common, however, was that one could—no, *wanted* to—dance to their music. Listening to this music over eighty years after it was recorded, one is startled by how fun, catchy—and, at times, *rocking*—it is. Listen to the horn section on Louis Armstrong's recording of "Dinah," and it is immediately evident that rock 'n' roll with its electrified instruments and amplifiers has nothing on it. As it evolved, swing became more subdued, respectable even. But that's not how it was in 1933.

Lyrics also expressed the Zeitgeist of the era. Yes, Al Jolson had crooned "Brother Can You Spare a Dime" in 1932. But the earnest, populist tunes of Woody Guthrie, for instance, hadn't yet made an impact. Again, the Depression was very real—in fact, the winter of 1932–1933, when construction of the fairgrounds was being completed, was as bleak as it got—but Americans then still seemed to prefer more playful music. There was a fun, slap-and-tickle element to songs, such as in Phil Harris and Leah Ray's "How's About It?" or "Shuffle Off to Buffalo" from the popular musical film, *42nd Street*. And sexual innuendo was common. The latter song is one long wink to a honeymooning couple who's going to be spending the trip in their private compartment on a sleeper. In "Harlem Camp Meeting," uber-cool Cab Calloway urged the "cats" to "Swing them sisters!" In another number from *42nd Street*, dapper Dick Powell sang of

> Little nifties from the Fifties
> So innocent and sweet
> Sexy ladies from the Eighties
> Who are indiscrete

Americans in 1933 knew how to have a good time. Our twenty-first-century understanding of them is so colored by the lens of the New Deal that we often miss this. The inauguration of Franklin D. Roosevelt as president of the United States in March 1933 heralded a new age in government. His "New Deal" for the American people was a bold rejection of what were perceived as the failed laissez-faire policies of previous administrations. FDR inspired many young people to believe in government, to become part of the solution, not just bystanders to history. There is no doubt that he was one of the greatest presidents in American history. He came of age politically during the Progressive era of the 1900s–1910s. The Prohibition era (though not Prohibition itself) was one long rejection of this earlier reformist, crusading period.

Now, middle-aged, the youthful progressives of yesteryear had taken over Washington and were poised to implement their version of what American society should be. By and large they were earnest, empathetic, well-meaning, serious people. They were also often boring, self-righteous prigs. For his part, FDR knew how to have a good time (even after being stricken with the scourge of polio), but he was surrounded by people who did not, and who did not particularly care for others having a good time either. It's worth re-calling that Prohibition itself had been championed by the progressives when it was up for ratification fifteen years earlier.

Thus, the new era that was dawning with FDR's presidency was going to move society in a new direction culturally, not just politically. Along with FDR becoming president, the repeal of Prohibition in the fall of 1933 would signal cultural change. With repeal, respect for the law would be enhanced, for one thing. The final signal of the cultural change that was about to oc-cur was the beginning, in 1934, of the strict enforcement of Hollywood's infamous Hays Code governing film content. But until then, the envelope would continue to be pushed.

At the fair that spring, visitors were drawn to the Midway just as they had been in 1893. The location was different—this time on the lakefront itself—but the ethos was not. The attractions of the *demimonde* mixed with the county fair to create a similar milieu as in 1893. Snake charmers and hootchy-kootchy dancers vied with rides, game booths, restaurants, and beer gardens for the fairgoers' dollars. Straightlaced Lenox Lohr might not have been a denizen of the dives, but he understood full well the financial implica-tions of the Midway concessions. The Fair Committee's share of the profits could spell the difference between a fair that paid for itself, and one that went into the red. Thus, a certain permissiveness reigned in its environs that would never have been allowed in the fairgrounds proper.

Nowhere was this more evident than in the Streets of Paris concession. Part exhibit, part cabaret, the "Streets" welcomed visitors with a stylized steamship façade meant to simulate a journey to distant lands. There was very little that was French about the concession, except perhaps the insinu-ation of a certain risqué allure. The undisputed star of the Streets of Paris was fan dancer Sally Rand. An out-of-work actress and dancer, Rand and her agent, Ed Callahan, conceived a plan to relaunch her flagging career by com-bining nudity, or near nudity, minimum props, and dance.[8] It was essentially performance art—or, rather, exhibitionism as performance art.

The curvy twenty-nine-year-old schemed with Callahan to get the pub-lic's attention right from the beginning of the fair. On opening night, May 27, 1933, she donned a cape and a long blonde wig (and nothing else), and mounted a rented white horse (with sidesaddle) to crash a posh party being given in the Midway's Cafe de la Paix. Her unexpected entrance had the desired effect. As historian Cheryl Ganz uproariously related:

> Beyond the gala's soft, warm ring of light, a virtually nude Lady Godiva disembarked unnoticed. She entered the gate and rode boldly through the Streets of Paris and onto the mini stage. Astounded, Chicago's merrymaking high society simply gaped, and then, seeing her as a novel addition to the planned entertainment, they burst into applause. The police arrested Rand for obscenity, but the horse remained to be photographed with the enthusiastic spectators.[9]

Sally Rand caught on camera splashing in Lake Michigan by a photographer from the *Chicago Herald and Examiner* (July 19, 1933). *Courtesy of University of Illinois Chicago Special Collections.*

Following the fair, Rand revived her career and returned to Hollywood for roles in a number of films in the 1930s. Sex sold. Starting in the early 1920s with the rise of the Prohibition-era "flapper," the Hollywood film industry began exploiting it in many of its films. Already by the early 1920s, nudity and sex were being—if not explicitly depicted—strongly hinted at by using creative camera angles, sets, and suggestive body language. With the rise of the "talkies" over the silent "movies" later in the Twenties, spoken dialogue could add heaps of sexual innuendo—and often did–in films such as *The Blue Angel* and *The Sign of the Cross*. In the latter, a classic of the sword-and-sandal genre by director Cecil B. DeMille, French-born actress Claudette Colbert cavorts quite clearly in the nude in a Roman bath in her role as the debauched Empress Poppaea. Then in her next line, she tells Dacia, another female character, "Dacia, you're a butterfly with the sting of a wasp. Take off your clothes. Get in here and tell me all about it."[10] This raised some eyebrows.

Hollywood had brought in a Presbyterian minister named Will Hays to draft a decency code that all of the studios bound themselves to, following an ugly scandal after a starlet was found dead after a drunken orgy. There was much earnest handwringing, but once the code was adopted, little meaningful effort was made to actually enforce it. To a certain extent, it was a bit like Prohibition itself.

The result was a period in film history (reciprocated to a very large degree by Broadway) where the prevailing mood seemed to be (as Cole Porter put it) "anything goes." Or at least anything as far as one was willing to push it. By 1933, under the influence of Hollywood, American society was probably "sexier" than it has ever been, before or since. This was not a sexiness that relied on explicit depictions of nudity and sex. It was more sophisticated than that. It understood that suggesting sex, or showing just a bit more than was publicly permissible—briefly—could be a tonic for one's imagination. Another aspect that stands out is that in 1933 there was nothing sordid or furtive about sex, and sexiness. Actresses of the era exuded a charm that frankly only that era could produce. And it wasn't just "cheesecake" that the studios were selling. Olympic swimming sensation Johnny Weissmuller, cast as Tarzan of the Apes by MGM, was one of many examples of "beefcake" depicted on screen, as well.

But in 1934, Joseph Breen gained control of the body tasked with enforcement of the code. Urged on by the Roman Catholic National Legion of Decency, Breen took his job very seriously indeed. Within months, a more puritanical climate took hold in Hollywood, and filmmakers, often grudgingly, had to change course. Twenty-first-century Americans are often shocked when they watch films from the early 1930s. The counterculture revolution of the late 1960s is often seen as the beginning of this country's sexual revolution. It doesn't seem possible that people living in such an antique age could be so, well, sexy. But they were.

That year, 1933, the first great blockbuster of the "talkie" era was released in theaters across the country. *King Kong* was to the Prohibition era what *Star Wars* was to Generation X. It was the must-see movie of 1933. It had its premiere two months before the fair opened, and was a competitor for Chicagoans' hard-earned entertainment dollars. The story centers around a love triangle between a woman, a man, and an ape of enormous size. Their adventures on the truly frightening Skull Island are later eclipsed by the final scenes atop the newly constructed, Art Deco–inspired, Empire State Building in New York. Actress Fay Wray's performance as Ann Darrow, the object of the affections of both man and ape, steals the film. Her character is so sexualized that it's hard not to see some connection between this film and the strict new enforcement of the Hays Code the following year. A cause and effect, if you will. And yet, Wray manages to convey an unaffected sweetness on film that saves it from being tawdry. The film has been remade on a number of occasions since, but no actress has ever come close to capturing the *je ne sais quoi* of Fay Wray's Ann Darrow. Why not? Only a woman of that era could combine these qualities to quite the same effect.

The film also featured aviation as the savior of civilization (New York City). In the final sequence, Kong, having abducted Ann Darrow, then climbs to the top of the Empire State Building to elude his enemies—but then, out of the blue, a squadron of fighter planes appears, looking both vulnerable and deadly at the same time. Kong can destroy one that gets too close to the building's spire, but the others pour bullets into the over-matched ape from a safe distance. Kong falls to his death. The aviators head back to base.

King Kong and the inauguration of FDR were the only two public spectacles that were on the same plane with the Chicago World's Fair in 1933. In retrospect, the film is full of racist and imperialistic overtones—but so was the age that produced it. It is also a very sexy film. So was the age that produced it.

—∞—

July 1933 was set to be one of the most consequential months of the entire World's Fair. Fascist Italy's intrepid air minister, Italo Balbo, was scheduled to arrive at the fair in the middle of the month with his armada of world-famous seaplanes. Generating excitement for visits such as this were part of what made the fair an ongoing event rather than a one-off proposition for

Fay Wray in *King Kong* (1933) exemplified the style, body language, attitude, and unaffected sex appeal of the era. *Alamy Images*.

Chicagoans. This is exactly what Rufus Dawes wanted. The fair needed to constantly be in the press, or else it risked becoming a passing fad before its allotted time was officially up. Balbo was a draw. There was no doubt about it. His journey would involve risk—and could also be milked for all the suspense it could generate in the press as well. For its part, Italy had made a serious investment in its contributions to the fair—a modernistic aviation-themed pavilion, and an installation in the Hall of Science. In these belt-tightening times, not all countries were willing or able to go all out in this manner. Italy wanted to make a statement.

To a certain degree, it seems that Benito Mussolini simply couldn't resist the opportunity the fair presented to boast. There were aspects of Italian society that, under his rule, had made strides. Aviation was the obvious example, but with its own attractive pavilion at the fair, Fascist Italy could more thoroughly develop a flattering, self-promoting narrative. The hope was that this in turn would favorably shape public opinion in the United States, an important country in Mussolini's estimation.* Italian designers certainly brought an original flair to the modernist/Art Deco theme of the fair. The aviation-themed Italian Pavilion invited visitors into a structure that was elegant, modern, and active.

Perhaps this could have described Balbo himself. He enjoyed immense popularity in the early 1930s, unlike his master. Surrounded by sycophants in his office in the ornate Palazzo Venezia, Mussolini felt secure in his own image of himself. Foreign papers, however, often had the effect of puncturing his narcissistic bubble. Italo Balbo was a useful tool when his successes were co-opted as Fascist Italy's successes, but his adoring press coverage in foreign papers was not something likely to please Benito Mussolini. As a result of Mussolini's megalomania, Balbo's upcoming expedition would require not only great leadership skills on his part, but also just the right amount of deference to his boss back in Rome. At the fair, few if any people would have understood this. Italy's marketing of itself was very slick. The thought that Benito Mussolini could possibly be so childish as to be jealous of a selfless and loyal patriot of his country would have seemed beneath the behavior of a statesman in the eyes of most Americans. But Mussolini was not a statesman. He was a clown and a bully.

---

* A handsome, full-color brochure was published in English for American visitors to the Pavilion to peruse. It included passages such as the following (with nary a hint of irony): "Foreign visitors to Italy over the past few years can vouch that the general renewal of the country was brought about and is still taking place in an atmosphere of order, discipline, and work without impairing the traditional calmness and gaiety of Italian life."

The aviation-themed Italian Pavilion at the 1933–1934 World's Fair. *Courtesy of University of Illinois Chicago Special Collections.*

As Chicago switched full on into deep summer, the fair's critical and commercial success seemed assured. Lenox Lohr and Rufus Dawes weren't going to leave things to chance, but they could rightly feel confident that the machine had been set in motion, and a bright future lay ahead for their creation. Each evening at dusk, in a repetition of the May 27 grand opening, light from the star Arcturus was harnessed to switch on the fair's multicolored lights. Fairgoers had quickly embraced the nightly light show in the fountain located between the two lagoons, with the Sky Ride's cables electrified and glowing above—another of Joseph Urban's many contributions to the fair he never was able to personally attend. Forty searchlights in five different colors lit up the night sky while a water show spurted from the fountain, with iridescent, multicolored cascades mesmerizing onlookers. It was truly the Rainbow City: fantasy, technology, and creativity combining to present a positive image of the world and the future. Given the grim realities that we correctly associate with the Great Depression, it's hard to believe that it really happened. But it really happened.

CHAPTER 9

Chief Flying Eagle

June 30, 1933. A summer night envelops the lagoon at Orbetello where an armada of giant white seaplanes rock gently at their moorings below Monte Argentario. The commander of this famous squadron, Italo Balbo, pedals a bicycle among the spartan quarters of his hundred-strong airmen, reminding them to turn in no later than 10:00 p.m. The months of training for the air voyage to Chicago are soon to be put to the test. The success of earlier air cruises with some of these same men doesn't lull their commander into a false sense of complacency. He knows that what they are about to do can turn deadly very quickly. Filled with nervous tension, recognizing the weight of responsibility that he is going to bear on his shoulders and his shoulders alone, Balbo can't sleep. In the early morning hours just before dawn, the airmen are awakened and ferried by launches to their preassigned seaplanes. Each new Savoia-Marchetti S.55 X is powered by two powerful engines*affixed to the top of each monoplane's wing, above the flight deck—one tractive, the other propulsive—generating 750 horsepower. As all fifty engines of the twenty-five seaplanes fire nearly simultaneously, the noise is deafening. The engines possess the growling, potent quality one associates with Ferraris or Bugattis. At 4:37 a.m. on July 1, Italo Balbo's lead plane heads out into the lagoon, leaving a silvery wake as it gathers speed, and lifts into the air, headed north toward the Swiss Alps.

Twenty-four seaplanes lift into the sky behind their leader; each carries four airmen (two pilots, a radio operator, and a mechanic). The "air armada" is composed of eight squadrons of three planes each (with a single seaplane in reserve). Each squadron is identified by a star or circle painted a

---

* Isotta-Fraschini Asso 750 engines.

particular color (black, red, white, or green) on the side rudders in the rear of the seaplanes. Balbo's lead squadron is identified by a black star.[1] They gain altitude and fly over northern Italy before ascending even higher as they near the Alps. The stunning majesty of these snow-topped peaks affects all but the most jaded. Even with the engines growling in their ears, the vista speaks to them of something akin to the eternal. Two and a half miles below, Sergei Rachmaninoff is in the midst of composing his "Rhapsody on a Theme from Paganini" in his villa on Lake Lucerne. The strains of his music lift, and lift the listener into someplace, something, rarefied. That morning, Italo Balbo and his men were living what Rachmaninoff was composing. A moment of transcendence? Perhaps . . .

Beginning to drop altitude, the Alps melt away and the course of the Rhine provides a guide northwestward toward the sea. The vineyards of the famous river had begun to produce the grapes that would swell and be made into famous Riesling wine, 1933 vintage. Cologne, with the steeple of its giant Gothic cathedral reaching skyward from another age, was visible to Balbo and his airmen. They were in the heart of Europe. Thus far the cruise had been nearly idyllic, but powerful wind gusts then reminded them of the seriousness of their undertaking. They leave the Rhine to descend toward the Zuider Zee (or what remained of it),* and the first stop on their journey— the city of Rembrandt—Amsterdam.

⸗∞⸗

Italo Balbo's epic flight to the United States—again with his air armada of flying boats, as in his 1930–1931 journey to Brazil—met with Mussolini's approval and great interest from the press in both Europe and America. This great fair had sparked something in the world, and by making Lake Michigan his destination, Italy's foremost aviator gave his imprimatur to the proceedings. He had to go! The technical, logistical, and navigational aspects of the flight were formidable. He and his team of pilots would fly via northern Europe, then Iceland and Canada before reaching the American heartland in Illinois. The loss of life and of aircraft on the preceding mission to Brazil hung over the expedition as it took off from Orbetello on July 1. This time they were flying the upgraded Savoia-Marchetti S.55 X, and instead of twelve seaplanes there were twenty-five aircraft. Soaring above the Alps en route to Amsterdam, the armada was beautiful to behold. Unfortunately, in the Dutch capital, tragedy struck.

---

* This inlet of the North Sea had been dammed at its mouth just the year before, and an ambitious land reclamation project had been undertaken.

As the armada descended onto the Zuider Zee, the seaplane piloted by Mario Baldini, coming in at too steep of an angle, flipped over in a violent accident, injuring the crew. More tragically, the craft's youthful radioman, Ugo Quintavalle, was trapped in the wreckage and drowned. It cast a pall over all of his former comrades. That could have been them, and they knew it. So much depended on precision. Balbo could not permit this loss to alter his course of action. That evening he met with Hugo Eckener's "girl Friday," Lady Grace Drummond-Hay, at the Amstel Hotel for dinner. The intrepid globetrotting journalist of course understood all too well the risks of air travel. As much as exacting training and technological innovation and competency had moved aviation forward, they were still to a large degree making this up as they went. This dissonance is what made this aviation's golden age. The heroic aspect of Lindbergh, Balbo, Eckener, and the Piccards was that they were aware of this, yet undaunted by it. To make air travel and space exploration "normal" took exceptional people. But Ugo Quintavalle also played a role in this. He was part of something truly special, he knew it, and he lost his life in the endeavor. And there were many Ugo Quintavalles in this era. Those of us living in the twenty-first century, who have the good fortune to take so much for granted in air travel, owe them.

The next day the giant white-painted armada ascended en route to Ireland, then on to the city of Reykjavik in Iceland. The Italians would spend more than a week in this far northern outpost of European civilization. The blonde Norse maidens were a source of endless fascination for Balbo's airmen. For their commander, planning the optimum moment for their departure occupied most of his waking hours. This was the most perilous part of the journey—a great leap over the forbidding gale-swept North Atlantic to Labrador. The distance—nearly fifteen hundred miles—the notorious fog, and the cold all presented grave challenges. And twenty-four seaplanes* had to be brought across, not just a single plane. The journey across the North Sea from Ireland to Iceland had already provided a preview of what to expect: the armada had been stuck in thick fog, and keeping formation had become a near impossible task. In the early-morning darkness of July 12, Balbo and his men bade farewell to their Icelandic hosts and pointed the noses of their aircraft west toward the New World and fame, with a whole lot of ocean below them and very little margin for error. Balbo biographer Claudio Segrè described the commander's state of mind as he "fortified himself with coffee and an occasional nip of cognac":

---

* After Baldini's craft had crashed, there was no longer a reserve.

In contrast to flying over land, flying over water, he fretted, stretched on interminably. The hours, especially the last ones, dragged on like months. With nothing for the eyes to focus on his imagination roamed freely and flying became a nightmare and an obsession. . . . Outside, fog banks varied from light and white to dark and opaque, so dark that he could only see the glow from his instruments.[2]

Balbo would later remark in an interview that this Arctic fog was "some of the worst weather I have encountered."[3] Climbing above it up into the chillier altitudes of blue sky risked the danger of ice forming on wings. In spite of this, Balbo ordered the armada to take the risk. This was as much (or more so) for the psychological effect on the pilots as it was for the aeronautical effect on the seaplanes. Onward on a southwesterly heading, the forty-eight engines powering the Savoia-Marchettis never once misfired, a testament to Italian engineering and workmanship.[4] Italy, the United States, and the world held their collective breath for news of Balbo. Then, at seven o'clock in the evening on July 12, the gleaming white phalanxes of flying boats appeared over Sandwich Bay in Labrador. To be fair, the Italian Air Force had played a supporting role for their airborne comrades by maintaining radio beacons and floating weather stations along the perilous route—but, in the end, it was the skill and discipline of the pilots and airmen that were the crucial factors in the crossing. It was no small achievement in scale. As aviation historian Robert Wohl explained: "To appreciate the magnitude of the Italians' achievement, one must realize that before their flight, only five aircraft had succeeded in making the North Atlantic crossing from east to west. That number now rose to twenty-nine, twenty-four of them being Italian."[5]

Hardy and intrepid members of the world press descended on this remote outpost located on the easternmost shores of the North American continent. Feeding the anticipation in the Windy City, the *Chicago American* scooped its competition by having photographs of Balbo's seaplanes afloat at their moorings flown directly to Chicago for publication. The caption beneath the aerial photograph reads, "Safe in American Waters."[6] Labrador was then part of the Dominion of Newfoundland, not yet annexed to the larger Dominion of Canada next door. To be the focal point for so much attention must have been quite a novelty indeed for the local residents. For his part, Italo Balbo first saw to the refueling of his seaplanes before attending to diplomatic niceties. But as he had demonstrated in South America earlier in the decade, Balbo could be a charming and articulate guest, the perfect representative for a regime whose image was normally dominated in the public's mind by a narcissistic bully frothing with bluster. Balbo showed that modern Italy could at the same time produce an urbane, intelligent man with a winning personality and genuine courage. Yet the black shirts Balbo and his men wore underneath their flight suits were a reminder of the ugly ideology they represented, if not embraced. Balbo's achievement was fascism's achievement, and this fact was not lost on more critical observers.

Fighting a storm as they flew southwest, Balbo's armada entered the Dominion of Canada on the morning of July 13, landing at the port town of Shediac, New Brunswick. Once again, Balbo won the crowd. The *Chicago Herald and Examiner* had sent correspondent Fred Glasby to Shediac in anticipation of the Italians' arrival. In his feature story, Glasby commented favorably on Balbo's linguistic ability, observing him "responding in Italian, English, and French."[7] New Brunswick's premier was on hand to welcome the aviators, and took the opportunity to "praise Mussolini's accomplishments in rejuvenating Italy."[8] A congratulatory telegram from German Chancellor Adolf Hitler also caught up with Balbo in Shediac, signed "with admiration." The next day the aviators were in Montreal, landing on the St Lawrence—ice free in the summer months. The population of this large and predominantly French-speaking city, built on the slopes of a promontory, enthusiastically came out to greet the visitors. And for the first time, an Italian immigrant community—replete with their own local black shirts and Fascist salutes—embraced their hero-brothers from the old country.[9] By this time, Balbo had become impatient, his diplomatic skills wearing thin under the strain and general lack of sleep. He understood all along that Chicago was the main objective, the raison d'être for his entire mission. He called off a planned dinner, disappointing local notables to concentrate on what the morrow would bring . . .

The Drake Hotel on Chicago's Gold Coast was built at the outset of the Jazz Age. When it opened its doors on New Year's Eve, 1920, it instantly became the premier hotel of the Midwest. As it had in the city as a whole, Prohibition had the effect of stimulating high society's social scene. This set made the Drake its preserve. In turn the Drake consciously cultivated its public image as an elite institution in the city as embodied in its Latin motto, *Aquila non capit muscas.** Even today, one can absorb some of the Zeitgeist of that era in the elegantly appointed Coq d'Or located below the hotel's lobby level. It was opened in 1933 during the time of the World's Fair.

---

* "The eagle hunts no flies" (i.e., a noble or important person doesn't deal with insignificant issues).

As Italo Balbo planned for the 870-mile journey that would have his armada "roar down on their goal, flying over Niagara Falls, skirting Toledo and Cleveland,"[10] the Drake prepared for its role as the expedition's official base of operations in the city of Chicago. The hotel was equipped with the capacity to receive radiograms from various locales on the lookout for Balbo's seaplanes, as well as Balbo himself. The flurry of these radiograms on the day of Balbo's arrival, documenting the seaplanes' movements in detail, first by the hour and then by the minute, vividly demonstrates the near hysteria of anticipatory suspense the city was under. Have they left Montreal? Is the weather going to delay them? When will they get here? The Drake's staff fed the hysteria being whipped up by the local press (five dailies locked in cutthroat competition). A sampling of these radiograms, now housed in the archives of the Chicago History Museum:

- THE FIRST BALBO PLANES HAVE PASSED PRESCOTT AT 12:33 PM E.D.T. THIS IS ABOUT 120 MILES FROM MONTREAL
- REPORT FROM GENERAL BALBO ADVISING THAT HE PASSED OVER PORTHURON AT 347PM EDT
- AT 457P CST TWELVE OF THE PLANES ARE CIRCLING OVER THE LOOP IN CHICAGO AND THE OTHER TWELVE ARE PLYING OVER THE LAKE IN A NORTHERLY DIRECTION. PERFECT FORMATION[11]

By the time the final radiograms were received, a crowd had gathered, described as "a seething mass of humanity" by the *Chicago American*. Within the fairgrounds "a hundred thousand persons were inside"; "Navy Pier was packed by more than 20,000, while all along the shore line from the far South Side other thousands gathered to witness the great spectacle." It was a "signal to the city to give vent to pent-up emotions."[12] On Saturday, July 15, at about 5:45 p.m. Chicago time, Balbo's brilliant white seaplanes appeared in the skies over the city. A gorgeous late afternoon on a mid-summer's day provided an idyllic backdrop for Balbo's crowning achievement. Adding to the splendor was the giant dirigible airship *Macon*, on hand to welcome the visitors, and a squadron of nearly forty U.S. army aircraft from Selfridge Field that had escorted the seaplanes after they entered American airspace earlier in the day. As the Italians descended the Americans flew in a formation above, spelling out I-T-A-L-Y for those on the ground to see.[13] The message was clear from the U.S. military: Welcome! But we possess potent aviation technology and skillful pilots as well.

Italo Balbo's seaplanes land flawlessly on Lake Michigan. *Getty Images.*

The roar of the engines and the giant propellers caught everyone's attention. So, too, did the perfect precision with which the formations appeared above the city's skyscrapers. It was the future coming to call in the Windy City. The enormous, expectant crowds that lined the lakefront were in for a treat. With red, white, and green Italian flags snapping to attention in the lakefront breeze, side by side with red, white, and blue American flags, the twenty-four Savoia Marchettis landed on Lake Michigan in a prearranged order meant to impress observers with the skill and discipline of the Italian pilots. Those who were there that day, whether man, woman, child, American, Italian, Fascist, or anti-Fascist, marveled at just how *beautiful* a spectacle it was. As Gus Lazzarini, an eyewitness, later recalled, "It moved everybody . . . people had never seen something like *that*."[14] College student Marie Nardulli was working as an official greeter at the fair and was similarly struck by what she witnessed: "It was noisy, you just had a lot of noise. . . . There was nothing like this, nothing like this. With the planes. I can still hear the roaring of the planes as they were coming through. It was very exciting. Very beautiful."[15]

To be fair, there were other observers who saw the foreign formations overhead and felt a certain unease, not unmixed with foreboding. The *Herald and Examiner* saw the spectacle as a lesson to the United States:

> It must have occurred to thousands yesterday to peer into the future. And it may have occurred to them to ponder a few thoughts. Suppose other planes, many more planes, would cross the sea on a mission that would be anything but goodwill. Chicago at least is air-minded now. It must realize the possibility of going from here to there, thousands of miles though the distance must be. And thus, I think, when Balbo set his ship down last evening, he completed the greatest lesson in aerial navigation that history yet records.[16]

Watching films of these giant seaplanes above Chicago in 1933, with their combined engines creating a very distinctive sound, one almost reflexively expects to hear next the equally distinctive whistle made by bombs descending on their targets. It's as if we have become conditioned to associating the one sound with the other because of what *we* know will soon happen in Europe later in this decade. It is an uncanny sensation. Chicagoans, in 1933, weren't preconditioned to this. Aviation's "golden age" seemed to offer more hope than dread, a brighter future for humanity. And people *wanted* to believe—this is important. The thought of another world war—this one involving aircraft as powerful as Balbo's—was simply too terrible a thought to dwell on. Better to see progress in those gleaming white seaplanes than a threat.

As Balbo emerged from his seaplane with black shirt and flying gear, he exuded a native charm that won over the crowd without even trying. But true to character, he thought first of his men and then their aircraft. There to greet him was Prince Potenziani, Italy's commissioner to the World's Fair, aboard the USS *Wilmette* (the Navy had thoughtfully sent the vessel as a staging point for the Italians to shower and change into their dress uniforms before having to face the crowds). Reporter Robert Wood, sent by the *Herald and Examiner* to get first impressions of the famous aviator, commented favorably on his first words to the Prince: "Before his first handshake . . . Gen. Italo Balbo wanted to know the latest word of the members of his crew who were injured in the crash of one of their planes in Amsterdam, Holland. 'How are the comrades we left behind?' . . . He seemed greatly relieved when told that Capt. Baldini and the enlisted men were recovering from their injuries in Rome."[17] Even before coming aboard the *Wilmette*, Balbo had waited: "For nearly two hours he stood on the wings of his ship, marked with a single black star, as it rode the waves in the harbor. He watched the maneuvers of

Balbo's seaplanes flying over the fairgrounds. *Courtesy of University of Illinois Chicago Special Collections.*

his charges until the last plane cleaved the water with its pontoons. Only then did he leave the ship."[18]

Balbo and his pilots were taken by motor launch down the shore to the Century of Progress Fairgrounds where the official reception was waiting for them near the Court of Honor of the Hall of Science. World War I ace Reed Landis had been placed in charge of the reception committee and had bungled the transfer of Balbo's men from their seaplanes to the *Wilmette*,[19] seemingly overmatched by the day's events, forced by his own mistakes into having to play catch-up. But he was there near the Court of Honor at the appointed time, and so were a throng of enthusiastic local blackshirts giving Balbo the Fascist salute, which he returned.[20] Harry S. New, U.S. commissioner to the World's Fair, officially welcomed the Italians to Illinois on behalf of President Franklin D. Roosevelt, while Governor Horner and Chicago's Mayor Kelly gushed over their visitors, with Horner comparing Balbo's air voyage to that of Columbus in 1492 and Kelly lauding (probably with an eye on the Italian American vote) Italy's "position in the front rank of the countries of the world, a nation of explorers, builders, scientists"[21] and not just gangsters—it was left unsaid, but the implication was clear. Balbo's speech in response was short and sweet, and carried live via radio back to Rome for Mussolini's ears:

> We have today accomplished the mission entrusted to us by our chief, Mussolini, in landing in the magic city of Chicago . . . I cannot find sufficient words to express the appreciation of myself and my men for this magnificent reception. The purpose of the flight was to bring the greeting of the new Italy to the United States. Viva Chicago! Viva America![22]

The crowd went wild in a torrent of mutual adulation. Mussolini back in Rome detected the proper amount of deferential sycophancy. In time he would try to convince his countrymen, and himself, that it was *he* and not Balbo who had achieved international aeronautical fame in Chicago. Regarding the latter, he seems to have been successful. Balbo and his pilots, meanwhile, piled into waiting convertibles to be taken to a popular reception at adjacent Soldier Field. As the motorcade, escorted by the city's Black Horse Troop mounted on coal-black chargers fitted with white reins,* carefully snaked its way through the mass of fairgoers, Chicago gave itself up to its new popular hero. The next day's edition of the *Herald and Examiner* prob-

---

* The "Black Horse" had no connection to the blackshirts. It was a special unit of the 106th Illinois Cavalry regiment, tasked with escorting visiting dignitaries.

ably described the Zeitgeist of that moment best: "The city like a gracious hostess, had donned her Summer best and strolled down to her great front yard to greet her guests."[23]

Soldier Field had been built in 1924 as the city's great enclosed open-air space. Its name (adopted in 1925) simply referred to the city's war dead (many of whom had perished in the recent war in Europe). Meant to hold tens of thousands of spectators and participants in public events, it features a neoclassical design that dominates the lakefront to the present day, with giant Doric columns and a portico with a triangular roof reminiscent of a Greek temple. By 1933, it had hosted millions for football games, political rallies, and cultural events. With the World's Fair just next door and on Northerly Island, the stadium was a natural complement to its activities. In the event approximately sixty thousand Chicagoans filled the stands to greet their hero,[24] none prouder than the city's many Italian Americans. Balbo addressed the crowd in Italian. His accomplishment was their accomplishment. He was of their blood. Regardless of the blackshirts and Fascist salutes that were evident, Balbo had touched something deeper with his Italian American cousins. Ideology was superficial (as the World War II experience for Italian Americans and Italians would largely bear out), but *patrie*, in the historical, linguistic, and cultural—if not necessarily political—context was felt on an emotional, instinctive level. As the sun began to go down behind the prairies of eastern Illinois and the floodlights were switched on, Soldier Field provided the setting for the embodiment of this bond. It was a wonderful moment for Italian Americans. The *Chicago Tribune* reported on the reaction of an Italian immigrant named Phil Gardini of Winnemac Avenue, who earlier in the day had witnessed Balbo's seaplanes landing on Lake Michigan: "he removed his hat from his graying hair. Tears were near the surface as he looked up and said with awe, 'Balbo's in one of those . . . planes.'"[25] Not all Italian Americans, however, felt this way. A pamphlet being distributed at this time was signed "Italian Socialist Federation and Italian League for Rights of Man" and highlighted Balbo's checkered, violent past, even implicating him in the murder and beheading of Giacomo Matteotti:

> It is a disgrace that this murderer and terrorist should be received by Democratic America as the official representative of the Italian people. This man no more represents the Italian people than Kaiser Wilhelm represented the German people. There should be no place in this free country for such tyrants. This terrorism continues today and the Italian born American workers protest against this infamy in the name of Matteotti and all our other murdered comrades. WE ask

the American people of all races to join us in protesting against the reception given to this murderer.[26]

Italian Consul General Giuseppe Castruccio countered this in an editorial written for the United Press and published in the *Chicago Daily Times* the day after Balbo arrived. No doubt the Socialist Federation and the League for the Rights of Man found his views laughable, if not ironic, when he claimed that Italy and the United States "form the cornerstone of protection of weak nations against the strong, the poor against the rich, and for the enforcement of a real and international justice."[27] One wonders if this is what Ethiopians thought Italy was fighting for less than two years later, when Mussolini ordered the invasion of that African nation?

Fortunately for Italo Balbo and his pilots, they did not have to face questions such as these. They left Soldier Field and went directly to the luxurious Drake Hotel where a reception put on by the Dante Alighieri Society awaited them, complete with replica seaplanes made entirely of red and white roses and green moss. To the chagrin of the Society members, who had been patiently waiting all evening, the Italian aviators "lingered only a moment or two, looked at the tea refreshments and joined six of their companions who were enjoying huge steaks in the main dining room."[28] Their commander went straight to his room to change into a fresh uniform, which included dress gloves and a natty walking stick. The Italians were, if nothing else, fashionable. The *Tribune*'s society editor, India Moffett, contributed a long list of who's who in early 1930s Chicago in the next morning's paper, but she singled out the Italian Consul's wife, Signora Castruccio, "a tall, willowy brunette" who never appeared smarter than she did in the "red, black, and plaid gown she was wearing," and Mrs. Howard Linn in her "simple, flowing robe of gray, with a red ribbon."[29]

It was a late night, and Balbo and his men were running on fumes. In fact, two days earlier Balbo had telegrammed Castruccio from New Brunswick begging for a respite: "I ask you to give me as much peace as possible, For we need rest. Cordial greeting to you in Chicago—Italo Balbo."[30]

On the other hand, the huge welcoming crowds, the "Pretty young 'sub-debs'" asking for autographs,[31] the Drake, the glittering representatives of Chicago Society, being in one of the richest, fastest, and most notorious cities in the world, must have kept the Italians going further than their normal constitutions would have allowed. But eventually the desire for sleep, precious sleep, drove them to their rooms where for nine sublime hours they had nothing to distract them except their dreams. For his part, Italo Balbo was comforted by the sight of the many plainclothes policeman outside the hotel, guaranteeing no appearances by intruders wishing him well or ill.[32]

—◦◦◦◦—

Sunday, July 16, dawned sunny and bright on the shores of Lake Michigan. After being served breakfast in their rooms by the curious Drake staff, a *Herald and Examiner* reporter found the aviators on the eighth floor wandering around in "gay pajamas from room to room, asking each other jovially if they wanted to start back on the long return flight at once. 'we want to see the fair first' was the usual reply."[33] However, as good Catholics (Mussolini after all had reached an accord with the Pope in 1929), Balbo and his men first attended mass at the Holy Name Cathedral. What Balbo's thoughts were, as a formerly ardent Republican,* are anyone's guess. After a quick refresher back at the Drake the men then headed for the fairgrounds—ostensibly their whole reason for being in Chicago—to meet with the fair's president, Rufus Dawes, and tour the grounds in person. More gushing praise and mutual adulation filled the day's events—everyone, it seemed, wanted to meet the Italian visitors.

Conspicuous in their uniforms and cossetted by their attendant entourage, the Italians saw the fair from a rather patrician perch. Mussolini did not want them mixing with the plebeian throngs enjoying the Midway. Fascist supermen were supposed to be above such amusements. It couldn't have been much fun. The welcome accorded to Balbo at the fair's Italian Pavilion, however, did have its rewards. Two Italian American maidens (one blonde, one brunette) each presented the conquering hero with roses.[34]

Decades later, historian Cheryl Ganz related the story of one of these young ladies in her book on the fair:

> Teresa de Falco, a resident in Chicago's Italian immigrant neighborhood and a cigarette girl at the Italian Pavilion, was proud to be chosen as one of the young women. . . . She felt it was a beautiful, joyous occasion with all of the pilots in their dress white uniforms participating in parades and festivities. . . . She joined several crew members at one of their banquet tables and toured the city with them by car.[35]

That evening, the Italian American community put on a spirited reception for Balbo and his men at the imposing Stevens Hotel overlooking Michigan Avenue. As they entered the grand ballroom, many of the approximately five thousand guests gave the Fascist salute and shouted Fascist slogans. The

---

* In the European, Leftist sense of the word.

Balbo received at the Italian Pavilion, July 16, 1933. *Courtesy of University of Illinois Chicago Special Collections.*

applause lasted fifteen minutes before the cheering died away. The jingoism was replaced by something more honorable when Balbo publicly called the roll of his airmen, with Quintavalle's name being called first; Balbo's simple tribute: "I salute him."[36] The speech that followed was less about what he and his men had accomplished, and more about the new Italy that had made it all possible: "I give all credit to Benito Mussolini."[37] This was exactly what his chief wanted to hear—the more cringe-worthy the sycophancy, the better. But as reports of Balbo's reception in Chicago began to filter back to him in Rome, Mussolini began to grow jealous of his younger protégé. Balbo was outshining him.* And the better Balbo did his job, the more pronounced it became. In this respect he was in an impossible position. No one back home was allowed to outshine Il Duce.

---

* Balbo even received an honorary degree from Loyola University Chicago.

The official festivities having concluded, Balbo's pilots had the opportunity to socialize with the guests in the Stevens' grand ballroom. Marie Nardulli, selected as a rose-bearing hostess, "danced with four or five of them"; as she later recalled, "they were very nice."[38]

Monday, July 17, was the second full day of the Italians' visit to the Fair. It proved to be probably the most eventful, unscripted, and—for lack of a better word— fun day that Balbo and his men had in the Windy City. For all of the talk of goodwill and international cooperation, there was often an earnest, stilted quality to much of the official interaction between the Italians and the Chicagoans. For Italo Balbo personally, it was the kind of day that most people fantasize about at some point in their lives, but never experience—a day when all the city was yours. And he was good-humored and enthusiastic enough to take advantage of the moment for all that it was worth.

The day began with another reception—this one at city hall—in which Mayor Kelly ceremoniously gave Balbo a golden "key to the city" and officially recognized East Seventh Street as hereafter to be known as "Balbo Avenue." It still is.* According to Bruce Grant of the *Chicago Daily Times*, "a woman crashed the police lines and did what every other woman wanted to do—kissed him."[39] From city hall, Balbo was escorted to Grant Park where he paid homage to his countryman, Christopher Columbus. The Italian American community erected a monument to the famous explorer and would affix a plaque to its base explicitly linking Balbo's air voyage with his predecessor's sea voyage.† Back to the Drake for a luncheon, then on to the fair where the most startingly original (if somewhat awkward) ceremony Balbo was to take part in took place.

As part of the 1933 World Fair's "cultural" exhibits, a group of Plains Indians led by Sioux Chief Blackhorn had come to the Windy City to represent Native American culture. By this time the "Cowboys and Indians" genre in popular literature and film had become ubiquitous, even back in Italy. Like most of the exhibits and cultural performances, the Sioux were viewed with a mix of curiosity, admiration, and denigration. The 1933 Fair had progressed to a certain degree beyond the blatantly racist tropes of its predecessor forty years earlier, but there was still plenty of racism evident, of both the academic and the leering varieties. And on the other side of the Atlantic,

---

* The street runs only a short distance between State Street and the lakefront. But it's a nice street, with a view of waves gently lapping at the sand where it ends.

† This monument would be removed in 2020 due to its glorification of a man many saw primarily as directly involved in enslaving Native Americans, and indirectly responsible for the eventual genocide of millions.

Hitler was ranting about the inherent superiority of Nordic (white) peoples. Eugenics was all the rage. Thus, the context for Balbo's famous meeting with Blackhorn is a complicated one. Balbo arrived at the "Indian Village" late in the afternoon, dressed in a gray double-breasted suit, effecting a dapper "man about town" air. Like everyone else at the fair, the Sioux visitors had been very impressed by the landings of Balbo's seaplanes on Lake Michigan two days before. The leader of such a magnificent mission must truly be a leader of men, one worthy of the title "Chief." With the press mesmerized by the spectacle unfolding in front of them, Blackhorn, in full tribal regalia, approached the nervous-looking Italian and placed a full Sioux war bonnet on his head, conferring the title "Chief Flying Eagle" on Balbo for all time. What could have been an undignified and circus-like ceremony was saved by Blackhorn's sincerity and Balbo's genuine, almost childlike, delight in receiving this honor.[40] As serious as Italo Balbo was about aviation, there was still also this "Peter Pan and the lost boys" aspect to his personality that was never more evident than on that afternoon.

That evening, the Congress Hotel was the site of another lavish dinner, followed by a dance at the fashionable Casino Club. For Balbo, the interminable round of receptions, speeches, and dinners had begun to wear thin. He wanted to *see* the fair—the real life that was going on outside the Drake, the limousines, and the rostrum. Enlisting the aid of fellow pilot Reed Landis,

THE INDUCTION OF CHIEF "FLYING EAGLE" (GENERAL ITALO BALBO) INTO THE SIOUX TRIBE,
INDIAN CEREMONIALS - AMERICAN INDIAN VILLAGES
A CENTURY OF PROGRESS 1933

Representatives of the Sioux Nation, and Chief Flying Eagle of Fascist Italy (1933). *Alamy Images.*

Balbo asked if he could arrange a late-night incognito visit to the Midway for the type of entertainment Mussolini had disparaged. Landis, this time up for the job (unlike his earlier ineffectiveness when Balbo and his men first arrived), discretely put together a small group composed of William C. Boyden, Mrs. Morton Schwartz, Mrs. Harold Strotz, a Mrs. Alexander of New York, a Mrs. Maxwell, and a fifth woman whose identity was never learned.[41] What Balbo and his escorts didn't realize was that they were being trailed by an intrepid *Chicago News* reporter (unfortunately, one without a camera). First stop, the "Auto scooters" where Balbo and his companions took turns chasing each other around. The next stop was the "African Dodger" dunking booth, where African American sitters could be dropped in the tub with a well-aimed ball at the target (needless to say, there were distinct racist overtones to this whole unfortunate setup); next came the "shooting gallery" where Balbo impressed his American friends by "knocking down seven squirrels."[42] The night ended at the "Manhattan Beer Garden" where the Casino escapees enjoyed a beer and music by the Ernie Young Orchestra. Whether Balbo found his way to see Sally Rand perform in her "Streets of Paris" revue isn't known.*

The final day of Balbo's visit was taken up with more receptions and reviews, and a final dance at the Tavern Club, but a seriousness of purpose would have reentered the lives of the Italian airmen as they readied for the long flight to their next destination—New York. Balbo had received an invitation to fly separately from New York to Washington, DC to visit President Roosevelt at the White House (Roosevelt, in fact, would belatedly bestow the Navy's Distinguished Flying Cross on Balbo for his achievement).[43] The city came out for one final expression of adulation as Balbo and his pilots were slowly driven down Michigan Avenue in a farewell parade; Chicagoans stood ten to fifteen deep on either side of the city's greatest thoroughfare. And then it was over. In New York, Balbo would be received by frenzied crowds of Italian Americans perhaps even larger in number than those that had welcomed him to Chicago. His message was simple: be proud to be Italian! The humiliation of the *emigranti* was at an end. Fascist Italy was ushering in a new age. That it would be a dark age, though, was clear to few at the time.

A giant rally in Madison Square Garden mixed Italian patriotism with Mussolini's chauvinism, alternately exciting or alienating New Yorkers depending on their ethnic and political backgrounds. The Garden later would

---

* In one day, Italo Balbo received a golden key to one of the great cities of America; had a street named after him while he was still living; was made a chief of the mightiest Indian tribe ever to ride the Great Plains; and, anticipating Audrey Hepburn's "Princess Ann" in the film "Roman Holiday," escaped his minders for a night on the town, riding an auto scooter with playful abandon—worth pausing to ponder.

be the site of the "America First" rallies led by Balbo's fellow aviator, Charles Lindbergh. By then, fascism could no longer claim a peaceful or progressive mantle. One had to make a choice: either to be cowed, to become an accomplice, or to resist.

———∞∞∞———

In the end, Balbo's arrival at the 1933 Chicago World's Fair was more than just great entertainment or a propaganda coup for fascism; it was an affirmation of the human spirit and the willingness to push the frontiers of the possible a little further for all of humanity. In this, perhaps no other event captured so assuredly the ethos of the fair itself.

Once ashore, Balbo's visit to Chicago took on an almost carnival-like momentum all its own, as everyone who was anyone, and many who were not, vied with each other to heap the most extravagant praise possible on the aviator. With the possible exception of the fictional Ferris Bueller, Chicago has probably never come out so spontaneously and affectionately for any single individual in its history. Parties, speeches, balls, diplomatic fetes, and

Fascist salute for Italo Balbo (center, in white uniform and cap), New York City (1933). *Getty Images.*

a rollicking parade down Michigan Avenue awaited the man from Ferrara. For Italian Americans, the pride felt in seeing one of their own taking center stage—not because he was notorious, but because he was skilled, daring, and dignified—generated near-euphoria that was hard to describe. But there were those who recognized that beneath the impressive gloss was a system that bullied, bragged, and glorified war. America later tried to erase the images of Italian Americans giving the fascist salute en masse as Balbo's motorcade rolled through Chicago, but it happened.

One of the endearing aspects of Balbo's visit to the fair was his willingness to join in the fun. Perhaps the most unforgettable moment was the ceremony in which the Sioux Nation awarded Balbo a war bonnet and gave him the honorary title, "Chief Flying Eagle." The Sioux representatives recognized something elemental and powerful in the white flying boats descending from the blue ether and landing so gracefully on Lake Michigan. And the press loved it.

Decades later, Italian aviation historian Gregory Alegi interviewed surviving members of Balbo's 1933 Air Armada. To a man, they were proud of their aeronautical achievement, but (though they themselves never articulated it explicitly) it came with a curse of sorts. For the rest of their lives there was a certain sense of anticlimax, that nothing they could ever do would surpass the unaffected glory and adulation of those champagne-filled days in Chicago and New York.[44]

CHAPTER 10

Waking from the Dream

Balbo's visit thrilled Chicagoans and visitors to the fair from across the country and the world alike. And the expected fall arrival of airship captain, Doctor Hugo Eckener, and his giant zeppelin from Germany generated continued excitement and anticipation. In the spring of 1933, before Air Marshal Balbo's famous trip to Chicago, German propaganda chief Joseph Goebbels had insisted that he go aloft in the *Graf Zeppelin* above Rome during its visit to the Eternal City. He understood the powerful propaganda value the giant airship possessed. In Chicago, among the fair's organizers, this bred no small degree of anxiety. If Hitler's poisonous ideology was able to attach itself to Eckener's dream, it could lead to trouble. But the upside, even given the risk, was also considerable. The *Graf Zeppelin*, then in Brazil on duty as a passenger liner between South America and Europe, was seen by the fair's organizers as a great prize. If the world's most famous airship and its equally famous captain came to Chicago, it would add even greater international prestige to the event. Eckener agreed on the condition that a special postage stamp be issued in the United States, sales of which would then be used to help offset the Zeppelin Company's costs in sending its flagship north to Chicago. But now, along with the traditional black, white, and red–striped German flag applied to its stabilizing fins, the airship would also include the swastika: symbol of Nazism.

For Chicago's Jewish community, Eckener's visit was fraught with peril. The ugly anti-Semitism loose in Germany would be seen to have official approval of a sort if the *Graf Zeppelin* came to the city. This generated denunciations and even violent threats. Eckener, for his part, was sensitive to this.* He had little respect for the ravings of Hitler or the thuggery of his followers. But zeppelins had become a symbol of German accomplishment and renewal, and like it or not, Adolf Hitler was now the leader of Germany. As the airship made its way inexorably north, Eckener was forced to confront his beliefs—beliefs that had no place in a country run by bullies, bigots, and psychopaths. His personal prestige was immense. But there was a limit to what Hitler would accept from the most admired German in the world. This was a moment of truth.

Eckener, of course, had previously brought the *Graf* to Chicago, during the final leg of his circumnavigation of the globe in 1929. Hundreds of thousands of Chicagoans had filled the lakefront and made as much noise as possible in greeting. In a city known for its civic boosterism, it was keen to out–New York, New York. Eckener recalled that "what we experienced in Chicago exceeded all our expectations and fantasies. . . . What the Chicagoans produced in the way of noise-making and other signs of enthusiasm on our appearance probably set a record that can never be beaten."[1] But that was then. Before the 1929 crash, before the Depression, and, most importantly, before Hitler.

Hitler's rapid accession to absolute power in early 1933 had caught the United States off guard, to a certain degree. But he hadn't come out of nowhere. Throughout 1932, Americans had been fed a steady diet in their newspapers from foreign correspondents about what was going on in Germany. Hitler and his "Brownshirts" were ugly and threatening, but at the same time clownish and seemingly out of their league politically. This was why the sudden about-face by Germany's more traditional conservative politicians to invite Hitler into the government was so unexpected. And now with the Reichstag a smoking ruin, and Hitler's Gestapo arresting political opponents and putting them in the new Dachau concentration camp, people were getting nervous. His rants against Jews added to the anxiety, and began to spark anger in many Americans. Who did this strutting, barking, madman think he was anyway! The mood in Chicago toward Germany had changed. That is not to say that the city's view of the great zeppelin captain, Hugo Eckener, had changed. But navigating the line between the two increasingly required nuance: a nuance that Hitler and his propaganda chief, Joseph Goebbels (whom Eckener referred to as the "wicked fairy"[2]) made more and more difficult to employ. To them, Germany and the Nazis were inseparable. One was either with Nazi Germany, or was not with Germany. Very

---

* Eckener, for instance, maintained a cordial professional relationship with the renowned Jewish economist, Edgar Salin (Eckener was, of course, himself a former economist).

intentionally, they didn't allow any space between the two. By dint of his well-deserved fame and the genuine esteem that so many millions of people the world over felt for him, Hugo Eckener could not be so easily brought to heel. But he was a German, and intended to remain so. This being the case, the Nazis ultimately held the trump card and, deep down, he must have recognized this on some elemental level.

What would you do if your country was highjacked by a gang of hate-filled racists? Would you leave? Could you leave? Might it not be better to just keep one's head down and hope for better days? Would you go along to a certain degree when you thought it was in your best interest to do so? If so, to what degree? Where was that line exactly? As enthusiastic as many Germans would come to be about Nazism, as Hitler put the unemployed back to work and forced a renegotiation of Germany's place in the world by tearing up the Versailles Treaty, it's important to keep in mind that not all Germans bought into this. But again, what would you do? This was the situation Hugo Eckener found himself in when the idea to bring the *Graf Zeppelin* to Chicago for the World's Fair was broached by Karl Eitel, the owner of the city's elegant Bismarck Hotel, and Henry Vissering, a back-channel contact to the Zeppelin Company. Perhaps recalling the *Graf*'s rousing reception in 1929, Eckener agreed, and the plan was set in motion that ultimately would force those involved to show their hand, even if it was done obliquely. In this, Eckener's visit to Chicago could be seen as the first public resistance to Hitler on the world stage (intended or not). Resisting isn't always as clear-cut and heroic as one might like—it can be awkward, in half-pints instead of full quarts—but it has to start somewhere. And one could make the argument that it started in Chicago.

———— ⬡ ————

The plan was to repeat the *Graf*'s earlier air voyage from Brazil to the United States via the Caribbean, first pioneered in 1930. Hugo Eckener, perhaps on a certain level sensing that this might be the final trip of the old regime—that is, a better time—before the full force of Nazism was brought to bear on Germany and the zeppelin project, seemed to be in fine fettle. Adding to the buoyant mood was the presence of eleven-month-old Billy Munson and his "big" sister (herself a young child).[3] Dorothea Momsen of the *New York Times* was aboard, and reported that over Trinidad, the passengers could clearly see sharks in the aquamarine waters below. Assessing the flight of the zeppelin from Brazil to the Caribbean, she remarked that "the technical conditions are satisfactory" and, furthermore, that the "children aboard are enjoying the trip. Even the baby looks out the window."[4] The airship skirted thunderstorms near Santo Domingo, and arrived in Miami on October 23.[5] The swastikas emblazoned on its port (left) side rear stabilizing fins were a glaring propaganda symbol, and magnet for those looking to make a statement opposing Hitler's policies, particularly those targeting Jews. In the event the *Graf* was moored at Opa Locka Naval Air Station, a dozen miles from the city center, under heavy security. Interest in the *Graf*'s return visit to Chicago were stoked by the city's dailies. Much as they had done three months before on the eve of Italo Balbo's arrival, the press outdid each other trying to get the inside scoop. In this, the *Herald and Examiner* had them all beat—hiring the mayor of Miami, E. G. Sewall (riding aboard the Zeppelin as a guest of honor) as its exclusive correspondent.[6] Another paper paid to have live radio dispatches relayed to its press room, in flight.

The trip north to Akron, the home of the Goodyear Company which had formed a separate airship unit with the Zeppelin Company in 1923, took thirty-three hours as adverse weather conditions forced a less direct route. Eckener had circled above Akron in a rainstorm waiting until the weather cleared to attempt a landing in the morning. When he was queried by a Goodyear engineer about why he had waited to land, Eckener had gaily replied, "I guess we could have . . . but it would have been impossible to dock the ship. Anyway, the baby [Billy Munson] had a bath up there."[7] This elicited a round of laughter. Eckener had a jovial and witty sense of humor that he could employ to make people feel at ease, yet another asset he could—and often did—employ to further the Zeppelin cause. He wasn't much with large crowds, but one on one or in smaller groups, his charm was unmistakable. And he enjoyed life. He couldn't have been more different than the "new" Germans rising to prominence under the Third Reich—a largely humorless lot whose insufferable arrogance and boorish insistence on carrying their point could spoil anyone's mood and test anyone's patience.

Eckener had already had an unpleasant experience with these "new" Germans in Brazil. It seemed that Nazi sycophants living abroad tried even harder than their like-minded cousins back home to press their views on those who disagreed with them. Later he would address, head on, what he termed the "tensions and divisions" that the local Nazis had caused within "the German colony in Rio," winning the gratitude of "distinguished Germans who had suffered from the terror of the local organization."[8] Thus, Hugo Eckener was under no illusions about the atmosphere that awaited him in Chicago. He'd already experienced it.

In Chicago itself, the city's large and influential German American community had been given control of the fair's German exhibition by the

A dapper Hugo Eckener greets the public in Miami en route to the Chicago World's Fair (1933). *Courtesy of University of Illinois Chicago Special Collections.*

organizers, and it had made a decision to very deliberately exclude any refer-
ence to Hitler or the Nazi regime. The swastika would not be permitted to
fly over a Century of Progress. As historian Cheryl Ganz pointed out, "The
German Americans viewed the fair as an opportunity to showcase German
music, art, and culture as well as contributions of Germans and German
Americans to the development of the United States"[9] (i.e., not Hitler). It is
important to keep in mind that Chicagoans of German ancestry made up
approximately one-quarter of the Windy City's population in 1933. Some
Chicago historians estimate that the figure might have even been higher, but
the anti-German persecution of the World War I era had convinced many
German Americans to "pass" into the larger English-speaking Anglo-Saxon
population. The roots of this German migration lay in the nineteenth century. These were troubled times in the German-speaking world; a time of
revolution, counterrevolution, and economic upheaval. The United States
offered a fresh start for those willing to put their shoulder to the wheel and
make a new life in a capitalist democracy. Some Germans brought radical
left-wing politics with them from the old country, most famously the leader
of the "Chicago 8," August Spies. But by and large, German Americans were
thrifty, hardworking, and law abiding. They prospered, not only in Chicago,
but in many other Midwestern cities (Cincinnati, Milwaukee, St. Louis).
The ugly blip of World War I–era xenophobia and anti-German hysteria
aside, the German American experience had largely been a successful one.
German Americans were, in fact, the "model minority" of that period.

For German Chicagoans, the philosophical, scientific, and creative
heritage of Kant, Hegel, Goethe, Schiller, Beethoven, Humboldt, Brahms,
and Wagner represented their culture—not the Brownshirts. But the anti-
Semitism of "new" Germans had antecedents in old Germans; most famously with the great composer of the Ring Cycle, Richard Wagner. Hitler,
in fact, loved Wagner's music, and saw his own rise and eventual fall as
some sort of fulfilment of a Wagnerian destiny. For their part, Jewish Chicagoans were keenly aware of the fragility of the successful place they had
carved out for themselves in the city. Like German immigrants, Jewish immigrants from the old country (primarily emigrating from the Russian and
Habsburg Empires) and their descendants had thrived in America, rising to
prominence in the arts, finance, and science. Yet the incurable disease of
European anti-Semitism seemed to have crossed the Atlantic and expressed
itself in coded admissions quotas to elite universities and "gentleman's
agreements" to exclude Jews from country clubs and America's "old boy"
network of white, Anglo-Saxon Protestant privilege. No group in Chicago
had as much at stake in resisting the attempts by Nazis, and Nazi sympa-

thizers, to make inroads at the fair. And no group more forcefully resisted the attempts by Nazis, and Nazi sympathizers, to highjack the World's Fair, than Chicago's Jewish population. Most prominent among these was the Chicago Women's Aid, an organization that had long-standing roots in the city and whose concerns could not be easily brushed aside. According to historian Willian Toll, Chicago Women's Aid was initially founded "to visit the Jewish sick" but then expanded to raising money "to bring Jewish nurses to Chicago." Additionally, as "genteel American women, they formed study circles to discuss literature."[10] They threatened to withdraw from the fair's Women's Day, scheduled to be held just a few days after the *Graf Zeppelin* visited the city, if the swastika were permitted to be flown at the fairgrounds. To be sure, Marie Becker of the German American Hostess Society showed solidarity with the Chicago Women's Aid and assured her Jewish sisters that Hitler's hated banner would not fly at any event or installation associated with the city's German American population.[11] And good as her word, the swastika was not welcome at the fair's German American Building. This was the only pavilion featuring German culture and themes because in the leadup to the 1933 Fair, Germany's Weimar government felt it lacked the funds needed to put on a worthy exhibit. The Depression had forced them to prioritize spending on more immediate concerns. The Nazis simply came to power too late to put their own stamp on the 1933 Chicago Fair. But they tried.

Inside Chicago, and elsewhere in the United States with sizeable German communities, the Nazis had created a layer of organizations and activities as pro-Nazi alternatives to more established groups and institutions. These tended to have special appeal to more recent arrivals from the Fatherland and, importantly, on the young. Hitler's unrestrained, tactless bullying excited immature minds. One of these organizations was the Friends of New Germany, whose members snatched the traditional German flag at a dedication ceremony held at the German American Building and replaced it with the swastika banner. Police were called, and the "Friends" were forced to back down, but . . . like it or not, the Nazis were now firmly in power back in Berlin. This emboldened those bent on further provocative acts. Joseph Goebbels's propaganda machine ultimately shipped a Nazi-inspired alternate German exhibit to Chicago after the fair had already begun, but the fair's Organizing Committee rejected its inclusion. Jewish Chicagoans had made absolutely clear how they felt. Organizing a mass rally of fifty thousand concerned citizens in Grant Park on May 10, two weeks before the fair opened, speakers and participants demanded that Goebbels not be permitted to come to the city as Germany's official representative.[12] Their message was heard:

In the ranks of the marchers were men and women who had come from every European land. Children and gray bearded men marched side by side. All professions were represented. The mass meeting was held in the plaza at Grant Park. Jewish members of the various posts of the American Legion marched in the lead behind a band. . . . Jacob Spiegel, the organizer of the protest movement and editor of the Jewish Daily Forward, was the first speaker. He called upon the Jewish people and all citizens of the city to unite against the appointment of Herr Goebbels as Germany's representative here. . . . He declared that Chancellor Hitler's persecution of Jews was a manifestation of militarism and a prelude to war. Of the burning of books by German authors he said that while books might be destroyed their ideals could never be seared out of Jewish minds. . . . Morris Siskind, labor editor of The Daily Forward, denounced the burning of Jewish books. "Hitler turned back history about 400 years in his burning of books of German Jews. . . . It is just like what happened when Catholics burned the books of heretics. Hitler should be destroyed."[13]

The original caption in the *Chicago Herald and Examiner* reads, "Jews Protest Hitler Regime. A general view of the parade of Chicago Jews who marched yesterday from Ashland Blvd. and Roosevelt Road to Grant Park at Congress St., where they held a mass meeting" (May 10, 1933). *Courtesy of United States Holocaust Memorial Museum.*

It is perhaps worth pausing and considering whether Hugo Eckener himself was anti-Semitic. He did grow up in a society that was anti-Semitic, though not yet of the murderous variety that the Nazis embraced. On the other hand, he was very cosmopolitan. Eckener maintained professional, not to say social, relationships with a number of prominent Jews, including the renowned economist Edgar Salin,[14] airship designer Karl Arnstein, and society reporter Bella From, who referred to him affectionately as her "good old gruff, upright, dry-witty bear."[15] Perhaps no other project embodied Eckener's cosmopolitanism more than the international radio broadcasts he endorsed. Chicago's German-language daily, the *Abendpost*, reported on this ambitious new concept in 1932:

> The idea of organizing an International Radio Forum for the purpose of international understanding and exchange of ideas was put into practice only a few weeks ago. This ingenious application of modern technique was first made in Paris, where a Trans-Atlantic transmitting service was organized. The idea has now gained a strong foothold in Germany. . . . The International Radio Forum, of which Committees already have been formed in France and America, and which now also will be extended into other countries, is not built either on a political or a business basis, but is intended only to serve as a means of fostering mutual understanding among nations.[16]

A list of prominent supporters of the International Radio Forum appears in the article with Hugo Eckener's name right next to that of Albert Einstein (one of the most famous people in the world in 1932, and also a Jew).

The far right-wing German daily *Völkischer Beobachtner* perhaps put it the most succinctly, but derisively when it referred to Eckener as "the friend of the Jews."[17] This wasn't intended as a compliment.

Thus, as Hugo Eckener prepared to lift off from Goodyear's base of operations in Akron, he was headed into a potential storm as rough in its own way as any of those he'd encountered from the Arctic to the tropics. People were fired up—and justifiably so. And there was no way for him to skirt the issue. To put it bluntly: the great achievement of his life (the *Graf Zeppelin*) had not one, but two, twenty-foot-tall swastikas emblazoned on it. There was no way to avoid it. En route to Chicago by train that very evening from Washington, DC, was Hitler's lickspittle ambassador to the United States, Hans Luther, and his staff. He was there to make sure that everyone (or at least everyone he could control) toed the official line from Berlin. He also could rely on those Chicagoans of German ancestry who had become intoxicated by Hitler's nationalist agenda. On the other hand, anti-Nazi/German sentiment was running high in certain quarters and producing results, as evidenced by the spread of a citizens' movement to boycott German-made goods. Both sides eagerly anticipated the *Graf Zeppelin*'s arrival and were no doubt interested to see which way Eckener would lean.

On October 26, with approximately two weeks remaining in the fair's 1933 season, the *Graf Zeppelin* appeared over Lake Michigan, dwarfing the Goodyear blimp and reminding fairgoers why the great airships inspired such awe.* The famous airship had left Akron late in the evening in order to arrive in Chicago at dawn. This was three hours earlier than the announced arrival time—a cleverly employed bit of misinformation to throw off the timing of any would-be agitators.[18] But Chicagoans were rising for work on a weekday, and as word would spread of the giant silver airship coming out of the lake as if from another world, eyes would turn skyward. According to an eyewitness account, Hugo Eckener anticipated this, and instead of turning to starboard and taking the most direct route north along the lakeshore to Curtiss-Reynolds Field, he continued in a wide northwesterly arc around—rather than straight over—the waking city.[19] Why do this?

One of those on the flight deck of the *Graf Zeppelin* that morning was Willy von Meister, the Zeppelin Company's U.S. representative. He asked the same question, "Why?" In interviews given many years later, he recalled Hugo Eckener's response: "And let my friends in Chicago see the swastikas?"[20] Ashamed of his country's new masters, Eckener had chosen to resist by diversion. His wide, looping route to Curtiss-Reynolds ensured that in the most populous part of the city, anyone looking up at the *Graf* that morning would have seen either its starboard (right) side, or its belly—not the port (left) side sporting the giant swastikas. The only emblem people would have seen was the traditional black, white, and red German flag. This maneuver by Eckener was a preview of what was to come the rest of that day. Hugo Eckener spoke without saying anything. Or did he? Reporter Robert Wood, covering the story for the *Chicago Herald and Examiner*, wrote: "The dark shadow of the Graf first appeared out of the fog and smoke of South Chicago at 6 a.m. It followed the shore line to the Loop and swung north-westward to Glenview Airport [Curtiss-Reynolds Field]."[21]

Wood's report seems to indicate a more direct route along the lakeshore, in which case the giant swastikas on the Zeppelin's port side would have been very visible to early risers in the city. However, his remark about a

---

* In fact, the U.S. Navy airship *Macon*, which was even larger than the *Graf*, had flown over the fair earlier in 1933.

swing "northwestward" would seem to indicate there was something to von Meister's story. The *Chicago News* reported that the *Graf* appeared "before 6, coming through a stiff breeze to the air field" and that later it "pointed its nose east into a stiff wind."[22] If this was indeed the case, it would indicate that the *Graf* approached Curtiss-Reynolds Field from the west, not the south—again, adding further circumstantial evidence to von Meister's later remarks. On the other hand, the weather report for October 26, 1933, in the *Chicago Tribune* predicted wind direction as coming from the south that day.[23] Francis Healy of the *Chicago Daily Times* reported that the *Graf* came "out of the southeastern sky . . . passed over its landing field, and swung around into the south wind."[24] In the final analysis, it's not definitive which route Eckener took that morning from Lake Michigan to Curtiss-Reynolds Field.* It partly comes down to wind direction, timing, and which eyewitness one chooses to believe. Willy von Meister was a long-time admirer and ally of Hugo Eckener, and therefore his objectivity has been questioned. But the story he told has a ring of authenticity to it—not just because he was there, but because it's just the sort of stunt that Hugo Eckener would have pulled to show up the Nazis.† October 1933 would be the last time he would be fully a "free agent" on the world stage. From this point on, Eckener would gradually become more and more compromised, by events and by his own decisions. But that morning he was still very much his own man.

The Chicago press failed to grasp the significance of Eckener's gesture (if it indeed occurred), instead focusing on the atmospherics of the Zeppelin's arrival—which seemed to never fail to captivate. Francis Healy, on the story that morning for the *Chicago Daily Times*, wrote: "Out of the red, cloud-flecked sky at dawn today the Graf Zeppelin. Germany's biggest dirigible which has flown 473,000 miles, came to Chicago."[25] Not to be outdone, the *Chicago News* had a stringer there as well: "Germany's leviathan of the air, the Graf Zeppelin, paid a visit . . . to Chicago today. . . . Coming out of the gray dawn the big ship settled at Curtiss-Reynolds airport at 6:55 this morning."[26] The emphasis was on the fact that Hugo Eckener would remain behind. The *Graf* would ascend back into the skies that morning to fly over

---

* Though Chicago could boast five English-language dailies in October 1933, they didn't always agree on details. For example, in the coverage of Eckener's stay in the city, one daily had him departing that evening for Goodyear's headquarters in Akron, by train; another had him departing by train the following morning, while a third had him catching a United Airlines flight to Akron the following morning. This provides a degree of insight into why the Graf's flight path in the early morning of October 26, 1933, can be characterized as not definitive.

† Hugo's grandson, Uwe Eckener, responding to a question from the author, pointed out that his grandfather had personally told him that he also had made this type of maneuver over other cities in 1933, for the same purpose.

the fair and the lake, and then on back to Akron. Ernst Lehmann, who had become Eckener's chief subordinate in piloting the Zeppelin, was given the responsibility to complete the mission. By reputation, Lehmann was a highly competent airship pilot with a bit of a daredevil streak. Later, he became a willing tool of Joseph Goebbels's propaganda. The extent of his commitment to the Nazi cause in 1933 isn't altogether clear—but he was certainly an opportunist. According to the *Herald and Examiner* and the *News*, Eckener had brought the *Graf* down with its nose facing to the east/southeast.[27] When Lehmann ascended skyward, then, the logical route to take would be southeast to the lakefront and then south over the fairgrounds, before coming about and making another pass traveling north before heading east back over the lake toward Ohio. Thus, the *Graf*'s starboard (right) side with fins featuring the traditional German flag would be visible to the fairgoers below—not the swastika. Whether Lehmann, given his later proclivities, would have been a knowing accomplice in such a plan is highly unlikely. But Eckener's positioning of the airship would have made any conspiracy largely unnecessary. As for Lehmann, to select any other route would have been illogical given where they were (Curtiss-Reynolds Field) and where he was going. Fortunately, the *Chicago News* had sent an intrepid photographer named Robert Stiewe to snap aerial shots from beside and above the *Graf*.[28] The photograph below provides conclusive proof that the *Graf*'s flight path over the fair kept its offensive swastikas facing the lake. It stands to reason that when it came about, the swastikas would still have not been visible to those below attending the fair. Again, whether Lehmann was conscious of this is largely a moot point—but perhaps Hugo Eckener was. For those perceptive enough, this might be a message as to where his true feelings lay.

As the *Graf* flew to the lakefront to thrill fairgoers, Hugo Eckener began one of the most eventful days of his life. First to emerge from the zeppelin after it touched down, sporting a heavy brown overcoat and a white cap, he was greeted by a crowd of well-wishers, reporters, and official dignitaries. Security was tight. To ensure order, a detachment of soldiers from nearby Camp Whistler were joined by Chicago police and sheriff's deputies in a show of force. Eckener was accustomed to this type of reception (though perhaps not the level of security), as he was famous in an age that invented celebrity. Cameramen crowded around the famed airship captain, bulbs flashing crisply in the autumn air. Playfully, Eckener said, "Just one more?" knowing full well they'd be on his tail for the next twenty-four hours. To the assembled throng, he said exactly what Chicagoans wanted to hear: "What a welcome. Compared to New York it is like a dollar to a penny. Eh, what?"[29] He had previously demonstrated a willingness to disappoint the press and

Photograph taken of the *Graf Zeppelin* by Robert Stiewe (October 26, 1933). To the left is one of the Sky Ride's giant towers and the "lagoon." To the right is Lake Michigan. At top right is the Adler Planetarium, which still stands. Note the swastika on the upper stabilizing fin of the Zeppelin, visible from the lake but not the fairgrounds. *Courtesy of University of Illinois Chicago Special Collections.*

public in any number of cities, but not Chicago. Not today. He was banking on his personal popularity to keep Chicagoans on the side of the zeppelin project; to not let goose-stepping morons sour them on his dream.

Stepping into a waiting motor car, Eckener joined the Hamburg-American Line's representative, the German Consul, and Karl Eitel, owner of the elegant Bismarck Hotel located adjacent to the Loop in downtown Chicago. Mayor Kelly, who had given Italo Balbo a "key to the city" just a few months before, bestowed the same honor on Eckener. The two hit it off immediately:

> "You talk like an Irishman" said the mayor. "Maybe it's because of the Irish whisky," replied Dr. Eckener, and both laughed. The Ger-

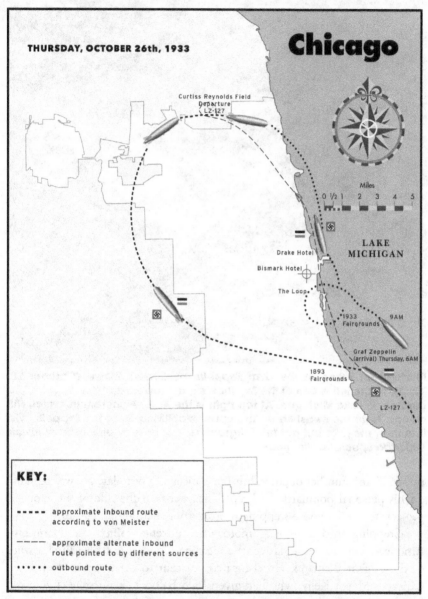

The *Graf Zeppelin*'s route over and around Chicago and the fairgrounds on the morning of October 26, 1933, according to Willy von Meister's account, and according to other contemporary accounts which place the route to Curtiss-Reynolds Field north along the lakeshore, which would have led to a very visible display of the Nazi swastika. *Illustration by Midori Tuzuki.*

man consul put his arm around Eckener and told him that during his last visit to Chicago with the Graf in 1929, a baby was born and they called it Hugo after him. "I'm afraid I wouldn't recognize the baby," roared the commander. "That reminds me of a story. Stop me doctor, if you've heard this one before," said Mayor Kelly. He told the commander a joke which ladies might object to—but there were no ladies.[30]

Eckener was a wine-drinking German,* but if he was already imbibing early in the day—and Jameson's, no less—it is a window into his state of mind. Take the edge off, enjoy the moment, stay loose.

A noon luncheon with German Ambassador Hans Luther must have been a trying experience. Luther had been a respected member of the Weimar government who had then thrown in his lot with the Nazis, lock, stock, and barrel. What's worse: spending the day with a fanatic, or a Judas? Next came a formal visit to the fair, and a face-to-face meeting with the dapper Rufus Dawes. The two hit it off immediately. Dawes had received plenty of forewarning about the potential hornets' nest Eckener might be stepping into; as in a memo written by the fair's protocol officer, Grant Smith, to Dawes two months before, it was clear that there was genuine concern:

> Dr. Yaeger, Acting German consul here in Chicago . . . stated that since this air-ship flew under the auspices of the German government, it would fly the flags of the German government including the Nazi flag and the Swastika, and asked for my comments upon this situation, realizing the protest that would be raised by Jewish citizens. I said to him in a visit of this kind that the State Department would answer any inquiries as to the proprieties of such a matter.[31]

But in the event, the public clearly differentiated between Eckener and Luther. At first, Eckener noticed a greatly diminished reaction from the large crowd that had gathered. But he soon realized that the frosty reception was reserved for Hans Luther and not for himself. As his name was announced and he appeared before the crowd, enthusiastic fairgoers cheered and waved their arms. They had made a distinction between Hitler's lackey and a great visionary.[32] One spouted arrogance and hate; the other quietly embodied cooperation and technological skill. The contrast was absolutely striking.

---

* He also enjoyed cigars, preferring Brazilian cheroots.

In the evening, a gala dinner was held at the Union League Club in Chicago. This was a bastion of the city's WASP old guard. Hans Luther, tone-deaf to the political atmosphere in the room, went on a nationalistic tirade in his prepared address, and much of the crowd remained stonily silent. The fair's chief, Rufus Dawes, invited to the dinner by club vice president Carl Latham,[33] leaned over to Eckener and remarked "If you were not here, they would have booed the speaker."[34] The doctor was embarrassed by his countryman's rant, but he maintained his reserved outward demeanor.

Despite a toast by Carl Latham in which (perhaps anticipating the "America Firsters" to come) he made a "plea for a friendly approach to mutual problems"[35] at a table draped with the stars and stripes and the swastika, the six-hundred-strong crowd fidgeted uncomfortably. When the "Star-Spangled Banner" was played, those in attendance sang with added emphasis on the closing line, "the land of the free."[36] The *Chicago Tribune* put it rather diplomatically, assessing the German Ambassador's performance: "Delicate as some of these subjects might appear to be, Dr. Luther seemed to be following the Nazi formula of leaving no doubt as to where Herr Hitler stood."[37]

Tactless, tone-deaf, insistent, and above all humorless, Hans Luther attacked the "Jewish" boycott, the League of Nations, and basically any criticism of the Nazis or their leader, Adolf Hitler.[38] Rufus Dawes, asked to make a toast of his own, raised *his* glass to Hugo Eckener:

> The weather beaten commander of the Graf smiled quizzically when Mr. Dawes paid tribute to his inventive genius and his courage, and thanked the audience haltingly when all arose in tribute to his character. He [Eckener] made no reference to political questions or the glories of Nazi-ism in his brief remarks.[39]

To say the dinner was awkward is an understatement. But it was the final event of the evening in front of a primarily German American crowd that would prove to be the climax of an increasingly tense visit.

The Medinah Temple was chosen as the site for a reception for the famed zeppelin commander, to be given by the city's pro-Nazi German American organizations. According to the *New York Times*, only six of Chicago's approximately five hundred German American societies chose to attend.[40] As Luther and Eckener entered the hall, 150 German youths stood and saluted them with right arm outstretched, palm down, in emulation of their Fascist counterparts in the Fatherland. Luther enthusiastically returned their salute in the same manner. But Eckener, walking with a deliberate step, offered no salute in response to this highly charged gesture.[41] He refused to be a part of this. Many in the large crowd kept their arms down too. Eckener's seeming ambivalence was keenly noted by the Nazis in attendance, most importantly by Fritz Gissibi, "the right hand man of Heinz Spanknoebel of New York, reputed chief Nazi propagandist in the United States."* The rally (because that's what it was) took on an air of ill-concealed menace.[42] This was real frothing-at-the-mouth fare. The pressure on Hugo Eckener, combined with the personal distaste he must have felt, made for a trying evening.

Decades later, historian Cheryl Ganz interviewed a Jewish American named Theodore Light, who as an enthusiastic young stamp collector had crashed the party at the Medinah Temple that night with a friend. He was hoping that he could get Hugo Eckener's autograph on some letters that he had mailed to himself with the special *Graf Zeppelin* stamp. Light recalled to Ganz how they found "the ushers all in storm trooper uniforms and across the stage was the biggest flag I have ever seen and it was the swastika."[43] They were truly pilgrims in an unholy land. Thinking better of the idea, Light told his friend, "Let's forget about autographs and get out of here."[44]

For his part, when he could slip away, Eckener returned to his room at the Bismarck Hotel and a well-deserved night's rest after the night flight from Akron and the long day in the Windy City. He had done the best he could to win the sympathy of the Americans—people he admired—for the zeppelin project. But there is no way he couldn't have realized how far things had drifted in an antagonistic direction since those heady days of 1929. There were important exceptions (particularly among the German American Bund crowd), but generally Americans didn't like Nazis, and there was no altering this fact, especially when their supporters and apologists in the United States behaved so boorishly. It was an uphill struggle, and it wouldn't get any easier as the decade progressed. Eckener sent a personal note to President Franklin D. Roosevelt speaking glowingly of the "friendly shores of America" and "the friendly reception and enthusiastic interest" of the American people,[45] but the times were changing.

Eckener took back command of the *Graf* in Akron, and set a course across the Atlantic for Seville, Spain; then home to Friedrichshafen on Lake Constance. But home wasn't home in the way it had been before. Most of

---

* Gissibi would later serve as a high-ranking SS officer in Nazi-occupied Poland. See Jeff Nichols, "In 1939 Nazis Rallied in Chicago to Make Germany Great Again," *Daily Reader*, March 11, 2016.

Chicago's German American community applauded him for his behavior in their city. But back in Germany, the mood was different. His lack of enthusiasm in Chicago was noted. Hugo Eckener's days as the undisputed leader of the Zeppelin Company were coming to an end. His new masters would continue to try to woo him to their cause, but his cooperation was elusive. Ultimately, his name would not be allowed to appear in print in his home country. Hitler was the most famous man in Germany now.

Eckener's appearance in Chicago marked the end of an epoch. The dream of Zeppelin flight as a peaceful, world-unifying enterprise was now compromised. The giant silver airships were co-opted by a cruel regime bent on world domination and racial hierarchy. People watching these beautiful examples of aviation technology now saw the obscene swastika, not their majesty. Triumphalism was in the air after Chicago. Its consequences would be enormous.

Meanwhile back in Chicago, as Eckener exited the stage the fair welcomed its next "A list" star, the internationally renowned violinist Jascha Heifetz. It was fitting that one of the most famous Jews in the world stole the spotlight from the Nazi instigators who had tried to highjack Eckener's visit. Heifetz's talent was legendary. Few have ever brought forth such depth of feeling from the instrument as he did. He was also a humanitarian, one who saw the worth in all people. And he never took a performance off; whether playing his Stradivarius for a packed house of *glitterati* or for an audience of one—as he famously did later on, on a rainy day during a tour of the western front in World War II[46]—he gave his all.

Born in Russia, Heifetz began his career at the Imperial Conservatory in St. Petersburg but fled in 1917 during the revolution and came to America. The one-time "boy genius," as the *Chicago American* described him, had become "one of the three or four top box-office musicians in the world."[47] Heifetz claimed he had nothing to say about politics, but earlier in the year he canceled a scheduled forty-five-date tour of Germany. The message was clear enough. Rufus Dawes personally welcomed him to the fair. But Heifetz wasn't particularly interested in formalities, preferring to view a new exbibit of paintings at the nearby Art Institute of Chicago. But he was a celebrity, "impeccably tailored . . . with his eyebrow-brush mustache . . . and his body guard-accompanists."[48] Heifetz could not move in the city in relative anonymity. He was one of the great musical stars of his day.

For Jewish Chicagoans, Heifetz's appearance at the fair provided a significant boost to both their civic and ethnic pride. What was happening in Germany could not be ignored—this was clear enough. But they had held the line in their city against further inroads by the Nazis and their sympathizers. Goebbels had failed in his attempt to use the World's Fair as a platform to spread his poison. The beautiful strains from Heifetz's Stradivarius had the last word in Chicago, at least that fall.

CHAPTER 11

Space Race

After his pioneering balloon flights into the stratosphere in 1931–1932, Auguste Piccard would pass the baton to his brother Jean. Working with Dow Chemical, the Goodyear-Zeppelin Company, and Union Carbide, among others, Jean Piccard looked to perfect the spherical gondola or "capsule" design his brother had ridden nearly into space. Two Nobel Prize–winning physicists—Arthur Holly Compton of the University of Chicago and Robert Millikan of Cal Tech—contributed their expertise in devising more accurate devices for measuring cosmic rays from inside the gondola. The disagreement between the two Nobel Laureates over the source of these rays provided a ready-made subplot for this next ascent into the heavens. And Chicago (Compton's home) and its great fair provided an ideal platform from which to promote this daring attempt to both set a new height record and settle the ongoing (and increasingly publicized) dispute between Compton and Millikan.* The fact that Compton had once been Millikan's student added further spice. He challenged his former mentor's conviction that, as science writer Mark Wolverton later explained, cosmic rays might "reveal the mind of God."[1] That this dispute was one beyond the understanding of most ordinary people mattered less than the dramatic tension it added to the narrative that the press was keen to develop. On one level, the 1933 Chicago World's Fair was seriously committed to demonstrating to the public the value of science in people's lives. On the other hand, the carnival-like aspect of the fair

---

* Essentially the dispute centered on the source of cosmic rays—did they originate in Earth's upper atmosphere, or were they coming from the deepest reaches of outer space to Earth? The larger significance of this question was that it could provide proof that the universe was subject to the second law of thermodynamics and would eventually burn itself out (Compton), or eternally re-create itself (insinuating a God-like quality to cosmic rays) (Millikan).

led organizations such as the fair's Science Advisory Committee to favor (as David DeVorkin in his excellent book on the 1930s race to the stratosphere described them) "stunts that would be wondrous for the twelve-year-old mind to behold."[2]

Lenox Lohr's head of concessions at the fair was one Forest Ray Moulton, professor emeritus in astronomy and mathematics at the University of Chicago. It was Moulton who initiated the fair's formal overtures to Auguste Piccard with an eye toward having him make a return to America to supervise, and possibly take a more direct part, in an *American*-based attempt at a new world altitude record. With his background, Moulton was certainly aware of Piccard's commitment to science, but as director of concessions, he also clearly grasped the potential for publicity and profit in having "Professor Calculus" recross the Atlantic and associate himself with the Chicago Fair. But though he would return briefly to America, Auguste made it clear that he was not available—his capable brother Jean, however, was. And it was with Jean that the fair's organizers would ultimately treat.

For Jean Piccard, the years following his once initially quite promising academic career spent in Chicago, Lausanne, and Cambridge, Massachusetts, had failed to materialize into a formal tenured position and he now found himself struggling to make ends meet working in research and development. The opportunity to play a leading role in the most heavily publicized high-altitude ballooning event in history was not simply a realization of a lifetime dream, but potentially an opportunity to capitalize on the inevitable fame that would follow, to secure a tenured position at a university and also financial security for his family. Both then and in the years since, Jean Piccard has been criticized as a petulant glory-seeker, jealous of his twin brother's success, using science as a convenient excuse to further his own egotistical aims. This is a decidedly ungenerous, not to say unkind, assessment of a talented, frustrated man, navigating what was for him a foreign (i.e., American) culture. His vision had its roots in his childhood with his brother. He was not an opportunist. He was a bold dreamer—and a man of science—with a long-standing interest in ballooning and stratospheric exploration. He was no fly-by-night huckster. But he was a foreigner dealing with a group of Americans drawn from the highest levels of industry, academia, and the military with their own agendas, often acting in concert. His leverage was the Piccard imprimatur—the Piccard name carried weight with, most importantly, the press. But he had little else. No money. Precious few contacts. Not even a balloon pilot's license. Thus, what ultimately transpired as a result of Forest Ray Moulton's overture to Auguste Piccard is really quite a fantastic story. It is a story of two people's creativity, courage, and above all, determination.

Lenox Lohr, Forest Ray Moulton, and Moulton's young protégé from the University of Chicago, a young chemist named Irving Muskat, made certain that the stratospheric ascent staged in conjunction with the fair would be an altogether more ambitious and far more highly publicized flight than that of Auguste Piccard and Paul Kipfer in 1931. And it would be undertaken, not by the Piccards, but by the U.S. Navy in the form of would-be soloist, Lieutenant Commander Thomas Settle. Why Settle? He was an American, and as a naval officer he had chosen to place himself in harm's way if called to do so. The fair's organizers clearly favored having an American boy—one nicknamed "Tex," no less—break the record rather than a foreigner. This was one of the few jingoistic gestures to mar the fair's legacy. In a Pathé newsreel from that summer, Jean Piccard is featured speaking to an assembled crowd from the open hatchway of the spherical capsule. He is tall, thin, lanky, dressed in white with his sleeves rolled up, shirt open at the collar. He has the look of a visionary, a savant. As he explains various features of the gondola's design, his heavily accented English is very noticeable. One has to listen carefully to understand what he is saying. Later in the film he has an awkward, staged conversation with a representative from Union Carbide (supplier of the hydrogen for the giant balloon).[3] For a provincial American audience—and Americans can be very provincial—he was not the ideal messenger in this new age of "talkies" and mass popular media. The reason given to Jean Piccard for the choice of Settle was Piccard's lack of a license from the National Aeronautic Association to actually fly a balloon, a deficiency that could have been readily rectified if the fair's organizers had genuinely wanted Piccard to fly. They didn't. To be fair, Settle was far more experienced in lighter-than-air aviation than Piccard, even having served as an observer aboard the *Graf Zeppelin* on its maiden trans-Atlantic voyage.[4] Be that as it may, Piccard accepted the decision with more grace than he was given credit for, but remained undaunted in his desire to someday ascend into the stratosphere as his brother had done.

The new gondola—based on Auguste Piccard's original capsule—was built using Dow Chemical's new lightweight, yet extremely strong, product known as "Dowmetal."* The giant balloon that would carry it aloft was constructed by Goodyear-Zeppelin, on the understanding that the cost would be offset by the official sponsors of the stratospheric ascent: the *Chicago Daily News* and the National Broadcasting Corporation (NBC).[5]

In the months leading up to the ascent, planned for the summer of 1933, it was still not altogether clear whether Jean Piccard would play a direct role

* A magnesium alloy.

Into the maelstrom: Jean Piccard signing autographs at the 1933 Chicago World's Fair.

inside the capsule. His work as an advisor to the large American concerns involved was crucial, in that he understood his brother's concept better than anyone else. But as the fair opened that spring, it had become increasingly clear that the "other" Piccard was to be elbowed out of the spotlight. It was Irving Muskat, now elevated to manager of the fair's Chemical Section,[6] who most bluntly and succinctly articulated the way the fair's organizers had refashioned their conception of the stratospheric ascent: "the flight will be made by an American pilot with a gondola made by an American manufacturer out of material developed by an American manufacturer and with a balloon designed and constructed by an American company."[7]

Jean Piccard was a naturalized American citizen, but, clearly, he wasn't American enough. In the event, Piccard did well to have steered clear of the proceedings of August 5, 1933. They were an embarrassment, and nearly proved fatal.

—⊶⊷—

As late as July 14, the *Chicago News* reported as a matter of fact that Jean Piccard would accompany Tex Settle as a science officer aboard the now-completed "A Century of Progress" Gondola. The article featured a photograph of Settle emerging from the hatch of the two-toned capsule, painted white on top and black on bottom.* The accompanying caption read: "Sealed in this metal ball with Jean Piccard, he will be carried eleven miles into the stratosphere in an attempt to bring the world's altitude record to the United States."[8] This no doubt would have come as a surprise to Piccard, who by midsummer understood he was considered an unwanted nuisance by fair organizers and the Navy. Meanwhile anticipation was built in the press to pique public excitement. Articles with photographs featuring the silk being prepared for the massive balloon that would take the gondola to the edge of space appeared, as did staged photos of Commander Settle (not Piccard) testing a radio with the NBC logo clearly in evidence. Later, the *News*'s Dempster MacMurphy claimed Jean Piccard would sensationally parachute out of the gondola "several miles above of the earth," quoting Tex Settle as his source: "The possibility of the fantastic vision of Dr. Piccard making a stork-like visit to a neighboring metropolis, however, is a constant, and chances are almost even that he will bail out."[9] This, of course, was ludicrous. It also made light of Jean Piccard as some sort of unnecessary baggage, whose main purpose, however unlikely, was to perform a wild stunt rather than conduct scientific experiments. The stratospheric ascent continued to be delayed as the wait for more favorable weather conditions kept putting it off. By July 25, the world knew that Jean Piccard would in fact not be going up with Settle—rather, it would be a solo affair. The irony of the *Chicago News*'s headline: "Settle to Go Aloft Alone in Piccard Flight" was positively Orwellian, cruel even. Arthur Holly Compton rationalized the solo effort by claiming that now additional apparatus for measuring cosmic rays could be installed inside the capsule.[10] Just who was going to be conducting these scientific observations was anybody's guess. Tex Settle would have more than enough on his plate trying to break the altitude record and get back to earth alive. Finally, in early August, fair weather descended on Chicago and preparations were made to stage the ascent (filling the giant balloon with hydrogen gas, preparing scientific instruments, selling tickets to the show). In the event it wasn't until the early morning hours that the paying public was able to witness the giant balloon being readied for liftoff. This was more Wizard of Oz than NASA.

With much fanfare, Tex Settle's balloon lifted off from Soldier Field in Chicago at 3:00 a.m. on August 5, 1933. Given an opportunity to think this

---

* Auguste Piccard had implemented this color scheme for his second stratosphere ascent in 1932. The white paint reflected the sun's rays on top of the capsule while the black paint insulated the underside of the capsule, exposed to the freezing temperatures of the upper stratosphere.

through again, Settle might have recognized that it was irresponsible, reckless even, to try and ascend in a balloon of that size from a semi-enclosed space (the stadium) full of thousands of onlookers—not to mention the giant towers of the Sky Ride and the fair's other tall buildings close by. This was a carnival act. Settle demonstrated skill in ascending and avoiding the dangerous obstacles nearby, but to the great disappointment of the onlookers, and Settle himself, the balloon rapidly descended to the ground soon afterward. A valve rope had caught in the balloon's fabric, and torn it. "A Century of Progress" descended to earth in the Burlington Railway Yards. According to David DeVorkin, "Before the launch, Settle had decided to ignore this problem because he felt pressured to hold to the launch schedule."[11] Italo Balbo, Hugo Eckener, and Auguste Piccard had all faced similar pressures. Tex Settle—a career Navy officer—acted out of character that night. Fortunately no one was hurt, and surprisingly the gondola and balloon were in fairly good condition as well. For Jean and Jeannette Piccard, the latter held particular significance as they had negotiated an agreement with all the parties involved that they would receive the gondola and the balloon when the fair had finished with them. But the fair wasn't finished with them.

❦

On the morning of October 1, 1933, Chicagoans awoke to the following jarring and unexpected headline in the *Chicago Tribune*: "RUSSIANS CLAIM BALLOON MARK." On September 30, Ernest Birnbaum, Georgi Prokofiev, and Konstantin Gudenoff ascended 11.8 miles into the sky, "the greatest height ever achieved by man."[12] Stalin's Russia—as previously demonstrated by its willingness to engage with the aviation exploits of Italo Balbo and Hugo Eckener—was keenly interested in the heavens. Given its technological attainment at that point in its history, a manned high-altitude balloon ascent was the most readily available means for the Soviet Union to make its mark in aviation exploration. According to that morning's *Tribune*, "The gondola in which they rode is shaped like a ball and is equipped with nine windows. When the takeoff was made it carried liquid oxygen enough to last three men 40 hours. In addition, there were numerous scientific instruments which functioned automatically."[13] That this stood in stark contrast to the fiasco of the American effort the month before, was evident to all. The same article closed with the following: "Commander T. G. W. Settle, America's famous balloonist, left today for Akron and was expected to go from there to Chicago to prepare for a second attempt to set a new altitude record."[14] This was serious now. The altitude record had not yet been confirmed by the Fédération Aéronautique Internationale in Lausanne, Switzerland, and the nature of the secretive totalitarian state lent itself to claims of suspicion and doubt. But for the United States, this was clearly now more than some sort of stunt at a fair. Planning immediately got under way for Tex Settle's second stratospheric attempt. The Soviet ascent was not Sputnik,* but it certainly anticipated it. The first tremors of what would eventually become the famous Cold War–era "Space Race" between these two giant adversaries began in 1933.

Settle tried again on November 20, this time with a copilot (U.S. marine Major Chester Fordney), and not from a Chicago stadium full of people, but rather, from an unobstructed launch site in Akron, Ohio, the base of operations for Goodyear-Zeppelin. It was now the Navy's show. The fair's organizers who had helped sideline Jean Piccard were themselves now sidelined. With the fair having closed its gates on November 12, a direct link to the ascent was tenuous anyway. As for Compton and Millikan, their scientific experiments were not prioritized. The altitude record was.

Settle and Fordney were successful in their endeavor, exceeding the heights reached by their Soviet rivals. One gets the sense that for Tex Settle, this was always what it had been about. The science was merely a cloak for pushing the envelope of human endeavor and exploration that much further—going where no man had gone before. Added to this was the satisfaction that what he was doing was *pro patria*. This unfortunate linking of nationalism and aviation/space exploration, most pronounced among the Fascists, was also used by their fellow totalitarians the Communists, as well as by democracies like the United States.

Jean Piccard had moved on by then. He had obtained work with the Bartol Research Foundation in Swarthmore, Pennsylvania. The foundation itself was associated with the prestigious Franklin Institute in nearby Philadelphia. Its director was the English physicist W. F. G. Swann, former head of the Carnegie Institute's Department of Terrestrial Magnetism. Like Piccard, Swann had military experience with balloons, serving with the U.S. Army Signal Corps and Robert Millikan in World War I.[15] Swann appreciated what Jean Piccard brought to the table. His encouragement, as well as his standing in the American scientific community, were absolutely crucial for Jean Piccard to use as a platform to achieve his stratospheric ambitions.

In an odd twist of fate, Tex Settle and Chester Fordney brought the "A Century of Progress" Gondola and balloon down in a swamp in southern New Jersey, not far from the Piccards' home at the time (it was well they did,

---

* The first satellite successfully launched into orbit around the earth, in 1957, by the Soviet Union.

as they came uncomfortably close to overshooting the Jersey Shore and coming down in the Atlantic and likely meeting almost-certain death). When Jean and Jeannette heard the news, they raced to the remote site: "We went over there and Jean waded through several feet of water till he reached the gondola. Then he stripped and swam the bayou to get to the balloon itself.* It was in beautiful condition."[16] Later the Navy retrieved the gondola, but left the balloon to be salvaged by a local strawberry farmer.[17] The Piccards were delighted. They had gambled that the capsule and balloon that Jean had helped design would still be flightworthy when the fair and the Navy were through with them. Now it was their turn.

—— ⚭ ——

Following the record American ascent, Jean and Jeannette Piccard startled the world by proclaiming that they would attempt to break Settle and Fordney's record in 1934, on their own, together. This last bit of news was the most startling. The plan was for Jeannette Piccard and her husband to ascend high into the stratosphere and continue the scientific experiments that his brother had initiated. It wasn't so much that Americans were shocked at the idea of a woman aeronaut—this was, after all, the era that produced Bessie Coleman and Amelia Earhart, among others. It was also the country that had produced the nineteenth-century acrobatic ballooning sensation, Leona Dare, who at the climax of her career had performed with none other than the "Great Spelterini" who had inspired the young Piccard boys to ascend to the skies in the first place.

What made Jeannette Piccard different was that—unlike Coleman, Earhart, or Dare—she was a mother. What kind of woman would place herself in a situation of such grave danger when she had three young sons back on earth who needed her? Clearly a double standard existed. Jean Piccard taking such risks might look reckless to a degree, but it also made him look like someone committed to loftier aims and, frankly, manly. What they were proposing turned all, or much, of this on its head. They had full trust in each other. They loved their children. But they also wanted their children not to be afraid. Fear paralyzes progress, and makes small people of us all. They were not afraid.

However, there was the issue of the balloon pilot's license that had earlier been raised when Jean Piccard had (at least officially) been considered for the

---

* It's worth noting that the November weather was uncommonly mild that year in Philadelphia/South Jersey, with the temperature on Thanksgiving Day exceeding 70 degrees. Otherwise stripping and diving into a swamp in November would seem rather rash.

Soldier Field ascent. Jeannette Piccard arrived at a solution—*she* would learn to fly, obtain a license, and then pilot the craft. This would have the doubly salutary effect of then freeing her husband to focus exclusively on the various scientific devices measuring and recording data. This was at a time when most women would never think of driving an automobile with an adult male in the passenger seat.* It was a societal given that a man's place was at the wheel. But Jeannette Piccard wasn't any woman. She was a true partner in her husband's life, and she was now going to train to be a partner in the attempt to fly higher than any human being had ever flown.

In order to achieve their objectives, sponsorship was an absolute must. Dow Chemical, on being informed that a mother of three was going to be piloting the craft with their corporate logo on it, backed out and required that it be removed. Goodyear-Zeppelin, a long-time supporter of the Piccards, also pulled out. In their attempt to secure a sponsor, the Piccards reached out to the National Geographic Society in Washington, DC. Jean Piccard entertained genuine hopes that the society would look favorably on their endeavor, but their proposal was treated with frosty indifference. Chicago—even though it was his wife's hometown, and her family was well connected there—was a dead end. They had burned too many bridges in the Windy City in the struggle for control of the Soldier Field ascent, and besides, Settle and Fordney had already established the world altitude record. Ultimately, it was one of Chicago's midwestern rivals that extended a hand to the daring couple.

Detroit in 1934 was one of the country's largest and most dynamic cities. The tragic inner-city decline and the riots it spawned were still decades in the future at that point. Henry Ford and Willian Durant (General Motors) had established Detroit and its environs as the center of the burgeoning American automobile industry. Even though the Depression had taken a bite out of its general prosperity, Detroit still was a wealthy, up-and-coming city. But for the Piccards, Ford was the key man. Like Swann, he enjoyed immense prestige, and his support encouraged others within his orbit to commit themselves. Finally, the Detroit Aero Club, the Grunow Radio Company, and the People's Outfitting Company (all of them based in Detroit) agreed to sponsor the record-breaking attempt. Ford offered the use of his personal air field for training purposes, and balloonist Edward Hill, winner of the Gordon Bennett Cup agreed to serve as Jeannette's instructor. She made rapid progress. Bold, intelligent, skillful, Jeannette Piccard possessed all of the attributes one looked for in a potential pilot—except her gender. Ford proved

---

* Except perhaps the fictional "Daisy Buchanan," and look how *that* turned out.

to be very progressive, in this instance. One afternoon, he invited a special guest to observe the would-be aeronaut's training. Orville Wright showed a keen interest in Mrs. Piccard's progress. Jeannette's young son, Donald (serving as a crew member at the air field), years later recalled shaking the flight pioneer's hand and the kindness the great man had shown toward him. Orville Wright had suffered serious injuries as a result of a flying accident years before and had no illusions about the dangers the young boy's mother was exposing herself to. But like Ford, Orville Wright was willing to lend his name and prestige to the endeavor. By June 1934, as the fair continued to draw huge crowds in its second summer, Jeannette Piccard flew solo for the first time in a balloon, and soon after was the first woman awarded a balloon pilot's license by the National Aeronautic Association. The famous gondola designed by the Piccards and flown by Settle and Fordney was suspended in a place of honor in the Hall of Science. But now it would be removed for its next mission into the farthest reaches of the stratosphere.

Even with sponsors and famous backers, the Piccards were still largely making things up as they went along. Jeannette Piccard was particularly

Jeannette Piccard's balloon pilot's license—the first ever issued to a woman by the National Aeronautic Association (1934). *Courtesy of Mary Louise Piccard.*

resourceful, launching a one-woman public relations campaign to generate enthusiasm—and additional funding—for the ascent. She personally designed commemorative stamps and brochures, and instead of couching her language in her responses to press inquiries (which more often than not focused on the dangers involved), she was bold, direct, provocative even. When asked about the possibility of a fatal mishap occurring, Jeannette responded, "If there's some accident, don't bother developing the film. The chemicals from our decomposing bodies will be enough."[18] She was not backing down. She wouldn't be shamed into returning to hearth and home, where many of the press and public felt she belonged. And she had a chip on her shoulder as well. Both she and Jean had felt disrespected, and easily dismissed, by the organizers of the Chicago Fair. This was an opportunity to stick it to them. It was also part of her competitive personal makeup. Later, she tried to explain this force that drove her into the stratosphere to her father: "There are many reasons, some of them so deep-seated emotionally as to be very difficult of expression. Possibly the simplest explanation is that we started along this road . . . and I cannot stop until I have won."[19]

In contrast to the Navy's November 1933 ascent—which only paid lip service to the importance of the various scientific apparatus aboard the gondola—Jean Piccard and W. F. G. Swann collaborated in a serious-minded effort to better understand cosmic ray behavior. To a degree, Swann's work in this field was a synthesis of the Millikan-Compton debate. Quantum theory had come up against a wall of sorts in trying to explain how cosmic rays were able to penetrate matter so deeply. As David DeVorkin explained, "most physicists at the time speculated that two particles might be involved: a new one producing cosmic ray 'showers,' and high-energy electrons that penetrated deeper than the laws of physics allowed. Swann thought that he could describe what was happening in terms of one particle."[20] But he needed proof. With this in mind, the Piccard Gondola would carry a series of Geiger counters and a heavy apparatus designed by Swann, known as a Stosse Chamber. This device incorporated a large pressurized spherical nitrogen gas tank, two electroscopes, and photographic cameras for recording the results.[21] Piccard and Swann tried to interest Robert Millikan in collaborating in the experiments, but his response was tepid. He had already thrown in his lot with the U.S. Army Air Corps–National Geographic Explorer stratosphere balloon, set for an ascent in the summer of 1934 from a site in South Dakota. It was a disaster. The balloon burst into flames on its descent, and Millikan's electroscopes were destroyed. Fortunately, the crew were able to parachute to safety, but for Millikan, who had long believed unmanned balloons were as effective as manned flights in gathering data, it seemed to confirm that he should not allow himself to be drawn too closely into the Piccard-Swann experiments. The U.S. Army's top aeronaut, Albert W. Stevens of Maine, later remarked on how impressed he was that the Piccards clearly knew that their attempt at a new altitude record (which he also knew was very important to them) would be greatly hampered by having so much scientific equipment aboard. Stevens, who had escaped a fiery death earlier in 1934 when he parachuted out of the Explorer, would turn out to be a quiet but generous ally of the Piccards in their stratospheric effort. Even though his had ended in quite spectacular failure, he didn't begrudge them their turn and he used the means at his disposal to help Jean test various features he was implementing in the Piccard Gondola.[22] This was in the best spirit of aviation in its golden age.*

—— ∞∞∞ ——

It's worth pausing a moment to consider what all of this meant to the general public. Unlike air travel in a seaplane or a zeppelin, the significance of balloon ascents into the stratosphere was more difficult for the average person to grasp. Men like Millikan, Swann, and Compton were almost like priests of an alien religion: physics. There was a vague understanding that all of this could very likely lead to something. But just what exactly that was, well . . . It took an editorial in a magazine called *Popular Mechanics* to articulate this to the masses. Its banner claimed that it was "WRITTEN SO YOU CAN UNDERSTAND IT." In the October 1933 edition, one year before the Piccard husband-and-wife ascent, it published "Why Explore the Stratosphere?" featuring a giant nighttime photograph of the failed Soldier Field ascent of August of that year. Few have articulated more cogently the answers to this question. It recognized the wonder of "this cold kingdom of mystery where there is no sound but the majestic music of the spheres, where the skies are deep blue, purple, and blue-black, where the sun shines forever, and the stars gleam with the cold ferocity of dagger points."[23] But then the article went on to raise a number of particularly prescient concepts: "the higher you rise the faster you fly, that speeds of five hundred miles an hour are not only practical, but highly desirable, that circumnavigation of the globe need require but two days of any man's time, and that all these things are now realizable if we apply our present-day knowledge"; "rockets will find their element in the thinnest atmosphere. Authorities predict altitudes of 1,000 miles and more, and the rocket's range will depend only on its ability to carry a fuel";

---

* Stevens could also be critical, but he was objective and fair. He understood the risks they were taking like few others could.

and "a Century of Progress wants more information on the blanket of ozone which is believed to absorb a great deal of the sun's ultra-violet energy before it reaches the earth."[24] What was happening was clearly important. That this is even more evident to us now looking back from the twenty-first century, certainly makes it no less so.

On October 23, 1934, Jean and Jeannette Piccard woke early and arrived at the airfield to find forty-five thousand spectators waiting for them. Their enthusiastic cheers mixed with an undercurrent of anxiety for the fate of the couple. This was underscored in dramatic fashion when the Piccards' young sons came forward with a bouquet of flowers for their parents. What if neither of them returned alive? To quiet these fears and add a bit of levity to the moment, the Piccards brought the family's turtle, Fleur de Lys, with them into the gondola along with "Angel" food cake, in case "they met any up there" to share it with.[25] Though it was no longer named "A Century of Progress," the spherical capsule with its balloon filling with hydrogen was to a large extent the final act in a remarkable World's Fair.

Albert W. Stevens was there, lending his professional eye to the proceedings. He was uneasy about the launch. A number of innovations made by Jean Piccard seemed unnecessarily risky.* The skies—predicted to be clear—were filled with a mass of low-hanging clouds, and Jeannette Piccard was an untried pilot. These were inauspicious portents, but the gods hadn't factored in the *sangfroid* and sheer determination of this remarkable pair of aeronauts. Auguste Piccard, as always a class act, had earlier cabled: "It would be nice, if the name of Piccard through Jeannette, would once more be placed on the record list of the F.A.I."[26] In making this statement, he was recognizing that the pilot would be given honor of place in the record books, and that Jean was essentially along for the ride. He would have had it no other way.

Inside the gondola, the Piccards signaled they were ready for the pyrotechnic launch. Blasting caps and TNT were used to release the lines and start the balloon on its way, and to remotely release external ballast from inside the craft. This was a revolutionary concept that eventually became standard practice under the director of NASA's manned spacecraft center, Robert Gilruth. Initially a crosswind caught the balloon, and a landline that

---

* For example, using controlled detonations to release the balloon's landlines, and leaving a space at the base of the giant hydrogen-filled balloon to allow for mixing of air and greater stability. Given the highly flammable nature of hydrogen gas, it comes as no surprise that Stevens was feeling somewhat unsettled that morning.

hadn't been successfully released by the detonation had to be released manually. In a Universal newsreel shot in the early-morning darkness during the launch, there is a palpable moment of genuine alarm as some of the ground crew hurry to push the gondola off before it collides with the ground.[27] Jeannette was visible outside the hatch to her sons and the tens of thousands of onlookers gazing anxiously skyward. Stevens piloted an airplane to observe the Piccards' ascent, but the cloud cover limited visibility. Up they shot into the air, through the clouds, and out of sight from those on the ground.

Official invitation to Piccard Stratosphere Flight (note the September 1934 date; delays pushed the flight into late October). *Courtesy of Bertrand Piccard.*

For Jeannette, seeing the giant hydrogen-filled balloon filling out to its full height and shape sixteen stories above her, spoke to the elemental—the spiritual even—reminding her of "a magnificent cathedral."[28] As they passed through a layer of clouds, the balloon was violently shaken side to side. To Jeannette's dismay, the rope controlling the vent valve at the top of the balloon had become obstructed. The line had to be freed, or else they wouldn't be able to valve gas when they needed to and as a result would effectively be unable to control the balloon's descent. Leaning out of the hatch and stepping onto the rigging connecting the massive balloon to the gondola, she reached to free the rope. Nearly ten thousand feet above Lake Erie, her foot slipped on some lead ballast that had been released earlier that morning.[29] Regaining her footing, she completed her task and re-entered the capsule through the hatch, only to receive a gentle, but puzzled, admonition from Jean, who was so engrossed in his work that he hadn't even noticed she was gone until just a moment before. They needed to seal the hatch and pressurize the cabin, as the air outside was becoming too thin to breathe.

They sped upward, ever upward, the altimeter steadily rising: 30,000, 40,000, 50,000 feet. The view from the craft was superior to those on earlier flights, as Jean Piccard had designed a frost-free window that he and Jeannette could look through. However, there was little to see below as the clouds stretched over a wide distance. This was cause for concern, because there was no way to know for certain where they were: how fast were they moving horizontally with the wind, as opposed to vertically? How long could they safely stay aloft and be confident they wouldn't drift over the Atlantic? Jeannette Piccard said later, half-jokingly, that her goal was to land the balloon on the White House lawn in Washington. Eleanor Roosevelt, no doubt, would've been tickled if Jeannette had been able to pull this off. But now just getting back to earth safely *anywhere* was the goal. It must have been nerve-wracking in the extreme. All the while, Jean Piccard carefully minded the instruments entrusted to him by Professor Swann. Finally, at 57,579 feet the balloon stopped, suspended for a moment nearly eleven miles above the Earth. Then it began its descent. Could they have pushed on and broken Settle and Fordney's mark, less than four thousand feet above? Perhaps. But in the final analysis, the added weight of the scientific instruments, the anxious uncertainty over just where they were above the map of the United States, and how much time they had left before the wind pushed them over the sea, decided the matter. But it wasn't as simple as just letting the balloon descend; it had to be a controlled descent, or disaster was still very much a possibility.

Jeannette Piccard's skills were tested to the utmost, as she needed to control the descent by shedding weight from the craft and using the ropes attached to the balloon to vent gas. As she later confided, there was a limit on what an aeronaut could reasonably hope to achieve regarding any kind of direction: "When you fly a balloon you don't file a flight plan; you go where the wind goes."[30] There it was: both the terror and the wonder of balloon flight. Her plan may have been to land on the White House lawn, but instead the couple landed in a grove of elm trees near Cadiz, Ohio. It was a rough landing—damaging the craft to a degree that its further use in stratospheric exploration would no longer be possible. Jean Piccard suffered cracked ribs, but he was jubilant over the record-setting ascent* and the scientific phenomena he was able to measure in the stratosphere. That he had done this with his wife, against all the odds, must have made it all the sweeter. What their pet turtle thought is unknown.

Jean and Jeannette tried to capitalize on their celebrity following their stratospheric ascent. There was genuine popular interest in what they had done together. But it was largely superficial. Jeannette Piccard admitted she felt shame at having not been able to pilot the balloon back to Earth in a more graceful manner.[31] She seemed to have forgotten what had happened to Tex Settle in Chicago—and he was supposed to have been one of the foremost aeronauts in the world! In the end, she was too hard on herself, not wanting to live up to the expectations of those who believed she was out of her depth, simply because she was a woman. On the other hand, she was awarded the prestigious Harmon Trophy in 1934 for her record-breaking ascent, joining the likes of her brother-in-law Auguste Piccard as well as Charles Lindbergh, Amelia Earhart, Italo Balbo, and Hugo Eckener. From a strictly scientific standpoint, Jean Piccard was later criticized for incomplete recordkeeping during the flight. On the other hand, no less prestigious a personage than Albert W. Stevens remarked to W. F. G. Swann that in terms of pure scientific value, the Piccards' ascent had been far superior to those of "A Century of Progress" or the ill-fated "Explorer," and he was shocked how little actual credit Jean Piccard had received for what he had done; "no one told the important facts . . . that the Piccards had successfully carried your Geiger counter and the Stosse Chamber to a very high altitude and had used it over a considerable length of time . . . I had all I could do to keep from getting up and stating these things."[32]

---

* Jeannette Ridlon Piccard became the first woman to pilot a balloon into the stratosphere, in the process setting an altitude record for a woman aeronaut that would stand until 1963.

On the other hand, first Robert Millikan (who in the end had ultimately been convinced to contribute some equipment for experiments) and Swann, either explicitly or implicitly, recognized that the data that Jean Piccard had collected was compromised by the fact that he had failed to properly account for the release of lead ballast during the Piccards' harried descent, and other factors. Given time, it was still technically possible to "do the math" and arrive at more accurate calculations. But these never came.[33] Looking at the October 23, 1934, ascent in a larger context, one can't help but feel that Jean Piccard was exhausted. He had tried for a not inconsiderable amount of time leading up to the ascent, going all the way back to 1932, to be all things to all people (husband, father, scientist, businessman, promoter, adventurer). Wasn't that enough? Apparently not. Science is an exacting master.

To a certain degree too, the public at large had begun to see manned balloon flights to the stratosphere as redundant. The novelty was still there, but the novelty was beginning to wear off—and the physics, despite the best attempts of science journalists, remained as abstract and remote as ever for the average person. For a brief moment in late 1934, Jean and Jeannette Piccard were the toast of the town; but it didn't last, melting away like Icarus's wax wings in the sun.

CHAPTER 12

City of Tomorrow

The aerial feats of Italo Balbo, Hugo Eckener, and the Piccards riveted the public's attention on aviation and space exploration. These events were milestones in the course of the World's Fair—unforgettable spectacles that shaped history. But what was getting the most attention on a daily basis were the "concessions" offering a night in Paris or Old Mexico, replete with music, food, and exotic dancers. At President Roosevelt's urging, Congress had already revised the laws pertaining to Prohibition* to permit the sale of beer, and the Pabst Brewing Company was quick to erect its own lakeside "Casino" near the entertainments. The fair's directors, Rufus Dawes and Lenox Lohr, were not above taking the concessionaires' money in the form of fees, and ultimately this had much to do with why the fair was a financial success. Walt Disney, then a young animation pioneer enjoying his first success with the Mickey Mouse character he had created, visited the fair and was drawn to both the scientific, futuristic halls and their displays, but also to the model cultural exhibits from throughout the world. The "Belgian Village" in particular made a deep impression on Disney.[1] He recalled his father regaling him with tales of his days helping build the structures of the great 1893 Fair, and its cultural expositions. The 1893 Fair too featured a sort of quasi-fair (the first "Midway") filled with amusements, many of them with foreign cultural themes. It was slightly salacious, very popular, and highly profitable. The possibility of combining the uplifting and culturally enriching aspects of exhibits on foreign countries with commercial success appealed to both the idealist and the businessman in Disney.

---

* In anticipation of the repeal of Prohibition altogether as a result of the Twenty-First Amendment, then well on its way to ratification at the state level.

The Midway. *Courtesy of University of Illinois Chicago Special Collections.*

The city of Chicago was all in on the fair. That potent elixir of profit mixed with genuine civic-mindedness and enthusiasm lent itself to creative collaboration. Major League Baseball, with two clubs in rival leagues calling Chicago home, decided to get in on the act and stage a "Midsummer Classic" in conjunction with the fair, pitting the top players from the older National League (founded 1876) against the more youthful American League (1901). The 1933 "All Star Game" was the first of its kind, and added a degree of glamour to the sport, the city, and the fair.

The location was Comiskey Park on Chicago's South Side. The park was home to the "White Sox," twice winners of the World Series in 1906 and 1917. Chicago's other professional baseball club were the North Siders (also known as the Cubs) who played their home games at Wrigley Field. They had twice won the World Series as well (1907, 1908). But the club that had dominated the Major Leagues since World War I were the mighty Yankees of New York, led by the great Babe Ruth. Ruth had been the American league's best pitcher with the Boston Red Sox before shifting his focus to hitting and becoming the greatest slugger in history with the Yankees. In an era when baseball players, boxers, and thoroughbred horses dominated the sports pages,* Babe Ruth was *the* sports hero of the age. Now on the down-side of a career filled with both laurels and dissipation, he was returning to Chicago to headline the big game. The previous October at Wrigley Field, Ruth was reputed to have pointed beyond the center-field fence in a World Series game versus the Cubs and "called his shot" before proceeding to hit a home run exactly where he had pointed. It was the stuff of legend. He arrived in Chicago, needless to say, with great fanfare.

For South Siders, the game's other great attractions were the starting third-baseman and centerfielder for the American League, Jimmy Dykes and Al Simmons, respectively, of the White Sox. Dykes and Simmons had rose to prominence in the game playing for Connie Mack's World Series–winning Philadelphia Athletics teams in 1929 and 1930. The White Sox poached Dykes and Simmons from the "A's" in the hope that their winning ways would rub off on their teammates. The White Sox hadn't been seriously competitive since the 1920 season, when eight of their players had been sus-pended from baseball for "throwing" the World Series the previous season, including the great "Shoeless" Joe Jackson—the greatest hitter in the game until Ruth.

An overflow crowd of 49,200 crowded Comiskey Park for the big game on July 6, 1933.[2] The North Siders had sent three of their own to play, in-cluding one of the National League's top pitchers, Lon Warnecke, and his catcher, Gaby Hartnett. But Babe Ruth was the star. In the third inning he hit a towering home run into the right-field bleachers off of St. Louis Car-dinals pitcher Bill Hallahan. Then, in the eighth inning of a 4–2 game, with the American League ahead, Chick Hafey of the Cincinnati Reds hit a shot to right field that looked like it was headed for the bleachers. With a runner on base in front of Hafey, a home run would have tied the game. But the aging Ruth had a bead on the ball and gracefully robbed Hafey of a home run by catching the ball in his mitt just as it was going over the fence! This ensured an American League victory, and added to Ruth's already prestigious legend. It would prove to be his swan song. He would be out of baseball by 1935, finishing his Major League career in a Boston Braves uniform. Ruth would have done better to depart Comiskey Park on July 6, 1933, and never look back. The baseball gods had granted him one last great day; there wouldn't be another.

Jean Shepherd recalled those days years later in a memoir of his child-hood growing up in Hammond, Indiana. His father was a die-hard White Sox fan, and Comiskey Park was conveniently located only about a half-

---

* The NBA didn't yet exist, and the NFL was a third-rate league.

Jimmy Dykes, "third sacker" for the hometown White Sox. *Author's photo.*

hour's drive in one of a series of old jalopies the "Old Man" drove, from their home in the extreme northwestern corner of Indiana. A selection of Shepherd's stories of his childhood were eventually made into the film, *A Christmas Story*, in 1983, fifty years after the fair opened. It's become an iconic part of holiday season Americana. But Shepherd's memoir actually is only partly set during the holidays, and it's not Christmas that becomes the obsession for Shepherd ("Ralph") and his brother ("Randy"), and their childhood friends—it's the Great Fair. To a certain extent the anticipation generated by the wondrous fairgrounds being constructed, then the news of its grand opening, exceeded actually visiting the fair itself. Shepherd described those first hints that something truly sensational was coming:

> "Yup. They're building a World's Fair." At that time the shore stretched empty and white, with little tufts of grass here and there, almost to Fields Museum and down to the cold water. . . . And, sure enough, a World's Fair began to grow. It spread outward like a mushroom patch . . . and grew and grew and grew. Month by month, year by year, great blue and yellow and orange buildings right out of the land of Oz blotted out the lake. . . . Mile after mile was covered with this fantasy, this wonderland, this land of real, genuine, absolute magic. . . . The Emerald City had come to the South Side.[3]

But going to the fair was a financial stretch for many families feeling the tight pinch of Depression era austerity, including Shepherd's own: "The word was out that we would go 'when the weather got warmer.' At least that was the explanation my brother and I got. No one talked to us too much about money. . . . The fair was all that anyone talked about for weeks, and a couple of my cousins had actually *been* there. It was impossible even to talk to them about it. They were speechless."[4] With admission of 50 cents for adults and 25 cents for children, the cost of just attending the fair wasn't onerous; but the rides cost a bit extra, there were the inevitable taffy apples, soda pop, and hot dogs, and the souvenir of course—a talisman to bring back to the far drearier "real" world to brandish in front of the uninitiated as proof that you had been there, and come back.

One of the most unique aspects of Jean Shepherd's memoir as it relates to the 1933 Chicago World's Fair is its ability to convey the sense of wonder it held for children. As inspiring, informative, and titillating as the fair could be for adults, the sheer sense of wonder it generated for children must have been exponentially greater. On a scale of one to ten, with one being the least wonder-generating and ten being the most, it would have been an eleven. And these children were going to grow up and, like Shepherd, they would remember what they had seen: a vision not of an idealized past, but of a streamlined, Technicolor future:

> I am looking at the flags and I see the Hall of Science. I am a tiny, tiny squirt, but it made a colossal impression on me, the first truly immense impression of my life. . . . The Skyride! The unreal Fantasy World's Fair architecture. World's Fair buildings have no relationship to real buildings. It was truly beyond all my expectations, whatever they were.[5]

Jean Shepherd's classmate "Flick," years later over a beer, asks him: "'Do you remember the robot?' 'What robot?' 'Well, they had this robot. That smoked cigars. My Old Man took me to see it. That's the only thing *I* remember.' 'That's the way it is with fairs. You never know what you'll remember.'"[6]

Gene Roddenberry was an eleven-year-old student at Berendo Junior High School in Los Angeles when the fair opened in May 1933, consuming a steady diet of Edgar Rice Burroughs's *Tarzan* and *John Carter of Mars* novels. He wouldn't attend the Chicago World's Fair, but from a distance, he was fascinated by it. He read everything he could on the new technologies, the great aviators, the odd but strangely moving buildings, and above all, the Piccard brothers (and in particular, Jean)[7]—those philosopher-princes of the land of science, aiming at no less than human exploration of outer space. It wasn't quite like that, of course, but that's the way it is with fairs, you never know what you'll remember.

For his part, after serving as an aviator himself in World War II, Roddenberry would go on to become a screenwriter and producer for television (another medium first introduced at the 1933 Chicago World's Fair). His signature work was the *Star Trek* series and its sequel, *Star Trek: Next Generation*. The original series, which aired for three seasons on NBC in the 1960s, was groundbreaking science fiction. Set in the twenty-third century, the starship *Enterprise* "seeks out new life and new civilizations" and goes "boldly where no man has gone before." Its multiracial cast set the tone for a progressive treatment of mankind's place in the cosmos, and our ability to use science to live up to our noble heritage. The futuristic sets and in particular the depictions of twenty-third-century architecture call to mind the buildings at the 1933 Chicago World's Fair. Then, over seven seasons in the 1980s and 1990s, Roddenberry continued the story into the twenty-fourth century with a new *Enterprise* under the command of Captain Jean-Luc Picard in *Next Generation*. These shows' influence on popular culture, public perceptions of science and space travel, and racial tolerance (whether

Official promotional poster for the 1933 Fair, featuring the U.S. Government Building.

through depicting interracial relationships or by introducing alien characters in important roles) has been enormous. Gene Roddenberry was a man ahead of his time, but it's important not to lose sight of the fact that he was also an adolescent *of* his time in the 1930s. The Great Fair's reach was wide. Who knows how many young people it touched, who never even visited the actual fair? Roddenberry is only the most famous.

Star Trek, as a reflection of Gene Roddenberry's own views, saw the future as a place where racial equality would be achieved, must be achieved. In an interview given later in his life Roddenberry explained his rationale: "if we don't have blacks and whites living together by the time our civilization catches up to the time frame our series is set in, there won't be any people."[8] He had a point. Roddenberry peopled his fictional *Enterprise* with blacks, whites, Asians, Russians (quite controversial at the height of the Cold War), and aliens (including the series' most memorable character—a Vulcan named Spock). He credited the context of his own education in 1930s Los Angeles—and the use of reason—for arriving at this view of humanity:

> It did not seem strange to me that I would use different races on the ship. Perhaps I received too good an education in the 1930s schools I went to, because I knew what proportion of people and races the world consisted of . . . I guess I owe a great part of this to my parents. They never taught me that one race or color was superior. I remember in school seeking out Chinese students and Mexican students because the idea of different cultures fascinated me. So, having not been taught that there is a pecking order of people, a superiority of race or culture, it was natural that my writing went that way.[9]

The contrast of Roddenberry's view of mankind, informed by the vision of the World's Fair, his family, and his own education, stood in stark contrast to the Hitler Youth. His contemporaries in Germany at the time were being fed—and eagerly consuming—the flattering lie that they were a superior "Aryan" race who would inevitably inherit a future where they would dominate the inferior and weak.

Gene Roddenberry also would pioneer, and advocate for, gender equality in his television series. He was aware of Jeannette Piccard's leading role in the 1934 stratospheric launch. She had proved herself to be both brave and resourceful. That women would eventually be considered for command of airliners and military aircraft seemed to Roddenberry simply a matter of time. As he said in an interview, "Those things strike me as so logical."[10] He even cast his future wife, Majel Barrett, in the role of second-in-command of the *Enterprise* in the original *Star Trek* pilot in 1964. Barrett later changed her hair color, and was recast as "Nurse Chapel" for the rest of the series. Roddenberry later admitted that featuring a Jeannette Piccard–type character in 1964 America was still too far ahead of its time: "The network killed that. The network brass at the time could not handle a woman being second-in-command of a spaceship. In those days it was such a monstrous thought to so many people. I realized that I had to get rid of her character or else I wouldn't get my series on the air."[11]

Two steps forward, one step backward—or some variant on that proportion—was the rule in mid-twentieth-century America. The 1933 Chicago World's Fair provided ample evidence of this.

For African Americans, even though the city of Chicago itself was a seething cauldron of racial unrest, the great 1933 World's Fair was for the most part fairly progressive-minded. The performance of Florence Price's Symphony no. 1 in 1933 was complemented by a historical exhibit featuring a replica of Jean Baptiste Point du Sable's original trading post that formed the basis for what eventually became Chicago,[12] and artist Charles Dawson's mural depicting the experience of those involved in the Great Migration—which had brought Florence Price to Chicago—was installed in the fair's Hall of Social Science. But on the Midway, blacks were more often than not depicted in a derogatory or ridiculous manner. Exhibits such as "Darkest Africa" only confirmed white fairgoers' worst prejudices about people of color. And black fairgoers were often made to feel unwelcome on the Midway. The "Streets of Paris" were officially open to all, but in reality looked to cater to an exclusively white clientele.[13] After a vigorous effort on the part of community leaders, a "Negro Day" was proclaimed at the fair. Talented artists such as Hubie Blake contributed to a musical "pageant" celebrating African American culture and history at Soldier Field. Two steps forward, one step back. The 1933 Chicago World's Fair would become known as the "City of Tomorrow" for its forward-looking technology and architecture, but for many, including African Americans, the moniker served as a frustrating reminder that in society at large, it was still the "City of Today."

For women, the fair also was a generally progressive-minded space where they were able to feature their contributions to society in a formal way. Louise Lentz Woodruff's series of sculptures and bas reliefs, *Science Advancing Mankind*, was the centerpiece of the entire fair, in fact. But a proposed "Temple of Womanhood" never materialized, and unlike the earlier 1893 Fair, there was no official women-specific exhibit hall. On the other hand, a highlight of the 1933 Fair was the visit of the dynamic new First Lady of the United States, Eleanor Roosevelt, on "Women's Day,"

October 31, 1933, held six days after the *Graf Zeppelin* sailed away over Lake Michigan. Her participation was billed as an "epochal event in A Century of Progress" featuring a "mass meeting."[14] Mrs. Roosevelt's feminist bona fides were impeccable. In rolling out the red carpet for her, Rufus Dawes very publicly demonstrated the fair's support for a more equal role for women in society.

Chicago and America loved "cheesecake," beauty pageants, and starlets too. Sally Rand certainly wasn't a one-off in a fair full of young women aspiring to fame, or at least a paycheck. The lineup ran the full spectrum from snake charmers[15] to actual actresses vying for screen tests in Hollywood.

Leggy starlets on display as car ornaments, 1933 Chicago World's Fair. Notice the featuring of both white and black swimsuit-clad beauties. Progress? It's in the eye of the beholder. *Courtesy of the* Chicago Tribune.

The messages were mixed: empower women, yes; objectify women, yes too. Two steps forward, one step back. Or some variant thereof. In this, Chicago and its fair were in no way out of step with the rest of the country. The high-minded and the less high-minded coexisted in a land of contradictions. And as Rufus Dawes no doubt would have concurred, it was all at the fair!

——— ✺ ———

The "City of Tomorrow," of course, wasn't meant to be ironic. It was meant as a beacon and an inspiration. Science was going to lead the world to a brighter future, and the fair would show the way. Ultimately, it was technology that defined the 1933 Chicago World's Fair for most of the millions who attended it. Model modern homes using revolutionary construction materials, an actual General Motors assembly line, and the first glimpse of television at the small, but popular Hudson-Essex exhibit in the Electricity Building were particular favorites. GE caused quite a sensation as well, using "microwave" technology to pop kernels of corn for fairgoers to consume for free. And everywhere one was surrounded by powerful, beautiful, and sometimes disturbing images, illuminated at night to even greater effect. One of the most moving was the two-story-tall relief sculpture of "Knowledge" in the form of a man destroying "Ignorance" in the form of a serpent. This was how the fair saw its role in the world. Whether it was cultural or scientific, the spread of knowledge and the embrace of new ideas and new technologies would free man from the coils of the dim past. No one who saw it was unaffected by it.

The fair was such a success that its organizers authorized a second, slightly shorter season in 1934. This decision wasn't without precedent. In 1900 the organizers of the Paris World's Fair added an additional season in 1901. It's a testament to the 1933 Chicago Fair's hold on the public imagination that a second season seemed a safe bet from a financial standpoint. To be sure, the exhibits changed to a certain degree, so there was some variety. Different companies competed with each other to stage the most impressive corporate exhibits—as opposed to cooperating with each other on industry-wide exhibits. There was also a noticeable shift to a less colorful fair, literally. As in 1893, white became a predominant color again. It tended to clean up the face of the fair after one busy season, and four months of winter weather had left it looking a bit down in the mouth. And where color was used in the 1934 version, it tended be in slightly more subdued hues than Joseph Urban's original exuberant vision. The light show at the central fountain still was a centerpiece of the fair experience for evening fairgoers. Millions more came before the gates were shut forever on October 31 of that year. The kaleidoscope of colored electric lights were switched off, and high above, Arcturus burned in the distant heavens.

CHAPTER 13

Lost Horizon

One year after the 1933 World's Fair closed, Benito Mussolini used a flimsy pretext to order the invasion of Ethiopia (then known as Abyssinia). This move, coupled with Japan's earlier invasion of Chinese territory in Manchuria,* tested the will of the international order erected by Woodrow Wilson at Paris in 1919. Without active U.S. involvement, the League of Nations did little more than investigate and condemn with words aggression that only would have respected force. Ethiopia's emperor, Haile Selassie, addressed the League at its impressive new headquarters in Geneva, appealing for assistance, but his plea fell on deaf ears. Fear of sparking a second world war in Europe over struggles in distant lands trumped doing the right thing. It was that simple.

Italo Balbo had returned to Italy in the summer of 1933 to a welcome that rivaled the triumphs held for victorious generals in ancient Rome. Mussolini indulged in an orgy of self-congratulatory Fascist spectacle. The official propaganda—which Balbo loyally parroted—was that the Chicago flight had been a demonstration of the superior will of Il Duce. One could easily forgive Italians of the time for thinking it was Mussolini, and not Balbo, who had led the seaplane squadron across the Atlantic to the Windy City. When the cheering faded away, Il Duce, recognizing that "there was room for only one eagle in the Fascist nest,"[1] dispatched Balbo to the rugged Italian colony in North Africa known as Libya to be its new governor. The

---

* For its part, Japan had staged a contest at the 1933 Chicago World's Fair for a roundtrip ticket to "Manchukuo." It was won by one Miss Francis Robinson of 2231 East 67th Street. No mention was made, however, of how the Japanese Army was trafficking opium to finance its operations in Manchuria, or about its plans to establish a secret biological weapons facility there to conduct experiments on live human beings.

Ministério da Aeronautica, which Balbo had painstakingly fashioned in his own image, was unceremoniously taken away from him. The official line was that it was a promotion for the Fascist aviator par excellence, but in reality this explanation fooled no one. Back in Chicago, the *Chicago American* made it crystal clear what most believed: "IL DUCE 'EXILES' BALBO TO POST IN AFRICA."[2] The *American*'s man in Rome, Guglielmo Emanuel, reported: "While there was no confirmation of reports abroad that Marshal Balbo was being shelved because of the immense popularity he won as a result of his aeronautical feats,"[3] it was commonly understood that this was in fact the case. For Balbo this was a crushing disappointment, but it couldn't have come entirely as a surprise. Mussolini was moving increasingly toward becoming a totalitarian dictator. With Hitler, Stalin, and Japanese militarists all ascendant and acting with less and less restraint, history seemed to favor Mussolini's megalomaniacal instincts. Emanuel reported: "With Il Duce scheduled to abolish the Chamber of Deputies in the near future and do away with all institutions even remotely linking fascist Italy to the tenets of democratic rule, he is now in a position to carry out his projected constitutional reforms virtually unhampered."[4]

As the new governor of Libya, Italo Balbo was more cheerleader than participant in the events that occurred in the ancient, mountainous country of Ethiopia in 1935. Despite a valiant defense, the Ethiopians were ultimately defeated. The use of poison gas and military aircraft greatly aided this show of Fascist might. It was undoubtedly better for Balbo's later historical reputation, in this instance, that he had been sent to Libya in 1933. If he had stayed as head of the Aeronautica, Balbo would have presided over the atrocities Italy meted out from the air on the Ethiopians. This would have greatly complicated things for Balbo's apologists who later on looked to position him historically as the "good" Fascist. This thesis has some merit. But in examining Balbo's role in history, one has to ask: would Balbo have said "no" to Mussolini when attacks on civilians were ordered, when the use of poison gas was authorized? But sidelined, his waist growing steadily thicker, Italo Balbo was not forced to make these decisions. As the world moved inexorably toward catastrophe, this talented man languished in Libya. His efforts, like so much water poured into the desert sand, were largely wasted in a backward land ruling over a surly, subjugated people. Meanwhile, Hitler—rapidly rearming in violation of the Versailles Treaty—looked to test his strength without fully committing Germany to all-out war. The civil war in Spain provided him with just such an opportunity. The Condor Legion, composed of German aircraft and pilots, gave nationalist leader Francisco Franco a decisive edge over his Republican opponents. Mussolini piled on. The year after Spain's capital city of Madrid began being bombed relentlessly from the air, the Japanese moved against mainland China and used similar aerial tactics in bombing Shanghai. That spring, the Condor Legion left Guernica in ashes.

At approximately the same time in central Europe, an emboldened Hitler absorbed his native Austria. Hysterical crowds of adoring Viennese gave him a welcome more closely associated in historical memory with that accorded the Beatles in a later decade. It was mass hysteria, giving lie to the postwar Austrian claim that they were having none of it. At the Munich Conference later that year, Hitler bullied the timid British prime minister, Neville Chamberlain, into conceding to the dismemberment of Czechoslovakia before absorbing all of it in March 1939. He next set his eyes on Poland. Mussolini, not to be outdone, looked greedily toward military conquests in Albania and the Aegean.

Americans, still locked in an isolationist mindset, looked on with grim fascination. Some recognized that the United States must abandon neutrality in a world that was becoming increasingly dangerous for democratic-minded nations. Others, led by hero-pilot Charles Lindbergh, argued that a policy of "America First" must be maintained and that Europe's problems would have to be sorted out by Europeans. The moral equivalency drawn by Lindbergh and others between Hitler's Third Reich and the British Empire had some merit, but was decidedly pro-Nazi on closer inspection. Other groups, notably the German American Bund and Italian American Fascist organizations, used pacifism as a mechanism to give Hitler and Mussolini free rein to do as they pleased abroad without fear of American military intervention.

It was during these years that James Hilton's novel, *Lost Horizon*, reached millions of readers across the globe. In 1937, as war raged in China and Spain, a film adaptation of the book was released in theaters. Hilton had hit a nerve. His story of a group of highjacked air travelers being brought to Shangri-La, where peace, learning, and civilization remained untouched, spoke to a yearning that many felt as they watched the world about them descend into a new darkness. Chicagoans recalling the Great Fair of 1933 could look back on it as a lost idyll at best, a lie at worst. The future didn't belong to the high-minded men of science and aviation and their contemporaries in the arts; it belonged to goose-stepping bullies marching in unison to force concessions by threatening to unleash war. Soon they would.

The final horrifying act in the story of the great zeppelins occurred in front of a large crowd at the airfield in Lakehurst, New Jersey on May 6, 1937. The images of the beautiful airship breaking into a giant ball of flame imprinted itself in the minds of those who were eyewitnesses, certainly, but

The *Hindenburg,* symbol of a cruel new order.

also in the minds of those who heard the live account of the tragedy unfolding on radio or who saw the graphic images of the tragedy blaring across the front pages of newspapers around the world. Many pointed to sabotage. There certainly was motive for such an act of terror. However, the evidence was elusive, and remains so. Hitler's henchman, Joseph Goebbels, had eagerly used the zeppelin commercial fleet as he had used the 1936 Berlin Olympics, as a propaganda tool to glorify the Third Reich and its "inevitable" rise to world domination. The fiery ball in New Jersey foreshadowed a different future for Germany.

For Hugo Eckener, the years after his return from the great Chicago Fair in 1933 had been awkward, even dangerous. Initially, Joseph Goebbels had been willing to put the full power of the state behind Eckener's vision of a larger zeppelin fleet and establish a regular trans-Atlantic service to New York/Lakehurst. The propaganda value of these ever-larger silver behemoths, now emblazoned with swastikas on *both* the port and starboard sides, was not lost on him. For his part, Hitler was not a fan—in fact, any talk of naming

May 6, 1937.

an airship after him was quickly quashed, as his superstitious nature worried that any accident could be perceived as an ill omen attaching itself to him personally.[5] The chief of the Luftwaffe, the ex-fighter pilot Hermann Goering, was also not a fan for obvious reasons. But Goebbels carried the day, and the construction of what would become the *Hindenburg* went ahead. The largest airship ever built was named for World War I hero and former president of the Weimar Republic, Paul von Hindenburg, who had died at the age of eighty-six in 1934.*

Goebbels and his master, Hitler, expected gratitude from Eckener. What they got instead was a continued oblique reticence to go along with the Nazi plan; his poking fun at the official "Heil Hitler" greeting expected between citizens of the Third Reich, for example. A foreign journalist had asked Eckener about this, and he had jokingly confirmed it: "Yes, that's right! When I get up in the morning, I don't say 'Heil Hitler!' to my wife, but rather 'good

---

* An interesting story relayed by J. Gordon Vaeth in his 1958 book on Eckener claims that a doctor attending Hindenburg in his final days was told by Hindenburg himself that in 1933, he had extracted a promise from Adolf Hitler to leave Eckener alone. On the other hand, what good were Hitler's promises?

morning.'"[6] When asked by the Nazi regime to make a public pronounce-
ment supporting Hitler's 1936 reoccupation of the Rhineland in violation
of the Versailles Treaty, he again demurred. This led to his being declared
persona non grata by Joseph Goebbels. The plebiscite that was put before the
German population to gain official sanction for the reoccupation was being
carefully stage-managed by the Nazis. At the zeppelin headquarters, Eckener
ordered that "election posters be removed from the hangar," and at a press
breakfast "the words 'Hail Deutschland' [and not "Heil Hitler"] were used
for the drinking greeting."[7] These might seem like small gestures for those
of us who have never lived under a totalitarian regime. But in a totalitarian regime there are no such things. The *New York Times* also reported on
Eckener's unwillingness to have his name used to push the plebiscite vote,
noting that he was "a man of rugged independence."[8] On the other hand,
the year after his Chicago appearance, Eckener made a public statement in
support of Hitler's 1934 plebiscite to the German people seeking approval
for his continued (and indefinite) dictatorial rule. Could the fact that Joseph
Goebbels had offered Eckener 2 million marks toward construction of his
next airship—to be the *ne plus ultra* in size and design—have been a deter-
mining factor? It's hard not to reach this conclusion. In the event, Hitler won
approval of 90 percent of votes cast. He didn't need Hugo Eckener's public
support to carry the German electorate. His popularity inside Germany was
enormous, and growing. However, a recognized moderate with name value,
coming out in support, lent a degree of respectability Hitler neither possessed nor deserved. Eckener himself later made it crystal clear that he understood the transactional nature of his relationship with him: "Herr Hitler
never did anything without demanding compensation either beforehand or
afterwards."[9] This was the price of continuing to be involved with the zeppelin project. Hugo Eckener would have to "play ball" to a certain degree—
and accept an increasingly diminished status, at least publicly, in the airship
program. But as the *Hindenburg* neared completion, it became more and
more difficult for Eckener to maintain his independence of mind on the one
hand, and continue to be associated with the great enterprise of his life on
the other. Privately he could confide, as he did to the Berlin-based American
journalist, Louis Lochner, that Hitler was a "venomous toad,"[10] but publicly
he was forced to be increasingly circumspect in his remarks.

He was infuriated when Joseph Goebbels, with Ernst Lehmann as willing
accomplice, cut the *Hindenburg*'s test trials short in order to use it in an aerial
display of Nazi political omnipotence. The airship was brought out of its
hangar in high winds and suffered damage to one of its lower fins. This first
experience with the *Hindenburg*—this magnificent piece of engineering—

being pimped out as a tool for Nazi propaganda, convinced Eckener that it "sailed under an evil star."[11] And so it did.

The night of the disaster in Lakehurst, Hugo Eckener was in Graz, Austria, a guest of the city's local aeronautical club. His celebrity in neighboring Austria at least had not been dimmed by Hitler's demotion. After the meeting, the famous sculptor Gustinus Ambrosi invited Eckener to his studio. Eckener had been an admirer of Ambrosi's work for some time. Ambrosi had gone deaf at the age of seven, but had overcome his disability to produce hundreds of works of sculpture that conveyed both physicality and emotion. Eckener later recalled his impressions on meeting the deaf genius: "in his expressive face there shone a pair of overpoweringly illuminated eyes in which there burned an almost mystical fire. And what was it he wanted to show me? It was a vision of Icarus plunging into the sea."[12] As he entered the space, Eckener, never one to embrace paranormal phenomena, was struck with an overwhelming sense of foreboding as he viewed a statue of a broken Icarus. Ambrosi wanted to convey the pain of Icarus's noble failure off the island of Crete. The son of Daedalus, torso impossibly twisted in pain as he hits an oncoming wave, was the image that met Eckener's eyes. In that moment, he was certain something was wrong—terribly wrong—but what? Later, a call in the middle of the night confirmed what he already suspected. Icarus *was* broken.

What was broken? The *Hindenburg*, the Zeppelin project as a whole, the dream of aviation as a force for global unity and progress: all of these. Immediately, the recorded public spectacle of the giant luxury liner of the skies being consumed by angry-looking flames jarred the public (and it was shown repeatedly). Herbert Morrison's famous description of the event—his distorted voice filled with both horror and empathy—became an icon of the radio age. Filmmaker Robert Wise's treatment of the explosion in his 1975 film is worth watching to gain a sense of what it must have felt like to be there witnessing it in person. His use of actual footage—replayed over a number of times for better effect—with the sound of the Naval Station's shrill klaxons blaring over the sounds of burning hydrogen gas and twisting metal, lends itself to nothing if not dread. It is very disturbing to watch. Something like that happening so publicly, being recorded and so widely distributed, doomed not just one ill-fated airship, but all airships. No one in their right mind after watching the film footage would purchase a ticket for travel on a zeppelin.

Falling Icarus, Gustinus Ambrosi (1937). *Courtesy of Dr. Uwe Eckener.*

Hugo Eckener didn't seem to grasp this at first. Even though he had been sidelined in official Germany,* he was immediately dispatched by Berlin to lead the German investigation of the disaster. His findings pointed not to sabotage, but rather to an electrical discharge igniting hydrogen gas that had leaked from one of the *Hindenburg*'s gas cells. Most serious studies of what happened in the decades since have generally concurred with Eckener's estimation. What if it had been helium in those cells instead? Eckener had been trying throughout the 1930s to convince Franklin D. Roosevelt to authorize the sale of helium to the Zeppelin Company. In fact, FDR's predecessor, Herbert Hoover, had been an ardent fan of Hugo Eckener—meeting with him in person and referring to him as a veritable Magellan of the skies.[13] If Hugo Eckener had exhibited a greater sense of urgency earlier, perhaps he could have convinced President Hoover to try to use his authority to move matters in this direction.† The United States at that time had a near-monopoly on this wonder gas. Its lift wasn't as great as that of hydrogen, but it was close, and more importantly, it was safe. However, the Roosevelt administration that came to power in 1933, peopled with left-leaning progressives—"New Dealers"—was in no hurry to sell helium to a company based in Hitler's Germany. As "Der Führer's" foreign policy grew increasingly aggressive, and his anti-Semitic rants became ever more unhinged, FDR's administration and many in Congress simply weren't interested in accommodating German interests, even if it involved a safety issue, as was so painfully evident after what happened over Lakehurst. There was sympathy for Hugo Eckener as an individual in his efforts to negotiate a deal for U.S. helium, but he was a German and there was little sympathy for Germany. In retrospect, this position could be seen as small, mean-spirited even, of the United States. Secretary of the Interior Harold Ickes in particular was intractable on this point.[14] Thirty-five passengers and crew had died in the *Hindenburg* disaster, as well as a member of the ground crew. Many more had suffered burns and other injuries. Airships should not rely on hydrogen for lift; it was simply too dangerous. By denying Eckener helium, the Americans were effectively killing the zeppelin project as a whole.

The *Graf* was completing what would be its final air voyage from South America when news reached the bridge of what had happened in New Jersey.

---

* It's worth noting that Eckener had been "rehabilitated" by the Nazi propaganda ministry following his successful crossing of the Atlantic at the helm of the *Hindenburg* on its maiden voyage to Lakehurst, in 1936. On the passenger list only his name appeared, without a title, even though he was commanding the airship. It was Ernst Lehmann—a reliable Nazi sympathizer—who was listed as "Captain."

† To be fair, Hoover was president for less than two months after Hitler became chancellor of Germany. Perhaps if Hoover had won re-election in 1932, he would have taken a similar stance as that of the Roosevelt administration.

Captain Hans von Schiller made the decision to keep it from the passengers until they had safely landed back in Germany.[15] Three years later, that amazing airship that had awed Chicagoans as it came out of the sunrise over Lake Michigan in 1933 was unceremoniously dismantled for scrap on the orders of Hermann Goering. Goering wanted the aluminum in its skeleton for use by the Luftwaffe, which had by then been unleashed on the rest of Europe by Hitler. Nothing could have been further from what the *Graf Zeppelin* had stood for at its best: that is to say, a better world.

CHAPTER 14

Into the Abyss

World War II took the lives of sixty million people, the overwhelming majority of them civilians. The magnificent roar of the propeller-driven engines of Italo Balbo's air squadrons above the skylines of Rio and Chicago took on a new, terrifying significance in the abyss of war. Once inspiring untold numbers of people to aspire to a better world, they now were associated with death and destruction meted out from the sky. What had begun in Madrid and Shanghai spread first to Barcelona and Guernica; then to Warsaw, Rotterdam, London, Plymouth, Leningrad, Hamburg, Dresden, Berlin, Tokyo, and, finally, Hiroshima and Nagasaki. The ideal of the Nietzschean "Superman" embraced by the futurists and put into action by men such as Italo Balbo and his black-shirted pilots, found its truest expression in the SS and its sinister implementation of Hitler's final solution to the Jewish "question."

To a certain extent Italo Balbo was absolved of much of this due to his publicly known discomfort with the German alliance Mussolini had created.[1] The former idol of Hitler had become his puppet, and the racial policies in particular that Mussolini now began aping, appalled Balbo. As early as 1937, Balbo *publicly* proclaimed: "I do not differentiate between Catholic Italians and Jewish Italians. We are all Italians."[2] To his everlasting credit, he made a particular point of inviting a number of Tripoli's most important Jewish families to attend a dinner he gave in honor of Reichsmarschall Hermann Goering's visit in 1938.[3] He enjoyed seeing the fat man squirm in his white uniform.

When war came in 1940, Balbo did his duty and organized the colony's defenses against an expected British attack from neighboring Egypt. On June 28, he was personally conducting reconnaissance in the vicinity of the naval base at Tobruk when he was shot down by friendly fire from the guns of an

Italian vessel, anti-aircraft batteries ashore, and possibly even small arms—or a combination of all three. The base had just been hit hard by a British Royal Air Force raid, and the all-clear signal had not yet been given. Balbo was unaware of this, and after his trimotor Savoia-Marchetti S.79 was hit, he and all those aboard (including three Italian airmen who had flown to Chicago with their chief in 1933) were consumed by flames. Italy mourned. Conspiracy theories pointing to an insecure Mussolini orchestrating Balbo's death are unsupported by solid evidence.[4] And Mussolini was such a buffoon that it's difficult to imagine him pulling off something like this, even if he had wanted to. The fact is, this was a tragic accident—a "perfect storm" of miscommunication, poor timing, and the fog of war.

Like Che Guevara (whom he resembled in more ways than one) in another epoch, Balbo died while he was still vigorous and relevant, unlike Mussolini, who had become ridiculous before his grisly demise. But does this absolve him? He allowed himself in his glory years at the Aeronautica to become a tremendously attractive apostle of an ugly ideology, with horrific historical consequences. An ancient column erected behind Soldier Field to the memory of his great 1933 flight remained (and remains) standing in Chicago, but the ideals so many wanted to believe lay in ruins.

<hr>

Hugo Eckener became an increasingly marginalized figure following the (unwanted) notoriety around the Hindenburg disaster. After returning to Germany, in 1938 his Nazi masters requested that he publicly endorse the Anschluss ("union") being forced on the Austrian government by Hitler. Within Austria, Hitler enjoyed wide, but not universal, support. Eckener, again, was useful as a recognized moderate voice to help provide a veneer of respectability to the annexation. In his memoir, Eckener clearly struggled with his decision to do as they requested: "I finally decided to give in to the terror, because nothing could now be done about the accomplished fact [Anschluss], and because I would not and could not be torn away from my life work at this critical moment."[5] In retrospect, this self-serving explanation is decidedly unsatisfactory. And to a large degree it informs our understanding of Eckener's actions during World War II. His life's work was the Zeppelin Company. He wanted to continue in at least some capacity at Zeppelin, and because of this, the Nazis had him. It's that simple. It's also very human. All of us have, or have had, a position, a project, a cause that we feel defines us. Without it, we feel a loss of purpose and identity. If those in charge recognize this, they can force compromise and concession. Pettiness often enters the equation. How much will we stand to keep what we have—or at least some of what we had? Where do we draw the line? That line continued to move further away from where Hugo Eckener had been when he visited Chicago in 1933 at the height of his fame and influence.

The Zeppelin Company, for its part, shifted from building and flying zeppelins to playing an important role in Germany's wartime armaments program. Like a number of well-known German firms, it was implicated in using forced labor to complete certain projects. Albert Speer, the slick, urbane Nazi chief of armaments, looked to supply Hitler's armies but also to produce a game-changing superweapon—the V2 rocket. Initially, a secret installation was established on the Baltic coast at Peenemunde to test and manufacture the V1 "buzz bombs" as they came to be popularly known in England (these were the precursor to the potentially far more deadly V2). Once Allied intelligence determined the location of the facility, it was heavily bombed, and Speer made the decision to relocate it to a new underground location in the interior of the country where Allied bombs couldn't penetrate. The specific location chosen for this vast new complex was inside and underneath a large hill in central Germany. It came to be known as Mittelwerk (the "Central Works"). It was a gigantic effort that utilized masses of slave laborers from the nearby Mittelbau-Dora concentration camp, and others. It is estimated that thousands of these forced laborers perished—essentially worked to death in hellish subterranean conditions.[6] The Zeppelin Company had become involved in the V2 project, and its facilities in Friedrichshafen, too, were bombed intensively. Hugo Eckener, still nominally in a position of leadership at Zeppelin, appeared to have been flattered when he was asked to consult on the project. Someone like Speer,* and his young protégé, Wernher von Braun, would have appealed to the science-minded Eckener. They weren't the usual grotesque clown-bully variety Nazi that he had dealt with earlier (Hitler, Goering, Goebbels). How much did Eckener know about the use of slave labor—and its fatal consequences? This is an important question. Some would argue that Eckener had been playing a double game all along, and was in fact much more in sympathy with the Nazi movement than has been widely understood. However, even a selective reading of the evidence we do have from the 1930s points to a pattern that is much more irregular. And even if he did know the worst of what was going on at Mittelwerk and Mittelbau-Dora, what could he have done to stop it? Any genuine influence

---

* Speer was later tried and convicted at the Nuremburg War Crimes Trials. He served his full sentence of twenty years at Spandau Prison. His sophistication and the contrition that he expressed led to a rehabilitation of his historical reputation, to a certain degree. But was that contrition genuine? He died a relatively wealthy man after publishing his memoirs.

he might once have exerted had long ago been eroded into irrelevance. He'd done it to himself. So, "continue to go along"; "pretend you're still continuing your life's work." In the final analysis, it's hard to escape the conclusion that Eckener was more pathetic than sinister in the context of Nazi-era Germany and World War II. That said, his association with Zeppelin in its wartime activities was not to his credit. At best, he was a compromised figure. But so was the whole country. That's the unfortunate truth.

Epilogue

Jean and Jeannette Piccard ultimately were able to find a long-term situation at the University of Minnesota in 1936. John D. Ackerman, the head of the Aeronautical Engineering department in the university's Institute of Technology, was an admirer of the Piccards' work. He offered Jean a position that would allow him to both teach and conduct further research. Piccard worked there until his death in 1963.[1] Albert W. Stevens would pilot the new "Explorer II" balloon to a world's record altitude of 72,395 feet in 1935,[2] thus giving this early round of the Space Race to the United States over the Soviet Union. Stevens's record stood for over twenty years. In 1957, the Soviets successfully launched the basketball-sized satellite *Sputnik* into orbit, taking round 2 of the Race.

The cutting-edge technology invented by Jean Piccard for the Piccard Gondola in 1934 would have uses in World War II and beyond. The frost-free windows, for instance, that he invented for the portals of the capsule were later adopted by high-flying American bombers in the war, and then for higher altitude jet travel after the war. The latter surprised him very little; he had predicted it. Jeannette Piccard earned her PhD at the University of Minnesota during the war, in 1942. All of their sons served in World War II. And the youngest of them, Donald Piccard, would go on to pioneer the sport of hot air ballooning. Looking back at his childhood, he once remarked of his mother, "she was fun." She liked to chop wood in the back yard, and always had projects going.[3]

—————— ∞∞∞ ——————

To its credit, the United States looked forward, not backward, after the war. Its willingness to continue to embrace a progressive futuristic vision for America and the world set it apart. Perhaps the fact that the American homeland had escaped destruction enabled the nation to more readily move on from the slaughter. Whatever the case, with the advent of the jet engine and advanced rocket technology first pioneered by the defeated Germans, the United States continued to look skyward. Wernher von Braun, who had once enjoyed attending Auguste Piccard's lectures, was brought to Huntsville, Alabama, in 1958 to lead the newly formed National Aeronautics and Space Administration's space rocket program. He had been a member of the Nazi Party (the American military had prioritized his talents over punishing him for his crimes—which included working slave laborers to death). American pilots such as Chuck Yaeger assumed the mantle of the prewar aviators willing to push ever faster, ever higher. In architecture, the United Nations headquarters building in New York was a giant, permanent expression of the vision and conception of the style that first manifested itself on such a breathtaking scale at the 1933 Chicago World's Fair. Cold War rivalries certainly played a role driving the Space Race in the 1950s and 1960s, with *Sputnik*, Yuri Gagarin, and John Glenn becoming household names. But it was more than this that inspired President John F. Kennedy to call for a moonshot by the end of the Sixties. Americans still believed in the promise of the future, of the heavens above, of outer space. Popular culture continued to equate technology and the future with the earlier, progressive vision of the 1933 Fair. And Gene Roddenberry's groundbreaking science-fiction series, *Star Trek*, continued to popularize this vision of the future.

There was a direct line between the Wright brothers' flight at Kitty Hawk in 1903 and the Apollo XI moonshot in 1969, pushing the limits of the possible ever further. NASA seemed to be doing what Roddenberry wrote for his fictional starship's mission: "To boldly go where no man has gone before." The two World's Fairs of the decade, in Seattle in 1962 and in New York in 1964, renewed America's outward- and forward-looking vision. The Space Needle's spire, reaching ever skyward toward the stars, was an expression of faith. And then something happened . . .

The cynicism of the 1970s infected interest in the future. In its place, nostalgia for a mythologized past caught the popular mood. Even space-based science fiction occurred "a long, long time ago," in "a galaxy far, far away." The last moonshot occurred in 1972. Even the more pragmatically minded space shuttle program has now been abandoned. The United States hasn't staged a World's Fair of consequence since 1965. Over eighty years on, we're now further away from the future envisioned on the shores of Lake Michigan than we were fifty years ago. We first rejected, then defeated, fascism, and the world was better for it. But, still, where are the Balbos, Eckeners, and Piccards today—those that inspire us to look upward, outward, forward?

Some would counter this pessimism by pointing to billionaire space flight pioneers Richard Branson, Elon Musk, and Jeff Bezos in the early twenty-first century. Reminiscent of billionaire-aviator Howard Hughes in the 1920s and 1930s, they are using giant fortunes to push the limits of aviation and rocket technology in the private sector. Then, of course, there is the splendid Mars "Perseverance" Rover produced and successfully landed on the "red planet" by NASA in 2020. There is even talk of the United States returning to the moon. But what would President Kennedy have said about this half a century after Apollo XI? Why haven't we already put human beings on Mars? Kennedy once said that we do the hard things "not because they are easy, but because they are hard."[4] Italo Balbo, Hugo Eckener, Auguste Piccard, Jean Piccard, and Jeannette Ridlon Piccard would all have understood this. We need their example now.

─── ∞∞∞ ───

Hugo Eckener lived through World War II and the military occupation that followed, to see the imminent advent of commercial jet travel. Even so, he never fully gave up his dream of zeppelins playing an important role in the future of aviation. After the war, J. Gordon Vaeth—himself a naval officer associated with lighter-than-air aviation—was sent by his superiors to locate the whereabouts of the once-famous commander of the *Graf Zeppelin*. He found him living in a village on Lake Constance, largely forgotten by his neighbors; a ghost from another time. Similar to Alberto Santos-Dumont, whom he so closely resembled in his worldview, he had become a relic of the past while he was still living. Seemingly flattered, but not surprised that the U.S. Navy had sent someone to find and question him, he suggested to Vaeth that "we talk in English. It will be easier for you. I am naturally out of practice."[5] He liked Americans. One of his favorite stories of his time in the United States was riding the subway around New York City, taking in art exhibits and other sights. At the time a universally recognized celebrity, he was always humored by how easily he could put his fellow subway riders off his trail by claiming, when asked if he was Hugo Eckener, "No, I'm his twin brother."[6]

Vaeth returned to the United States and reported to his superiors on his interactions with Dr. Eckener. One of those being briefed was T. G. W. "Tex" Settle, now risen to the rank of Admiral in the U.S. Navy. Goodyear also was interested in what Eckener might have to say. Eventually, the seventy-eight-year-old zeppelin captain was invited to return to America. He still believed a lighter-than-air ship, using helium for lift, could be an attractive alternative to the loud engines of commercial airliners. Vaeth left us a memorable description of Eckener in his twilight years: "In his favorite haunt, a small pavilion near the shore, the old man would sit by the hour, puffing on a cigar, and looking out over the lake. Nighttime passersby knew he was there by the red glow which alternately brightened and subsided as he sat smoking, thinking, reminiscing."[7] Did he regret the path he followed after his country was highjacked by Adolf Hitler? Should he have emigrated to the United States to maintain his independence of thought, speech, and action? Albert Einstein and Marlene Dietrich, for instance, were other famous residents of Germany who refused to live under the hooked cross. Eckener was well connected and viewed in a favorable light by powerful people—none more so than President Roosevelt himself. However, though Hugo Eckener was an internationalist, he was also a German patriot. He didn't feel these two things were incompatible. The Nazi era taught him otherwise. And he had a family. His now-grown children would have careers, families of their own back in Germany. Might they not face retribution if their famous émigré father made forceful anti-Hitler statements from the safety of New York or Washington? Given the Nazis' track record, it would appear likely. No, where he had gone astray was in refusing simply to let go of his "dream." The Nazis would twist it into a nightmare. But for a moment in the late 1920s and early 1930s . . . it had been beautiful.

⋙

There is still a place one can go to share in the vision of that fair nearly ninety years ago. Walt Disney's "Experimental City of Tomorrow" incorporates both the cultural mélange of the earlier fair his father helped build, and the refreshing optimism and technological wonder of the fair he personally witnessed himself as a young man. Millions of people from both the United States and abroad pass through EPCOT's gates each year, experiencing a French *boulangerie* or a simulated flight to Mars. At the park's entrance is the giant, futuristic geodesic dome enclosing "Spaceship Earth." In the evenings, the vast, centrally located lagoon is the site of a spectacular light and fireworks display emphasizing our common humanity and the distance we have come as a species, not just in time, but technologically. The selective use of colored lighting lends an unearthly aspect to the setting, harkening back to the "Rainbow City." Walt Disney's gift to the country and the world is

Hugo Eckener (center) in better days, at a reception (1928) with his daughter Lotte (with curly blonde hair) on his left. *Getty Images.*

that he never lost faith in that future he glimpsed in Chicago. Perhaps we need to recapture it.

In 1963, Jean Piccard died on the birthday he shared with Auguste. Auguste had died the year before. Jean's son, Donald, and Auguste's son, Jacques, had followed in their fathers' footsteps, embracing lives of science and exploration. Jacques had worked with his father to design a bathyscape to descend to the deepest depths of the ocean. Donald, of course, as a balloon pilot, was also following in his mother's, not just his father's, footsteps. By this time, he was a famous aeronaut in his own right. In that same year—1963—Soviet cosmonaut Valentina Tereshkova broke his mother's altitude record inside a capsule launched into orbit around the earth on a Soviet R-7 rocket.

Jean Piccard had wanted to return to the stratosphere after 1934. His work at the University of Minnesota was closely linked to his interest in ballooning and high-altitude aviation. In the late 1930s, his work on the Pleiades project hoped to achieve flights of one hundred thousand feet using a lightweight gondola carried aloft by double clusters of small balloons. On October 18, 1937, Piccard made an experimental flight more modest in scale than what he ultimately hoped to achieve. It was the only flight, but it stirred people's imaginations. Films such as *The Red Balloon* and *Up* featured these same cluster balloons taking the protagonists aloft. For all of the noise he had to contend with in Chicago in 1933, Jean Piccard's life's work stands as the best testament and response. Robert Gilruth, the first director of NASA's Johnson Spaceflight Center, was Piccard's aeronautical engineering student at the University of Minnesota: "I learned many things from him, ways of looking at problems. He had a way of simplifying things, in talking [about how his devices worked] . . . learning about the gondola and how he managed it, [which was] just 20 years ahead of designing the Mercury capsule."[8] Considering the source, this was high praise indeed. Piccard was named one of Minnesota's greatest living men. A speaker at the ceremony honoring him finished his remarks thus, "I think one of his colleagues has summed up the feelings of us all when he said, 'Jean Piccard is simple, mild,—and brilliant.'"[9]

Gilruth, whose respect for Jean was equaled by his respect for Jeannette, hired her as a consultant to the burgeoning NASA program after Jean's death. In addition, she became a spokesperson for the Mercury, Gemini, and Apollo programs: supporting the feasibility of manned space flight, generating interest in the moonshot. Jeannette Ridlon Piccard was America's first priestess of space travel. She spent long, idyllic summers in a cabin on an island that she had purchased with Jean in 1935 on a remote lake in Minnesota. Her children and grandchildren often joined her for weeks at a time. In all, five generations of her family spent time on the island. Her granddaughter, Mary Louise, recalled long afterward looking up at the Milky Way at night talking with her about life, the stars, the future. She never forgot her grandmother telling her more than once: "Darling, never forget that women are the stronger sex."[10] Throughout her life she was a champion for the rights of women and their capacity to achieve anything that a man could achieve. Mary Louise Piccard grew up as part of her father Donald Piccard's ground crew, while ballooning nearly every weekend . . . earning a place next to her father in the basket while working toward her balloon pilot's license. Later, she worked as a stuntwoman in New York.[11]

In 1963, Donald Piccard attended the Fédération Aéronautique Internationale Conference in Mexico City. His mother was unable to attend. The world's first female cosmonaut, Valentina Tereshkova, however, was in attendance. He later recounted telling her:

"Comrade Tereshkova when I told my mother I was perhaps going to meet you. She asked me to greet you." Tereshkova said, "Thank you, very much." I replied, "Perhaps you don't know who my mother is. My mother is Jeannette Piccard, who piloted a balloon to 57,579 feet in 1934, more than two miles into physiological Space. And she wanted me to congratulate you on your marvelous achievement, and on behalf of all the women in America to welcome you to Space." Tereshkova said, "I know very well who your mother is."[12]

Author's photo.

Chronology of Events

1783	Montgolfier brothers' balloon makes first ascent
1868	Hugo Eckener is born
1884	Auguste and Jean Piccard are born
1893	First Chicago World's Fair (Columbian Exposition)
1895	Jeannette Ridlon is born
1896	Italo Balbo is born
1900	First test flight of a zeppelin
1901	Alberto Santos-Dumont circles spire of Eiffel Tower in powered dirigible
1903	Wright brothers' first successful flight in heavier-than-air craft at Kitty Hawk, North Carolina
1914–1918	World War I
1919	Versailles Treaty
1922	March on Rome
1927	Charles Lindbergh flies solo across the Atlantic
1929	*Graf Zeppelin*'s around-the-world flight
1931	Italo Balbo's trans-Atlantic seaplane squadron cruise to Brazil
May 1931	Auguste Piccard reaches stratosphere
1932	Franklin D. Roosevelt elected president of the United States

1933	Adolf Hitler named Chancellor of Germany
May 1933– October 1934	Second Chicago World's Fair (A Century of Progress)
July 1933	Italo Balbo's trans-Atlantic seaplane squadron cruise to Chicago
October 1933	Hugo Eckener brings *Graf Zeppelin* to Chicago World's Fair
November 1933	Tex Settle and Chester Fordney set new altitude record in gondola and balloon designed by the Piccards
October 1934	Jeannette and Jean Piccard reach stratosphere
1935	Italy invades Ethiopia
1936	Hitler reoccupies the Rhineland
1937	Hindenburg explodes over Lakehurst, New Jersey
1939–1945	World War II
1940	Italo Balbo shot down and killed
1954	Hugo Eckener dies
1962	Auguste Piccard dies
1963	Jean Piccard dies
1963	Valentina Tereshkova successfully launched into orbit by a Soviet R-7 rocket
1969	Apollo XI moonshot
1981	Jeannette Piccard dies
1982	EPCOT theme park opens in Orlando, Florida

Notes

Chapter 1: On the Edge

1. Joseph Goebbels, quoted in *People's Century: Master Race*, produced by Peter Pagnamenta (WGBH, 1997).

2. *Airship Over "The Eternal City"!* (newsreel, British Pathé, 1933).

3. Claudio Segrè, *Italo Balbo: A Fascist Life* (Berkeley and Los Angeles: University of California Press, 1987), 345.

4. Balbo, quoted in Piers Brendon, *The Dark Valley: A Panorama of the 1930s* (New York: Alfred A. Knopf, 2000), 143.

5. Clarence K. Streit, "Civilian Air Parley Starts at Geneva: Experts of 13 Nations Gather Under League's Auspices," *New York Times*, July 9, 1930.

6. Segrè, *Italo Balbo*, 180.

7. Ibid., 203.

8. R. J. B. Bosworth, *Mussolini's Italy: Life under the Dictatorship 1915–1945* (New York: Penguin Press, 2006), 295.

Chapter 2: White City

1. Donald L. Miller, *City of the Century: The Epic of Chicago and the Making of America* (New York: Simon & Schuster, 1996), 492.

2. Ibid., 498.

3. Leonard Mosley, *Disney's World: A Biography* (New York: Stein & Day, 1985), 25–26.

4. Patrick Meehan, "The Big Wheel," *UBC Engineer* (1964), reprinted in *Hyde Park Historical Society Newsletter*, Spring, 2000.

Chapter 3: Black Shirt

1. Claudio Segrè, *Italo Balbo: A Fascist Life* (Berkeley and Los Angeles: University of California Press, 1987), 5.
2. G. Ward Price, quoted in Segrè, *Italo Balbo*, 5.
3. Max Gallo, *Mussolini's Italy: Twenty Years of the Fascist Era* (New York: Macmillan Publishing, 1973), 9.
4. Segrè, *Italo Balbo*, 16.
5. Ibid., 22.
6. Gallo, *Mussolini's Italy*, 53, 86.
7. Segrè, *Italo Balbo*, 27.
8. Margaret Macmillan, *Paris: 1919* (New York: Random House, 2002), 294–95, 304.
9. Robert Wohl, *The Spectacle of Flight: Aviation and the Western Imagination 1920–1950* (New Haven, CT: Yale University Press, 2005), 55.
10. Gallo, *Mussolini's Italy*, 177.
11. Ignazio Silone, *Bread and Wine* (New York: Harper & Brothers, 1937), 30.
12. Ibid., 145.
13. Wohl, *The Spectacle of Flight*, 3.
14. Segrè, *Italo Balbo*, xiii.
15. Guido Mattioli, quoted in Wohl, *The Spectacle of Flight*, 51.
16. Schneider Trophy History: 9th édition, November 1926, https://www.hydroretro.net/race1926.
17. Wohl, *The Spectacle of Flight*, 69.
18. Segrè, *Italo Balbo*, 208.
19. Wohl, *The Spectacle of Flight*, 46.
20. *The Aviators: Fellowship of the Air*, directed by Tim Kirby (BBC Two, 1998).
21. Segrè, *Italo Balbo*, 223–25.
22. *Lo Stormo Atlantico* (Cinematografia sonora dell'Instituto Nazionale, 1931).
23. *Azas Italianas sob os céos do Brasil* (newsreel, Ottorino Pietras, 1931).
24. Wohl, *The Spectacle of Flight*, 74.

Chapter 4: Zeppelin

1. Douglas Botting, *Dr. Eckener's Dream Machine: The Great Zeppelin and the Dawn of Air Travel* (New York: Henry Holt, 2001), 41.
2. Ibid.
3. Ibid., 37.
4. Hugo Eckener, *My Zeppelins* (London: Putnam & Company, 1958), 12.
5. Ibid., 14.
6. Eckener quoted in Botting, *Dr. Eckener's Dream Machine*, 62.

7. Ibid., 18.

8. *The Aviators: Fellowship of the Air*, directed by Tim Kirby (BBC Two, 1998).

9. Eckener, *My Zeppelins*, 23.

10. Ibid., 25–26.

11. Ibid., 27.

12. Ibid., 30.

13. Botting, *Dr. Eckener's Dream Machine*, 106–7.

14. Wolfgang Lambrecht, "New York to Berlin Via Zeppelin," *American Traveler's Gazette*, June 1933.

15. "To Europe in 3 Days: Regular Zeppelin Services for Passengers, Mail, and Cargo," circa 1933, University of Illinois Chicago Special Collections.

16. Eckener, *My Zeppelins*, 36–37.

17. Ibid., 39.

18. Ibid.

19. Ibid., 40–41.

20. "Notes, News and Notions," *The Practical Clock and Watchmaker*, November 15, 1929.

21. Eckener, *My Zeppelins*, 79.

22. Botting, *Dr. Eckener's Dream Machine*, 167.

23. Eckener, *My Zeppelins*, 86–87.

24. Ibid., 91.

25. Ibid., 106.

26. Charles Lindbergh, "Future of Air Transport: By Three Leaders," *New York Times*, May 4, 1930.

27. Hugo Eckener, statement to League of Nations' Committee on Communications and Transit, in Clarence K. Streit, "Civilian Air Parley Starts at Geneva: Experts of 13 Nations Gather Under League's Auspices," *New York Times*, July 9, 1930.

28. Italo Balbo, statement to League of Nations' Committee on Communications and Transit, in Streit, "Civilian Air Parley Starts at Geneva."

29. Eckener, *My Zeppelins*, 124–25.

30. Ibid., 128–29.

31. Ibid., 143.

Chapter 5: Up!

1. Bertrand Piccard (chairman, Solar Impulse Foundation, Lausanne, Switzerland), personal interview.

2. Lena Young de Grummond and Lynn de Grummond Delaune, *Jean Felix Piccard: Boy Balloonist* (New York: Bobbs-Merrill Company, 1968), 81.

3. Ibid., 107.

4. Ibid., 118.

5. Ibid., 190–91.

6. Ibid., 131.

7. Jason Kelly, "Jeannette Piccard, SM'19 (1895–1981): A 'Pioneer of the Skies,'" *University of Chicago Magazine*, May–June 2011.

8. Mary Louise Piccard (Los Angeles, California), personal interview.

9. Ibid.

10. Jeannette Piccard, quoted in Young de Grummond and de Grummond Delaune, *Jean Felix Piccard*, 142–43.

11. Ibid., 145.

12. Tom Cheshire, *The Explorer Gene: How Three Generations of One Family Went Higher, Deeper, and Further Than Any Before* (New York: Marble Arch Press, 2013), 17.

13. Ibid., 12.

14. Michael G. Smith, "A Race to the Stratosphere in 1933: Long before the Cold War, Soviets and Americans Dueled to Reach the Top of the Atmosphere," *Air & Space Magazine*, August 24, 2015.

15. Cheshire, *The Explorer Gene*, 32.

16. Auguste Piccard, quoted in "Ten Miles High in an Air-Tight Ball," *Popular Science Magazine,* August 1931.

17. Cheshire, *The Explorer Gene*, 48.

18. *10 Miles Above the Earth* (newsreel, British Pathé, 1931).

19. Cheshire, *The Explorer Gene*, 62.

20. Bertrand Piccard, personal interview.

Chapter 6: Crash

1. Cheryl R. Ganz, *The 1933 Chicago World's Fair: A Century of Progress* (Urbana and Chicago: University of Illinois Press, 2008), 42.

2. Ibid., 46.

3. Lauro de Bosis letter, in Piers Brendon, *The Dark Valley: A Panorama of the 1930s* (New York: Alfred A. Knopf, 2000), 144.

4. Ibid.

5. Brendon, *The Dark Valley*, 144.

6. Ibid., 143.

7. Ganz, *The 1933 Chicago World's Fair*, 39–40.

Chapter 7: A Single Beam of Starlight

1. "The Star Arcturus," 1933, University of Illinois Chicago Special Collections.

2. Lisa D. Schrenk, *Building a Century of Progress: The Architecture of Chicago's 1933–34 World's Fair* (Minneapolis: University of Minnesota Press, 2007), 13–14.

3. Ibid., 87–88.

Chapter 8: Rainbow City

1. Lisa D. Schrenk, *Building a Century of Progress: The Architecture of Chicago's 1933–34 World's Fair* (Minneapolis: University of Minnesota Press, 2007), 44.

2. Joseph Urban Collection: New York Series, Columbia University, n.d., http://www.columbia.edu/cu/lweb/eresources/archives/rbml/urban/.

3. Cheryl Ganz, *The 1933 Chicago World's Fair: A Century of Progress* (Urbana and Chicago: University of Illinois Press, 2008), 61.

4. Ibid.

5. Charles Collins, "World's Fair Colorist and Follies' Designer Was Genius of Decoration," *Chicago Tribune*, July 16, 1933.

6. Paul Johnson, *A History of the American People* (New York: Harper Collins, 1997), 662–63.

7. Robert Abbott, "The Week," *Chicago Defender*, June 24, 1933.

8. Ganz, *The 1933 Chicago World's Fair*, 9.

9. Ibid., 10.

10. *The Sign of the Cross*, directed and produced by Cecil B. DeMille (Paramount, 1932).

Chapter 9: Chief Flying Eagle

1. Michael Pratt, *Italo Balbo's Transatlantic Flight (1933): 24 Italian Seaplanes in America* (Montreal: Bibliothèque et Archives nationales du Québec, 2019), 13.

2. Claudio G. Segrè, *Italo Balbo: A Fascist Life* (Berkeley: University of California Press, 1987), 240–41.

3. Robert Wood, "Proud to Bring Friendship Message, Says Balbo," *Chicago Herald and Examiner*, July 16, 1933.

4. "Balbo's Own Story of Amazing Flight," *Chicago Herald and Examiner*, July 16, 1933.

5. Robert Wohl, *The Spectacle of Flight: Aviation and the Western Imagination 1920–1950* (New Haven, CT: Yale University Press, 2005), 93.

6. "Safe in American Waters," *Chicago American*, July 14, 1933.

7. Fred H. Glasby, "Balbo Fleet Flies 800 Miles; Ready for Montreal Honors," *Chicago Herald and Examiner*, July 14, 1933.

8. Ibid.

9. Pratt, *Italo Balbo's Transatlantic Flight (1933)*, 45.

10. Ibid.

11. Radiograms reporting the progress of Italo Balbo's squadron of seaplanes from Montreal to Chicago, July 15, 1933.

12. "24 Italian Planes Land on Lakefront to End 7,000 Mile Flight," *Chicago American*, July 15, 1933.

13. "Chicago Welcome for Fascist Leader," *Chicago Tribune*, July 15, 1933.

14. Gus Lazzarini, quoted in *The Aviators: Fellowship of the Air*, directed by Tim Kirby (BBC Two, 1998).

15. Marie Nardulli-Doody, quoted in *The Aviators: Fellowship of the Air*.

16. "Flight a Lesson to U.S.," *Chicago Herald and Examiner*, July 16, 1933.

17. Wood, "Proud to Bring Friendship Message, Says Balbo."

18. Ibid.

19. "Scramble for Launches," *Chicago Herald and Examiner*, July 16, 1933.

20. "General Gives Fascist Salute to Throng," *Chicago Herald and Examiner*, July 16, 1933.

21. Ibid.

22. "General Gives Fascist Salute to Throng."

23. "24 Plane Armada Lands, Completes Daring 6,100-mile Mission on Lakefront," *Chicago Herald and Examiner*, July 16, 1933.

24. "Italian Airmen Given Rousing Welcome in Soldier Field," *Chicago Tribune*, July 16, 1933.

25. "Italian Flyers," *Chicago Tribune*, July 16, 1933.

26. "Who Is Balbo," pamphlet of the Italian Socialist Federation Italian League for the Rights of Man, University of Illinois Chicago Special Collections, 1933.

27. Giuseppe Castruccio, "Italian Consul Sees Peace Link in Balbo Flight," *Chicago Daily Times*, July 16, 1933.

28. India Moffett, "Society Folk Meet Balbo at Saddle and Cycle," *Chicago Tribune*, July 16, 1933.

29. Ibid.

30. Italo Balbo, telegram to Dr. Giuseppe Castruccio, Italian Consul General in Chicago, reprinted in the *Chicago Daily Times*, July 14, 1933.

31. Moffett, "Society Folk Meet Balbo at Saddle and Cycle."

32. Segrè, *Italo Balbo*, 243.

33. "Fliers Arise to Explore City," *Chicago Herald and Examiner*, July 16, 1933.

34. "Rose of Victory," *Chicago Herald and Examiner*, July 17, 1933.

35. Cheryl R. Ganz, *The 1933 Chicago World's Fair: A Century of Progress* (Urbana and Chicago: University of Illinois Press, 2008), 135.

36. "5,000 Acclaim Balbo Flyers at Italian Dinner; Throngs Mass on Michigan Ave. to See Airmen," *Chicago Tribune*, July 17, 1933.

37. Ibid.

38. Marie Nardulli-Doody, quoted in *Chicago Stories—A Break in the Clouds: Chicago's 1933 World's Fair*, produced and written by Mike Leiderman (WWTT, 2000).

39. Bruce Grant, "Balbo Proclaimed 2nd Columbus at Statue Unveiling," *Chicago Daily Times*, July 17, 1933.

40. Segrè, *Italo Balbo*, 244.

41. "General Balbo Plays Hookey to Ride Scooter at Fair," *Chicago News*, July 18, 1933.

42. Ibid.

43. Franklin D. Roosevelt letter to Italo Balbo, May 16, 1935, courtesy of Gregory Alegi.

44. Gregory Alegi, Libera Università Internazionale degli Studi Sociali "Guido Carli" (LUISS), Rome, personal interview.

Chapter 10: Waking from the Dream

1. Hugo Eckener, *My Zeppelins* (London: Putnam & Co., 1958), 92.

2. Ibid, 161.

3. *Chicago News*, October 25, 1933.

4. Dorothea Momsen, "Graf Zeppelin Due at Miami Today," *New York Times*, October 23, 1933.

5. "Graf Zeppelin Leaves Miami, Chicago Bound," *Chicago Tribune*, October 24, 1933.

6. "Gale Keeps Graf Cruising Around Akron All Night," *Chicago Herald and Examiner*, October 25, 1933.

7. Hugo Eckener, quoted in "Zep Due to Reach Chicago in Morning on Fair Flight," *Chicago News*, October 25, 1933.

8. Eckener, *My Zeppelins*, 152–53.

9. Cheryl Ganz, *The* Graf Zeppelin *and the Swastika: Conflicting Symbols at the 1933 Chicago World's Fair* (Dayton, OH: National Aerospace Conference Proceedings, Wright State University, 1998), 59.

10. William Toll, "Club Movement in the United States," in *Jewish Women: A Comprehensive Historical Encyclopedia* (Brookline, MA: Jewish Women's Archive, 2009).

11. Ganz, *The* Graf Zeppelin *and the Swastika*, 59.

12. "50,000 Jews Unite in Chicago Protest," *New York Times*, May 10, 1933.

13. Ibid.

14. Hugo Eckener, note to Dr. Edgar Salin, July 17, 1931, Basel University Library, Switzerland.

15. Bella Fromm, *Blood and Banquets* (New York: Harper, 1942), 219.

16. "Prominent Persons on the German Committee of the International Radio Forum," *Abendpost*, April 19, 1932.

17. "Is Mischief Starting Again?" *Völkischer Beobachtner*, June 23, 1926.

18. Ganz, *The* Graf Zeppelin *and the Swastika*, 60.

19. Robert Wood, "Fair Honors Eckener, Graf on Brief Visit," *Chicago Herald and Examiner*, October 27, 1933.

20. Hugo Eckener to Willy von Meister, from a 1976 interview of Willy von Meister by Cheryl Ganz, quoted in Ganz, *The Graf Zeppelin and the Swastika*, 56. Also, Hugo Eckener to Willy von Meister, from a 1973 interview of Willy von Meister, quoted in Henry Cord Mayer, *Airshipmen: Businessmen and Politics 1890–1940* (Washington, DC: Smithsonian Institution Press, 1991), 203.

21. Wood, "Fair Honors Eckener, Graf on Brief Visit."

22. "Graf Flies Over City Salutes Fair," *Chicago News*, October 26, 1933.

23. *Chicago Tribune*, October 26, 1933.

24. Francis Healy, "Graf Lands Here Goes Back East," *Chicago Daily Times*, October 26, 1933.

25. Ibid.

26. "Graf Flies Over City Salutes Fair."

27. Wood, "Fair Honors Eckener, Graf on Brief Visit"; "Graf Flies Over City Salutes Fair."

28. "Friedrichshafen to Chicago," *Chicago News*, October 26, 1933.

29. "Graf Flies Over City Salutes Fair."

30. Healy, "Graf Lands Here Goes Back East"; "Graf Flies Over City Salutes Fair."

31. Grant Smith, letter to Rufus Dawes, August 30, 1933, University of Illinois Chicago Special Collections.

32. Ganz, *The Graf Zeppelin and the Swastika*, 60.

33. Carl R. Latham, vice president, Union League Club of Chicago, invitation to Rufus Dawes, October 23, 1933, University of Illinois Chicago Special Collections.

34. "Rufus Dawes to Hugo Eckener," in Hugo Eckener, *Im Zeppelin*, 473, in Ganz, *The Graf Zeppelin and the Swastika*, 61.

35. "Luther Backs Nazi Policies," *Chicago Herald and Examiner*, October 27, 1933.

36. "German Envoy Expounds Nazi Aims in Chicago," *Chicago Tribune*, October 27, 1933.

37. Ibid.

38. Ibid.

39. Ibid.

40. "Nazi Clash Greets Eckener in Chicago," *New York Times*, October 27, 1933.

41. Ganz, *The Graf Zeppelin and the Swastika*, 61.

42. "Nazi Clash Greets Eckener in Chicago."

43. Theodore Light to Cheryl R. Ganz, October 25, 1993, in Cheryl R. Ganz, *The 1933 Chicago World's Fair: A Century of Progress* (Urbana and Chicago: University of Illinois Press, 2008), 147.

44. Ibid.

45. Hugo Eckener, letter to Franklin D. Roosevelt, October 26, 1933.

46. *God's Fiddler: Jascha Heifetz*, directed by Peter Rosen (EuroArts, 2011).

47. "Heifetz Brings Strad, Acclaim to Chicago," *Chicago American*, October 30, 1933.

48. Ibid.

Chapter 11: Space Race

1. Mark Wolverton, "How the First American Science Writer Found (Then Lost) God in the Cosmic Ray," *Distillations*, October 8, 2019.

2. David H. DeVorkin, *Race to the Stratosphere: Manned Scientific Ballooning in America* (Washington DC: Smithsonian Institution, 1989), 50.

3. *Professor Piccard* (newsreel, Pathé, 1933).

4. Gordon J. Vaeth, *Graf Zeppelin: The Adventures of an Aerial Globetrotter* (New York: Harper & Brothers, 1958), 62.

5. DeVorkin, *Race to the Stratosphere*, 57–58.

6. Ibid., 58.

7. Muskat quoted in DeVorkin, *Race to the Stratosphere*, 71.

8. "Here for World's Highest Hop," *Chicago News*, July 14, 1933.

9. Dempster MacMurphy, "Pilot of Stratosphere Balloon Admits Professor May Be Dumped," *Chicago News*, July 17, 1933.

10. Dempster MacMurphy, "Settle to Go Aloft Alone in Piccard Flight," *Chicago News*, July 25, 1933.

11. DeVorkin, *Race to the Stratosphere*, 81.

12. "Russians Claim Balloon Mark," *Chicago Tribune*, October 1, 1933.

13. Ibid.

14. Ibid.

15. DeVorkin, *Race to the Stratosphere*, 108.

16. Mrs. Jean Piccard to William Rosenfeld, November 28, 1933, in DeVorkin, *Race to the Stratosphere*, 91.

17. Ibid.

18. Jason Kelly, "Jeannette Piccard, SM'19 (1895–1981): A 'Pioneer of the Skies,'" *University of Chicago Magazine*, May–June 2011.

19. Jeannette Piccard, quoted in Ian A. Moule and David J. Shayler, *Women in Space—Following Valentina* (Berlin and Heidelburg, Germany: Springer, 2005), 25.

20. DeVorkin, *Race to the Stratosphere*, 113.

21. Ibid.

22. Ibid., 119.

23. "Why Explore the Stratosphere?" *Popular Mechanics*, October 1933.

24. Ibid.

25. Lena Young de Grummond and Lynn de Grummond Delaune, *Jean Felix Piccard: Boy Balloonist* (New York: Bobbs-Merrill Company, 1968), 160.

26. Auguste Piccard to Jean Piccard, in DeVorkin, *Race to the Stratosphere*, 109.

27. *Piccards in Cloud Hop* (Universal Newsreel, 1934).

28. Kelly, "Jeannette Piccard, SM'19 (1895–1981)."

29. "Jeannette Piccard—First Woman to Reach the Stratosphere," NASTAR Center, n.d., www.nastarcenter.com/jeannette-piccard-first-woman-to-reach-the -stratosphere.

30. Jeannette Piccard, quoted in Paul Sorenson, "Looking Back," *AEM Magazine*, University of Minnesota Institute of Technology, 1998–1999.

31. "Mrs. Piccard Tells of Flight Thrills," *New York Times*, October 24, 1934.

32. Albert W. Stevens to W. F. G. Swann, in DeVorkin, *Race to the Stratosphere*, 123.

33. Ibid., 124–25.

Chapter 12: City of Tomorrow

1. "Walt Disney and the World's Fairs, Part 1," Bureau International des Expositions, September 18, 2013, https://www.bie-paris.org/site/en/blog/entry/walt -disney-and-world-s-fairs-part-1.

2. "1933 All Star Game," Baseball Almanac, n.d., https://www.baseball-almanac .com/asgbox/yr1933as.shtml.

3. Jean Shepherd, *In God We Trust, All Others Pay Cash* (New York: Broadway Books, 1966), 104–5.

4. Ibid., 106.

5. Ibid.

6. Ibid., 110.

7. Producer Robert H. Justman to Mary Louise Piccard, in 1991; Mary Louise Piccard, personal interview.

8. David Alexander, "Interview of Gene Roddenberry," *The Humanist*, March–April 1991.

9. Ibid.

10. Ibid.

11. Ibid.

12. Cheryl Ganz, *The 1933 Chicago World's Fair: A Century of Progress* (Urbana and Chicago: University of Illinois Press, 2008), 115.

13. Ibid., 112–13.

14. "Sets Fair's Women's Day," *New York Times*, October 21, 1933.

15. "Serpent Dancer with Python," *Chicago Tribune*, October 29, 1933.

Chapter 13: Lost Horizon

1. *Aviators: Fellowship of the Air*, directed by Tim Kirby (BBC Two, 1998).

2. Guglielmo Emanuel, "Il Duce 'Exiles' Balbo to Post in Africa," *Chicago American*, November 6, 1933.

3. Ibid.

4. Ibid.

5. Hugo Eckener, *My Zeppelins* (London: Putnam & Co., 1958), 158.

6. Ibid., 153.

7. "What is Going to Happen to Eckener?" *Pariser Tagblatt*, April 5, 1936.

8. "Eckener Refuse Election Plea from Hitler; Name Banned from the Press as a Result," *New York Times*, April 3, 1936.

9. Eckener, *My Zeppelins*, 149.

10. "Aboard the Airship Hindenburg: Louis Lochner's Diary of Its Maiden Flight to the United States," May 6–14, 1936; postscript May 30, 1937 (Wisconsin Historical Society).

11. Eckener, *My Zeppelins*, 165.

12. Ibid, 167.

13. Vaeth, *Graf Zeppelin: The Adventures of an Aerial Globetrotter* (New York: Harper & Brothers, 1958), 108.

14. Eckener, *My Zeppelins*, 180–81.

15. Vaeth, *Graf Zeppelin*, 196–98.

Chapter 14: Into the Abyss

1. Claudio Segrè, *Italo Balbo: A Fascist Life* (Berkeley and Los Angeles: University of California Press, 1987), 356–58.

2. Ibid., 346.

3. Ibid., 358.

4. Gregory Alegi, "Ninety Seconds over Tobruk," *The Aviation Historian*, no. 13, October 15, 2015.

5. Eckener, *My Zeppelins* (London: Putnam & Co., 1958), 178.

6. Michael J. Neufeld, "Mittelbau Main Camp: In Depth," in *Holocaust Encyclopedia* (Washington, DC: United States Holocaust Memorial Museum, 2021).

Epilogue

1. Gayla Marty, "Heaven and Earth," *CE + HD Connect*, July 2019.

2. David H. DeVorkin, *Race to the Stratosphere: Manned Scientific Ballooning in America* (Washington, DC: Smithsonian Institution, 1989), frontispiece.

3. Don Piccard, quoted in Marty, "Heaven and Earth."

4. John F. Kennedy, "Rice University Speech," September 12, 1962.

5. J. Gordon Vaeth, *Graf Zeppelin: The Adventures of an Aerial Globetrotter* (New York: Harper & Brothers, 1958), 222.

6. Ibid., 129.

7. Ibid., 225.

8. Robert Gilruth, quoted in DeVorkin, *Race to the Stratosphere*, 109.

9. Lena Young de Grummond and Lynn de Grummond Delaune, *Jean Felix Piccard: Boy Balloonist* (New York: Bobbs-Merrill Company, 1968), 192.

10. Mary Louise Piccard (Los Angeles and Santa Monica, California), personal interview.

11. Ibid.

12. "Jeannette Piccard—First Woman to Reach the Stratosphere," NASTAR Center, n.d., www.nastarcenter.com/jeannette-piccard-first-woman-to-reach-the-stratosphere.

Selected Bibliography

Books

Balbo, Italo. *Stormi in volo dell'Oceano*. Italy: A. Mondadori, 1931.

Bosworth, R. J. B. *Mussolini's Italy: Life under the Dictatorship 1915–1945*. New York: The Penguin Press, 2006.

Botting, Douglas. *Dr. Eckener's Dream Machine: The Great Zeppelin and the Dawn of Air Travel*. New York: Henry Holt, 2001.

Brendon, Piers. *The Dark Valley: A Panorama of the 1930s*. New York: Alfred A. Knopf, 2000.

Cheshire, Tom. *The Explorer Gene: How Three Generations of One Family Went Higher, Deeper, and Further Than Any Before*. New York: Marble Arch Press, 2013.

Cord Mayer, Henry. *Airshipmen: Businessmen and Politics 1890–1940*. Washington, DC: Smithsonian Institution Press, 1991.

de Grummond, Lena Young, and Lynn de Grummond Delaune. *Jean Felix Piccard: Boy Balloonist*. New York: Bobbs-Merrill Company, 1968.

DeVorkin, David H. *Race to the Stratosphere: Manned Scientific Ballooning in America*. Washington, DC: Smithsonian Institution, 1989.

Duggan, Christopher. *Fascist Voices: An Intimate History of Mussolini's Italy*. Oxford (UK) and New York: Oxford University Press, 2013.

Eckener, Hugo. *My Zeppelins*. London: Putnam & Co., 1958.

Fromm, Bella. *Blood and Banquets*. New York: Harper, 1942.

Gallo, Max. *Mussolini's Italy: Twenty Years of the Fascist Era*. New York: Macmillan Publishing, 1973.

Ganz, Cheryl. *The* Graf Zeppelin *and the Swastika: Conflicting Symbols at the 1933 Chicago World's Fair*. Dayton, OH: National Aerospace Conference Proceedings Wright State University, 1998.

Ganz, Cheryl R. *The 1933 Chicago World's Fair: A Century of Progress*. Urbana and Chicago: University of Illinois Press, 2008.

Johnson, Paul. *A History of the American People*. New York: Harper Collins, 1997.

Larson, Erik. *The Devil in the White City*. New York: Vintage Books, 2004.

Macmillan, Margaret. *Paris: 1919*. New York: Random House, 2002.

Miller, Donald L. *City of the Century: The Epic of Chicago and the Making of America*. New York: Simon & Schuster, 1996.

Mosley, Leonard. *Disney's World: A Biography*. New York: Stein & Day, 1985.

Moule, Ian A., and David J. Shayler. *Women in Space—Following Valentina*. Berlin and Heidelburg, Germany: Springer, 2005.

Neufeld, Michael J. "Mittelbau Main Camp: In Depth," In *Holocaust Encyclopedia*. Washington, DC: United States Holocaust Memorial Museum, 2021.

Okrent, Daniel. *Last Call: The Rise and Fall of Prohibition*. New York: Scribner, 2011.

Pratt, Michael. *Italo Balbo's Transatlantic Flight (1933): 24 Italian Seaplanes in America*. Montreal: Bibliothèque et Archives nationales du Québec, 2019.

Schrenk, Lisa D. *Building a Century of Progress: The Architecture of Chicago's 1933–34 World's Fair*. Minneapolis: University of Minnesota Press, 2007.

Segrè, Claudio G. *Italo Balbo: A Fascist Life*. Berkeley: University of California Press, 1987.

Shepherd, Jean. *In God We Trust, All Others Pay Cash*. New York: Broadway Books, 1966.

Silone, Ignazio. *Bread and Wine*. New York: Harper & Brothers, 1937.

Ten Years of Italian Progress. Rome: E.N.I.T. (Italian State Tourist Department), 1933.

Toll, Willian. "Club Movement in the United States." In *Jewish Women: A Comprehensive Historical Encyclopedia*. Brookline, MA: Jewish Women's Archive, 2009.

Vaeth, J. Gordon. *Graf Zeppelin: The Adventures of an Aerial Globetrotter*. New York: Harper & Brothers, 1958.

Wohl, Robert. *The Spectacle of Flight: Aviation and the Western Imagination 1920–1950*. New Haven, CT: Yale University Press, 2005.

Journals and Magazines

"Aeronautics: Zeppelining." *Time*, September 16, 1929.

Alegi, Gregory. "Ninety Seconds over Tobruk." *Aviation Historian*, no. 13, October 15, 2015.

Alexander, David. "Interview of Gene Roddenberry." *The Humanist*, March–April 1991.

Kelly, Jason. "Jeannette Piccard, SM'19 (1895–1981): 'A Pioneer of the Skies.'" *University of Chicago Magazine*, May–June 2011.

Marty, Gayla. "Heaven and Earth." *CE + HD Connect*, July 2019.

Meehan, Patrick. "The Big Wheel." *UBC Engineer*, 1964. Reprinted in *Hyde Park Historical Society Newsletter*, Spring 2000.

"Notes, News, and Notions." *The Practical Watch and Clockmaker*, November 15, 1929.

"Science: Millikan to Compton." *Time*, February 13, 1933.

Smith, Michael G. "A Race to the Stratosphere in 1933." *Air & Space Magazine*, August 24, 2015.

Sorenson, Paul. "Looking Back." *AEM Magazine*, University of Minnesota Institute of Technology, 1998–1999.

"Ten Miles High in an Air-Tight Ball." *Popular Science Magazine*, August 1931.

White, April. "Hulking Airships Rise Again, Slowly." *Smithsonian Magazine*, December 2019.

"Why Explore the Stratosphere?" *Popular Mechanics*, October 1933.

Wolverton, Mark. "How the First American Science Writer Found (Then Lost) God in the Cosmic Ray." *Distillations*, October 8, 2019.

Documents

"Aboard the Airship Hindenburg: Louis Lochner's Diary of Its Maiden Flight to the United States." May 6–14, 1936; postscript, May 30, 1937. Wisconsin Historical Society.

Carl R. Latham, vice president, Union League Club of Chicago, invitation to Rufus Dawes, October 23, 1933. University of Illinois Chicago Special Collections.

Communications received from General I. Balbo, Dr. Hugo Eckener, and Colonel Charles A. Lindbergh. League of Nations, Committee for Communications and Transit, Air Transport Cooperation Committee, 1930. Harvard Law School Library.

Franklin D. Roosevelt, letter to Italo Balbo, May 16, 1935. Courtesy of Gregory Alegi.

Grant Smith, letter to Rufus Dawes, August 30, 1933. University of Illinois Chicago Special Collections.

Hugo Eckener, letter to Franklin D. Roosevelt, October 26. 1933. University of Illinois Chicago Special Collections.

Hugo Eckener, note to Dr. Edgar Salin, July 17, 1931. Basel University Library, Switzerland.

Italo Balbo, note to *Chicago Herald and Examiner*, July 1933. University of Illinois Chicago Special Collections.

Italo Balbo, telegram to Dr. Giuseppe Catruccio, Italian Consul General in Chicago. Reprinted in the *Chicago Daily Times*, July 14, 1933. University of Illinois Chicago Special Collections.

John F. Kennedy, "Rice University Speech," September 12, 1962. Transcript.

Lenox R. Lohr Collection of Official Photographs, "A Century of Progress International Exposition, 1933–1934." University of Illinois Chicago Special Collections.

Official Invitation to Piccard Stratosphere Flight, September 1934. Courtesy of Bertrand Piccard.

Radiograms reporting progress of Italo Balbo's squadron of seaplanes from Montreal to Chicago, July 15, 1933. Chicago History Museum.

"The Star Arcturus," 1933. University of Illinois Chicago Special Collections.

"To Europe in 3 Days: Regular Zeppelin Services for Passengers, Mail, and Cargo General Representatives of the Luftschiffbau Zeppelin Hamburg-American Line," circa 1933. University of Illinois Chicago Special Collections.

"Who Is Balbo," Italian Socialist Federation Italian League for the Rights of Man, 1933. University of Illinois Chicago Special Collections.

Periodicals

Abendpost
American Traveler's Gazette (University of Illinois Chicago Special Collections)
Chicago American (University of Illinois Chicago Special Collections)
Chicago Daily Times (University of Illinois Chicago Special Collections)
Chicago Defender
Chicago Herald and Examiner (University of Illinois Chicago Special Collections)
Chicago News (University of Illinois Chicago Special Collections)
Chicago Tribune (University of Illinois Chicago Special Collections)
Daily Reader
Los Angeles Times
Minneapolis Star Tribune
Münchener Neueste Nachrichten
Münchener Post
Münchener Zeitung
New York Times
Pariser Tageblatt
Völkischer Beobachtner

Interviews

Barry Sears, Guide, Chicago Architecture Center
Bertrand Piccard, Chairman, Solar Impulse Foundation, Lausanne, Switzerland
Gregory Alegi, Libera Università Internazionale degli Studi Sociali "Guido Carli" (LUISS), Rome, Italy

Hans-Paul Stroehle, Leiter Abteilung Passagierservice/Luftschiffkapitän, Deutsche
  Zeppelin-Reederei GmbH, Friedrichshafen, Germany
Mary Louise Piccard, Los Angeles, California
Uwe Eckener, Konstanz, Switzerland

Films

10 Miles Above the Earth. Newsreel, British Pathé, 1931.
Airship Over "The Eternal City"! Newsreel, British Pathé, 1933.
American Experience: Chicago City of the Century. Produced and directed by Austin
  Hoyt. WGBH, 2003.
The Aviators: Fellowship of the Air. Directed by Tim Kirby. BBC Two, 1998.
Azas Italianas sob os céos do Brasil. Newsreel, Ottorino Pietras, 1931
Century of Progress, 80 Years Later. Produced by John Owens. Chicago Tribune,
  2013.
Chicago Stories—A Break in the Clouds: Chicago's 1933 World's Fair. Produced and
  written by Mike Leiderman. WWTT, 2000.
Flying Down to Rio. Directed by Thornton Freeland. RKO Radio Pictures, 1933.
God's Fiddler: Jascha Heifetz. Directed by Peter Rosen, EuroArts, 2011.
Graf Zeppelin Flies over World's Fair. Newsreel, British Movietone, 1933.
Hell's Angels. Produced and directed by Howard Hughes. United Artists, 1930.
The Hindenburg. Produced and directed by Robert Wise. Universal Pictures, 1975.
Octave Chanute: Patron Saint of Flight. Directed by Paul Nelson, 2020.
People's Century: Master Race. Produced by Peter Pagnamenta. WGBH, 1997.
Piccards in Cloud Hop. Universal Newsreel, 1934.
Professor Piccard. Newsreel, Pathé, 1933.
Prohibition. Directed by Ken Burns and Lynn Novick. Florentine Films, 2011.
The Sign of the Cross. Directed and produced by Cecil B. DeMille. Paramount, 1932.
Lo Stormo Atlantico. Cinematografia sonora dell'Instituto Nazionale, 1931.

Websites

"1933 All Star Game." Baseball Almanac, n.d. https://www.baseball-almanac.com
  /asgbox/yr1933as.shtml.
The Drake. n.d. https://www.thedrakehotel.com/explore/history.
"Florence Price: Symphony No. 1 in E Minor." Brian Dowdy.com, 2021. https://www
  .briandowdy.com/v2/2020/06/10/florence-price-symphony-no-1-in-e-minor
  -1933/.
"Harmon Trophy." Everipedia, n.d. https://everipedia.org/wiki/lang_en/Harmon
  _Trophy.

"Hit Songs from 1933." YouTube, December 1, 2018, https://www.youtube.com /watch?v=khbVRovcplg&feature=emb_logo

Jeannette Piccard: Blazing a Trail to the Stratosphere. Fédération Aéronautique Internationale (World Air Sports Federation), March 26, 2019. https://www.fai.org /news/jeannette-piccard-blazing-trail-stratosphere.

"Jeannette Piccard—First Woman to Reach the Stratosphere." NASTAR Center, n.d. https://www.nastarcenter.com/jeannette-piccard-first-woman-to-reach-the -stratosphere

Joseph Urban Collection: New York Series. Columbia University, n.d. http://www .columbia.edu/cu/lweb/eresources/archives/rbml/urban/

"Schneider Trophy History: 9th édition November 1926." n.d. https://www.hydro retro.net/race1926.

"Shifting Grounds: The Armory Years—Black Horse Troop." Shifting Grounds, 2021. http://www.shifting-grounds.net/armory/black-horse-troop.html.

"Walt Disney and the World's Fairs, Part 1." Bureau International des Expositions, September 18, 2013. https://www.bie-paris.org/site/en/blog/entry/walt-disney -and-world-s-fairs-part-1.

Acknowledgments

This was an ambitious book to write; without the help and generosity of spirit of knowledgeable guides, I would have no doubt stumbled from the outset. I would like to extend my most sincere thanks to Marilyn Bergante at the University of Illinois Chicago's Special Collections, as well as her staff. They were unfailingly patient and helpful. The time I spent in the Sharon Hogan Reading Room at UIC represented the most important component of my research. Frankly, this book couldn't have been written without it. I would also like to thank Lesley Martin of the Chicago History Museum for sharing the radiograms received at the Drake Hotel on July 15, 1933. Collectively these documents conveyed the breathless quality of the anticipation in Chicago on that long-ago day in a way that nothing else could. I'd also like to thank Ms. Martin for pointing me to the UIC archives. Without her suggestion, that treasure trove might have eluded me. Principal Stephen Locke at Joliet High School was generous with his time on a busy school day to show me the original artwork by one of the school's famous alumna, sculptor Louise Lentz Woodruff, for the 1933 Chicago World's Fair. Getting to see this in person made a deep impression on me. Kathleen McCarthy of Chicago's impressive Museum of Science and Industry provided me with detailed photographs of the interior of the Piccard Gondola that now hangs high above the museum's aviation gallery, and is thus inaccessible. Guide Barry Sears, of the Chicago Architecture Center, explained Art Deco architecture on a frigid day, touring buildings from the 1920s and 1930s. Thanks to Mr. Sears, the whole concept of Art Deco (something that had escaped me up to that point in my life) finally "clicked." Thanks also to the CAC's Zachary Whittenburg for suggesting the tour, and helping me grasp the 1933 Fair in the larger context of the city's development as a whole; and historian, Cheryl

221

Ganz, for generously sharing information about sources that I was having difficulty identifying. Catherine Uecker of the University of Chicago Library took time to point out useful resources for German-language Chicago newspapers. This turned out to be very helpful. Josephine Burri, director of philanthropy at the Shipley School in Bryn Mawr, Pennsylvania, provided me with a high-quality copy of Jeannette Ridlon's graduation photograph, which I very much appreciated. Thank you, Lilo Peter of Harwood Watch Company, Ltd., for sharing the photograph of Lady Grace Drummond-Hay (It's Magnificent!). Mike Zickus took time to explain the existing original architecture of the old Bismarck Hotel, on his last day on the job as engineer after more than forty years. I'd also like to thank the city of Chicago in general for maintaining its history so well. It can be a loud, fast city with an edge to it—even for a New Yorker—but there's an honesty to Chicago's sense of self that is refreshing (but pay attention crossing the street!).

Closer to home, I would like to thank the Lakehurst Navy Historical Society for offering free, informative tours of the naval air station's historical sites. The U.S. Navy also deserves a great deal of credit for maintaining this history at what is, after all, an active military installation. As always, the Morris County (New Jersey) Inter-Library Loan program was indispensable. My next-door neighbor, Angela Notari, took the time to try to convey to me Italo Balbo's Italian prose, while also sharing insightful pieces of information on him that she researched. I would also like to thank Stella Han (Columbia University '24) for her internet research on Italo Balbo, Hugo Eckener, and the Piccards, in various online archives. She located many useful sources. It also has been a great comfort to know that my supervisor at Stuyvesant High School, Jennifer Suri, understands and appreciates my work as an author. I am lucky. I'm also lucky to have someone I can rely on in Paris to hunt down documents and rare photographs: *merci* Claire Khelfaoui.

I am also very fortunate to have connected with individuals whose own stories have connected in intimate ways with the story that I was telling. First, Bertrand Piccard and his cousin, Mary Louise Piccard, were willing to share their recollections from their grandparents Auguste, and Jean and Jeannette, respectively. These discussions brought home to me as nothing else could how the spirit of science and exploration were passed from one generation to the next in this remarkable family. Mary Louise's father, the pioneering balloonist Donald Piccard, had very recently passed away when I first reached out to her. This was a very difficult time in her life. Her willingness to talk to me then, in particular, is something for which I will always be grateful. Hans-Paul Stroehle of Deutsche Zeppelin was absolutely the most informed and gracious guide to the world of the giant airships, of which he is intimately aware. *Danke Schoen*. Cruising in a zeppelin above Lake Constance was an experience I will never forget, and one that I hope to repeat. *Danke* also to Dr. Uwe Eckener (with the assistance of his daughter, Nikola) for fielding my questions about his grandfather, and for sharing the photograph of Ambrosi's powerful and evocative statue. I also would like to thank Colonel Gene Gay, U.S. Air Force retired, whom I met at a speaking engagement at the Army and Navy Club in Washington, DC, in 2018. It was he who introduced me to a former colleague of his, the former Italian air attaché in Washington, Major General Stefano Cont. Cont then introduced me to Gregory Alegi—the foremost living historian on the life and career of his countryman, Italo Balbo. Alegi spent an afternoon taking me on a tour of the Aeronautica Militare's headquarters building in Rome. His knowledge and passion for Italian aviation are infectious. Our official host was Staff Seargent Peter Bevilacqua of the Italian Air Force, who was patient in answering all of my questions about the magnificent murals that adorn the building's interior. One could feel his pride in sharing this aspect of the Aeronautica Militare with a foreign guest. Likewise, it was author and journalist Tom Cheshire who so generously provided an entrée to the Solar Impulse Team in Lausanne, Switzerland. I likely would never have spoken with the Piccards without this generous act on his part. Thank you. Authors Alex Rose and Michael McCarthy—whose recent books overlap to a degree with my own—were also generous in pointing out various sources that clarified important aspects of the chapters dealing with Hugo Eckener. I must confess that I haven't read either of their books (*Empires of the Sky* and *The Hidden Hindenburg*, respectively). I have a standard modus operandi that I will not read recent books by my contemporaries on topics similar to those on which I am writing. I need to be confident that my ideas are my own ideas, and that I reach my own conclusions.

I am very fortunate to have had two author mentors who encouraged me to stick with my vision for this book, because they felt it had merit: George Daughan and the late Thomas Fleming, who saw what a long list of agents and editors did not see. Thank you. Lastly, I would like to give my heartfelt thanks to my agent, Andrew Stuart. His unflagging efforts on my behalf, even when all the signals said "Stop," allowed me the chance to write this book. His confidence in me as a writer, and in my vision for how I wanted to tell this story, made it possible. Without him, there is no book. The same can be said of Jake Bonar at Rowman & Littlefield. His enthusiasm for this subject matter was a shot in the arm. His patience as it took me nearly a year longer than anticipated to complete the book (due to restrictions on travel to Europe as a result of the pandemic) was greatly appreciated as well. My hope is that this book is worth the wait.

Index

Note: Page numbers in *italics* refer to photographs.

About the Author

David Hanna teaches history at Stuyvesant High School in Lower Manhattan. He is a recipient of the *New York Times* Teachers Make a Difference Award and the University of Chicago's Outstanding Educator Award, and is the author of *Knights of the Sea: The True Story of the Boxer and the Enterprise and the War of 1812* (2012), which *New York Magazine*'s "Approval Matrix" categorized as "high-brow, brilliant," and *Rendezvous with Death: The Americans Who Joined the Foreign Legion in 1914 to Fight for France and for Civilization* (2016). As a result of his work on the latter book, he was invited to become a "publishing partner" of the United States World War One Centennial Commission. Both books are currently in print. Hanna has been a featured speaker at the Smithsonian's National Portrait Gallery, the Independence Seaport Museum in Philadelphia, the Maine Maritime Museum, the Rhinebeck Aerodrome Museum, and the American School of Paris, among others. He lives in Morris County, New Jersey, with his wife and two children.